Pelican Books

**Reflections
on the Revolution
in France: 1968**

Reflections
on the Revolution
in France: 1968

Edited by Charles Posner

Penguin Books

Penguin Books Ltd, Harmondsworth,
Middlesex, England
Penguin Books Inc., 7110 Ambassador Road,
Baltimore, Maryland 21207, U.S.A.
Penguin Books Australia Ltd, Ringwood,
Victoria, Australia

First published 1970
Copyright © Charles Posner, 1970

Made and printed in Great Britain by
C. Nicholls & Company Ltd
Set in Monotype Plantin

'What can possibly be wrong? You are in Paris,
the capital of a prosperous country, part of a
world slowly curing itself of those hereditary
illnesses it used to treat like family heirlooms:
misery, hunger, death, logic. You are opening
what may well be the most important turning-point
in history since the discovery of fire. What
troubles you? Are you frightened of Fantomas?

Do you, as they often say, think about yourself
too much? Or without knowing, do you think too
much about others? In your confusion you may
sense that your destiny is connected to their
destiny, that both fortune and misfortune are
secret societies, so secret that unknowingly you are
members of both, and that somewhere you shelter a
voice you do not hear which says:

So long as there is misery, you are not rich,
So long as there is suffering, you are not happy,
So long as there are prisons, you are not free.'

Chris Marker (*Le Joli Mai*)

Contents

Acknowledgements

We wish to thank the following for allowing us permission to publish the following articles: *Le Monde* for 'The student commune' by Edgar Morin and 'Create!' by José Pierre; 'L'homme et société' (Éditions Anthropos) for 'The May movement at the Lycée Pasteur' by Y.L.; *Les temps modernes* for 'CGT 1968: Subjectivism to the rescue of the status quo' by André Barjonet; Editions Christian Bourgois for the extract from 'Stratégie et révolution en France 1968': by André Glucksmann (a complete English version appeared in the *New Left Review* No. 52). And the Action committees: Paris-Vincennes-Sorbonne for 'The Monetary Putsch'. Special thanks to Katie Furness-Lane, Paulet Cahen, Claude Angeli, Maud Mannoni and 'A' and 'F' for their help and advice.

The Events

1. Introduction

What happened in France in May 1968? The newspapers and television spoke of student demonstrations and strikes, riots, civil disorder and the traditional French propensity for revolution. A few days before, bemoaning the economic stagnation of Britain, they held up France as a shining example of what could be accomplished by a Government 'with guts' and a population willing to work hard. Clearly they have missed the point. To tell us what really happened, a group of French writers, journalists, trade unionists, teachers and students have prepared this volume. They all feel that the events of last May in France marked both a decisive break with the past and heralded the beginning of a new political era. The movement of students and workers that suddenly emerged during the May events destroyed the widely-shared assumption that in a complex and modern society, with its many built-in safety valves, its abundance of consumer goods and increase in leisure time, a revolution is impossible. But the movement did not stop there. It also unveiled possible solutions to the problems of democracy, democratic control, and the purpose and meaning of work which plague all industrial societies. Hitherto these solutions have been discussed in the abstract; the May events put them to the test for the first time.

All of the contributors to this volume feel that if May was not a fully-fledged revolution, it was, at the very least, 'a dress rehearsal – what the sociologist would call a pre-revolutionary situation'. The May events herald profound changes not only in who exerts power but how power is to be exerted and for what ends. The institutions of contemporary society, from primary schools to factories, universities and cultural centres, were forced to take a long hard look at what they were doing and the purposes which governed their activities. The very ideas that society held to be self-evident, like the need for hierarchical rule, the need for personal initiative, the need for an economic system based on monetary gain, etc., will never be self-evident again to the French population. When the contributors to this volume speak of society trembling and established order on the verge of collapse, they mean that by the end of May France was on the threshold of something new – a vast experiment in building a new kind of society with new institutions and ideas. If France is an example of an advanced industrial society, the May movement, the questions and problems it raised, the perspectives it opened, and an account of what happened from the time of the first demonstrations on 3 May until the demonstration of 1 June is extremely important to all other advanced industrial societies. An old nineteenth-century adage ran: 'When France has a cold, all of Europe sneezes.' One of our purposes in this volume is to describe the nature of this cold and to say to what extent it is a passing seasonal illness or likely to reach the proportions of an epidemic.

All the writers of the present volume share a series of assumptions. One of the most important, and least clear for the British reader, is that the May events completely altered the way we look at ourselves, that is, how a society goes about selecting its cultural values, seeks to distribute them amongst its peoples, and enforces and endeavours to maintain that distribution. For André Jeanson May meant seriously rethinking the purpose of trade unionism in modern society. For André Barjonet it raised the need to consider new forms of political action. For the lycée pupils it destroyed the notion that education is neutral. For Maud Mannoni it showed that the problem of adjusting people to society could probably be better solved by adjusting society to people. To José Pierre it showed that people must rethink everything taken for granted in their daily lives and find some way of restoring creativity to their daily tasks. To the average Frenchman caught in the events, May was a time when all his ordinary landmarks were swept aside and he was called to build new ones collectively, discover new forms of human relationships and think about his urban and industrial environment as he never had before. During May an interesting inversion took place. What was once assumed was questioned, and what was once impossible became feasible. Many of contemporary society's illusions about how it works were dispelled. Our societies maintain that they have the ability to absorb and integrate all of their disparate elements because ultimately everyone accepts the same norms and values or the rule of a social elite invested with the power to impose these norms and values and translate them into rules, regulations and laws. These rules and laws derived their cogency from the fact that they both described and compelled. The May events revealed just how great this compulsion was, how subtle the techniques used to secure compliance had been, and the lengths to which a modern society was willing to go to impose its will. May saw savagery in the name of freedom and butchery in the name of maintaining traditional liberal values. This revelation has destroyed these many cherished illusions.

It is true that May was destructive. But it was not physically destructive: when the Left Bank of Paris was evacuated by the police after 13 May the crime rate dropped considerably. During the worst of the riots not one shop was looted and not one shop window broken by the demonstrators. Its destruction was both constructive and educative. May showed that contemporary society, far from living up to its chosen image of a monolithic machine, subject to no more than short periodic breakdowns to be cured by legislation and Government decrees, was extremely vulnerable where and when it least expected. The system received its rudest shock when the first to reject its fondly held premises were those who supposedly benefited most from its rules and those responsible for instilling these norms by means of education and the mass media. Once recovered from the initial trauma of its own mortality, the regime stripped off its mask. It first attacked the 'irresponsibility' of the movement, crudely in the words of Georges Pompidou, the then Prime Minister, as the *pègre* (scum), and more elegantly in the words of some academics, as 'generational conflict' accompanied by the traditional irresponsibility of youth, the unintegrated sowers of wild oats with too much time on their hands, too much money in their pockets, who derived their inspiration from a group of over-intellectualized middle-class pundits trying to enact their own true version of the great proletarian revolution when the proletariat no longer existed.

From the Gaullists to the PCF (Communist party) leaders chastised students and young workers for their refusal to make the traditional demands of the consumer in the traditional way. When they discovered to their horror that their ideological presuppositions were not accepted and inadequate to the task, they resorted to less subtle means of persuasion.

May not only taught people about how their society functioned; it also changed the way in which we ask questions about ourselves and our societies. The question of how much we choose was discarded. Instead people asked questions about *how* and *why* we choose, or in the language of the contributers to this volume, *qualitative* rather than *quantitative* questions. What is the sense of working, they asked? What is the satisfaction gained in owning a particular good? What is the sense of accumulating? What is the purpose of possessing? By raising these questions and making new demands, the very framework within which contemporary society allows us to choose was challenged. When the normal system of political bartering, the basic ideas underpinning a social system and what it sets out to do are challenged, what can be more revolutionary?

May also asked a series of more complicated questions. We have invented social sciences, as René Lourau points out, to tell us about ourselves. Yet our social sciences have also fallen far short of the mark. They could not predict the explosion. In fact, one week before the occupation of the Sorbonne by the students, an American political scientist published a study in which he claimed that France was one of the two most 'stable' countries in the world. Moreover, social sciences hardly raise the question of quality. Some writers in the social sciences have reached the point where they admit that there must clearly be reasons why a certain range of choice is allowed and enforced and why people sometimes appear to be irrational in the light of established values. But they fail to go on to discuss the subversive implications of such statements. The reason they stop at this point is that they do not question the established system of values. Indeed, social sciences, rather than dealing with these problems as they should, tend to base their research and methods on the view that certain ideas, values and patterns of behaviour are just sheer commonsense. How very convenient for some people that these values and patterns of behaviour coincide with the norms enforced by contemporary society!

During May it was no accident that these questions of purpose and value, banished for so long to the slagheap of 'private opinions' and 'personal views', were most frequently asked by those rigorously schooled in the quantitative disciplines, supposedly the new knights-in-white-armour of a technologically advanced society: technicians, engineers, scientists, social scientists and particularly students revolting against what Edgar Morin calls the 'disease of the questionnaire'. Their *livres de combat* were written by those who dealt with qualitative problems: like Paul Nizan, who was concerned with bankruptcy and the purposelessness of an increasingly absurd society; Wilhelm Reich, who dealt with the relation between individual and social oppression; Henri Lefebvre, who wrote about the exploitation found in daily life which is accepted as 'inevitable' and as 'commonsense', and surrealist writers who exaggerated the sheer waste and folly of a rampant disorganized urban environment that pretends to be rational, reasonable, etc.

That France was on the verge of a revolution, that immense changes in the way French society looked at itself occurred in a very short period, and the fact that these changes were beyond the understanding of those organizations like the PCF (Communist party) the FGDS (Federation of the Left) are the points stressed in this volume. For the most part what we say is descriptive. We describe what happened, how the movement developed in the schools, the universities, the factories, the professions and the arts, how people acted and what form their action took. Why were these questions first asked in France? Why did the May event happen? Why were they initiated by what Morin calls 'daddy's little darlings'? Finally why did the movement not succeed? These are the questions I want to raise here.

Before I approach these problems, it is necessary to clear up some widely held misconceptions about modern France. French society has recently been taken as an example of a modern and efficient consumer society. Writers have stressed her rapid development, her ability to change, the advances made by French management, the efficiency of the French work force and French administration. These statements are only partially true. France is both highly developed and also very much underdeveloped. France is clearly one of the most industrially advanced countries in Europe, having made use of the most up-to-date industrial and managerial innovations. But these innovations have not been widely adopted. They have never penetrated beyond a few leading firms. Not only is France still one of the least urbanized countries in Western Europe but she has yet to develop the large enterprises and financial markets characteristic of an intensive economy. The Gaullists have taken steps in this direction but, as we will see, they have been blocked by their own followers. Merging small enterprises has been strenuously resisted by the CNPF (the French Confederation of Industries) largely dominated by relatively small provincial interests. The attempt to turn Paris into a banking centre to rival the City of London has met with no more than the suspicion of a French bourgeoisie which prefers hoarding gold bars and investing in property to buying shares and bonds. In recent years, France has built some of the most modern urban industrial complexes in the Paris region, in Rennes, Grenoble, etc., whilst also maintaining a large backward rural and small-town population with a surprisingly large political influence. France has pioneered the most successful administrative and planning system in Europe, the *Commissariat au Plan*, a range of associated and subsidiary agencies for development and research, an extremely efficient informal network between private industry and the Government, and State financial and advisory services which to many foreign industrialists and social scientists are the hallmark of the modern industrial state; whilst alongside one finds a weakened but still vigorous political system, out of touch with modern developments and requirements, still living in the nineteenth century. France has some of the most proficient technological institutions in the world in the *grandes écoles* preparing administrators, civil servants, managers and technologists alongside one of the most archaic university systems, churning out increasing numbers of disillusioned graduates whose qualifications are irrelevant to social needs. In the eyes of many European industrialists and planners from Franz-Josef Strauss in Germany to Barbara Castle in Britain, France is the country which has most nearly perfected the ideal administrative system. Since coming to power in 1958, the Gaullist regime has streamlined the administration, removed parliamentary blocks to efficiency and clearly delineated responsibility. Yet this supposedly efficient system depended on the acquiescence of a large traditional middle class more interested in small immediate profits and speculation than in planning for the future and long-term industrial expansion.

The May events themselves only add to our list of paradoxes. Contrary to the statements of Raymond Marcellin, the Minister of the Interior, the events were not 'engineered'. Contrary to expectations, neither the PCF nor any other organization based on the manual working class was behind the movement. The events were precipitated by an unexpected combination of groups and organizations led by university students, lycée pupils, their teachers, technicians, engineers, white-collar workers, artists, and professional workers catalysed by the young – supposedly the most pampered, politically apathetic and highly-refined product of the modern consumers' society. Nor was the May confrontation a traditional confrontation: the events were not planned by any single organization; the organized political parties of the opposition, the PCF, the FGDS and the PSU (Left-wing Socialist party) had no inkling of what was happening during the first two weeks of May. They were as fully stunned as the Gaullists by the mounting crescendo of events around them. Nor was the movement led by a vanguard or an elite, the groups of conspirators rising from the depths and the foreign agents that M. Marcellin and the head of the

Parisian police, M. Grimaud, seemed to see everywhere. Finally the sit-in strikes and factory occupations that spread across France after 13 May until they involved over ten million workers were very different from the strike movement of 1936, as both André Jeanson and André Barjonet point out. The strikers, unlike those of 1936, were clearly dissatisfied with the bread-and-butter concessions granted by the Government and the CNPF. To get the strikers to return to work took all the available skill of an alliance of convenience between the Government and the powerful CGT (the Communist-dominated trade-union federation). The strike movement itself, despite proddings from Left and Right, a hostile press, and radio was not finally broken until the end of June. How can we begin to understand these paradoxes?

First of all France has changed enormously since the War. In 1945 France was still a rural country with over 35 per cent of her population directly employed on the land. Her industrial sector was small and concentrated in a very few areas. She was largely dominated by a small-town bourgeoisie. Yet from 1945 to 1966 the percentage of people employed in agriculture declined from 35 per cent to under 15 per cent, a drop greater than any recorded in a comparable period of any Western country in the throes of industrialization. France became an industrial country almost overnight and was changed beyond recognition. She has also undergone a political revolution, the Gaullist *coup d'état* of 1958, the purpose of which was to solidify the great economic gains made during the 1950s for the middle class and to give France the kind of efficient political system that went along with her new aims.

These aims themselves have been fostered by something the French have called rational or indicative planning. Planning became the official ideology of her industrial expansion. Economic planning was supposed to be the definitive solution to all the political problems which hounded France in the past. The general view was that France had been politically unstable because not enough care was taken in making decisions. Planning would expand the economy, make available a greater number of consumers' goods and thereby lessen tension. If the economy were planned, the heads of the *Commissariat au Plan* emphasized time and time again to allay the fears of the small businessmen, politics would cease to be contentious and violent. Hence planning assumed that political stability, social satisfaction *and* the modern industrial state's crying need for stable markets and a pliant labour force could be married successfully. In practice things never worked out this way.

Planning is less than useful as a means to decide what is good for a society as a whole. Planning can no more than indicate 'how to' once 'what one wants to do' has been decided. But 'what one wants to do' is the essence of politics. In France, the planners glossed over this problem with the assumption that value and social utility were determined by some inexorable, indeed metaphysical, laws of natural progress. That is, they stated that people do not and cannot decide what they want; only the 'market' can. In the cold light of day, planning required not only the effective neutralization of the trade unions, but was controlled by a meritocracy from which trade unionists were excluded. Under the planning system, the State occupied a role closely aligned to the new industrialists. Amongst its many duties, it had to guarantee and guide investment, which the private sector could no longer do, provide those services and social measures to maintain, equip and train a modern labour force, assure the means of enforcing these policies as well as a network of educational and cultural facilities required by the modern industrial society. The State readily made use of its immense financial powers and of the large nationalized sector to secure expansion, stability, keep down wages and buttress the private sector. But the Fourth Republic did this badly. It was open to too much influence from those opposed to these changes. For the industrialists and the new generation of managers and planners, the old Gaullist theory, enunciated as early as 1944, of an association between capital and labour was not only a useful slogan to describe their aims but Gaullism was a movement in which they could actively take part. By stressing the need to rejuvenate the 'outmoded and stultified political institutions' of the Fourth Republic, Gaullism paraphrased their ideas about bringing the administrators to power. General de Gaulle's ambiguous rhetoric not only complemented the day-to-day work of the new technocrats labouring behind the scenes like Jacques Chirac and Jacques Foccart but also appealed to the traditional middle class brought up on the profit motive, notions of strict economy and the patriarchal State. This strange combination of the old and the new brought de Gaulle to power in 1958 and his ability to manoeuvre between these camps kept him in power.

Economically and *socially*, the post-1958 Gaullist governments have depended upon the close cooperation between the new industrial sector and government administrators. But *institutionally* and *politically*, Gaullism has depended upon the traditional French middle class. By appealing to continuity, order and tradition, Gaullism secured the support of the traditional middle class and by window-dressing its major decisions with a mask of rhetoric, and in periods of crisis, like the Algerian War, pointing out that the alternative to Gaullism was chaos or the 'totalitarian danger' from the Left, the Gaullists put the seal to an alliance of mutual convenience between two very different groups with very different ambitions.

Gaullism's attraction and power have been based upon a shot-gun marriage. What was the rule of the expert to one group was the rule of tradition and stability to the other. To maintain its alliance, Gaullism tried to make every social and political institution respond to each partner. These institutions were designed to smother the gaping contradiction between the integrated economy sought by the planners and the liberal economics and liberal State espoused by the traditional middle class.

The university was the hothouse of these contradictions. On the one hand, the planners envisaged a revamped university as the training centre for a new generation of scientific managers and demanded it be equipped with a modern curriculum and research facilities. People like Marc Zamansky, the Dean of the Science Faculty in Paris, and Rector Capelle called for a technologically-based university system. On the other hand, the traditional middle class saw the university as a kind of 'finishing school' where it was not vital to spend vast sums of money on equipment or on revising the classical liberal arts education given by university faculties.

After much pressure from the planners, the secondary-school system was made more vocational. As part of the reform the *baccalauréat* (combination of leaving certificate and entrance examination to university) was slightly changed. But because funds were earmarked for the French nuclear deterrent, to satisfy the vanity of the traditional middle class, there was no provision for financing the reforms and by 1968 the lycée system was in a state of disorganization.

In the eyes of the planners, the traditional notion of representative democracy was outmoded and inefficient and called for changes either through the direct representation of interest groups or by strengthening the hand of the executive and administration. But in the eyes of the traditional middle class Parliament guaranteed a tried and tested system of compromise and bargaining. The Gaullist compromise was to maintain the parliamentary system but with greatly reduced powers.

In its prime the Gaullist State succeeded in discrediting the parliamentary democracy of the Fourth Republic and, more importantly, converted the Communist and Socialist opposition from an opposition that challenged the legitimacy of a capitalist society into a 'loyal and official opposition'. These parties never challenged the basic assumptions of the planners. They merely demanded that the benefits of the consumer society be more widely distributed. They never questioned what was meant by a higher rate of growth and increased productivity. Their trade unions bargained for wages and never considered the question of increasing their role in running their factories and workshops. Because they gave up the idea of changing society, they were geared to assuring peaceful bargaining over wages and conditions in the factory. Whether intentionally or not, the result was that power was kept out of the hands of the rank-and-file unionists to an extent greater than in most other European countries. It is little wonder that trade-union membership has declined since the war, that trade unions have found it difficult to enroll young workers and that France has one of the lowest rates of trade-union membership in Europe (only 20 per cent against 48 per cent in Britain and 35 per cent in Germany). But so long as Gaullism maintained a tolerably high rate of growth, the trade-union leaders were reasonably satisfied and the ordinary worker seemingly apathetic. One of the assumptions of this volume is that the traditional opposition ceased to oppose the values of the established political system. It worked within the system and accepted the reforms initiated by the Gaullist regime.

One should not lose sight of the fact that the Gaullist state clearly failed to satisfy the immediate bread-and-butter demands of the great majority of manual workers. Except in the great strikes of 1947 they have not been able to coordinate their actions and in the private sector have been little problem to management.

But the new groups we have mentioned, technicians, white-collar workers, students and those working in the arts and communications could not be satisfied within the framework of the consumer's society. They refused to accept its basic assumption that happiness can be gained by consuming an increasing variety and quantity of goods: not only cars and fridges but books, paintings, *objets d'art*, cinema and theatre. 'Commodities are the opium of the people', they declared throwing down the gauntlet in May. These groups were the first to criticize and the first to act. They constituted a new kind of opposition that did not accept the rules of the game and that challenged every assumption and institution of the modern state. Paradoxically, they are well paid, have good financial prospects and the cultural opportunities about which the manual working class dreams. Why should they have been in the vanguard of a revolutionary movement?

Marx once wrote that those who lead a revolutionary movement and those who spark off a revolutionary situation are not the most exploited, the poorest and most uncertain about what the future holds in store for them. The 'catalysers' are those who are the most aware of the contradictions of their society and those who through their daily experience of these contradictions are spurred to action.

It may appear that I am now saying that the May events were

made by the students and the workers in the advanced industries. This is far from the case. In this volume we argue that they were only the pacesetters. Why they acted and why the traditional opposition did not act is what I want to explain. André Barjonet goes to great lengths to absolve the PCF and the CGT of being traitors to their past. People act as they do because of the way they see the world around them. As Maud Mannoni states, every group has a view of the world and tries to act in accordance with that view. A point which takes some explaining is that the PCF and the CGT both acted rationally in terms of the way they saw the world around them and in terms of their aims.

To make this clearer I will show how their views arose from the way they understood their social, cultural and political background. Each of the groups I have discussed is rooted in a different historical tradition or a different phase of industrial, economic and social development. They each have their own languages, aims and experiences. To answer the question posed above I will first highlight these phases and then show how French society is a bizarre combination of these different traditions and developments.

The workshop and the urbanizing phase

The workshop phase is the first sign of industrial development. In most European countries it occurred at the beginning of the nineteenth century. In France it occurred somewhat later and in many areas still persists. It is marked by the rise of the individual entrepreneur, like those celebrated by Mrs Gaskell in *North and South*. It is governed by a *laissez-faire* state that does away with the shackles of feudalism and protects the entrepreneur's economic interests by allowing scope for his dealings. Such a society is dominated by the idea that hard labour and the suffering it embraced are moral necessities, whilst enjoyment, called idleness by the nineteenth-century industrialists, was not a right but only a fruit of one's labour. That very few people were in a position to savour these fruits was no longer a moral question in their eyes. Gone indeed were the days when, as Carlyle observed, work and enjoyment were indistinguishable. England was the only country where this middle class actually came to power. Wielding power it could easily make concessions and absorb the challenge of the large-scale industrialists which developed after 1860. But in France this middle class not only did not gain power but was challenged by the new industrialists before it could make concessions. Whereas the small entrepreneur could easily be absorbed in Britain, he was still spreading his net from one agrarian community to another in France as late as 1910. In those areas of France, particularly the centre and the south, still untouched by mechanization, the small entrepreneur retains his importance. Incapable of understanding the workings of a modern industrial system, incapable of understanding trade unionism, incapable of forming a permanent alliance with the large-scale industrialists, he has remained an extremely potent political force on his own and the key to the control of many middle-sized market towns. The fact that France never really industrialized during the nineteenth century and that where she did industrialize she did so haphazardly led to the continued strength of a middle class that all but disappeared in Britain before 1914. With its beliefs in a limited state, localism, self-reliance supplemented by opposition to anything new and a fierce and intense nationalism, this middle class has not only been unyielding in its opposition towards trade unionism but equally adamant in its opposition to industrialization and a national economy. Its aims are framed through Catholicism and a celebration of France's past glories. Where industry has made inroads its reaction has been strong and one Right-wing movement after another has taken root. In those areas still unscarred by factories and factory farming, the remnants of the Catholic party, the MRP, and the *indépendants* are not easily dislodged.

Manufactured goods are produced by an artisan class labouring in small workshops usually close to their living quarters. Except in some mines and the rare textile mill, an artisan craftsman fashioned the goods from the initial to the final stages of production. This gave him a feeling of accomplishment, control and pride. But the rhythm and pace of his labour, the design and use of what he produced were dictated by a capricious market rather than by his own creative will. Paradoxically the artisan, particularly in industries built on moderately large workshops, had to fight to work and when he found work, fight to find release from long hours and onerous conditions. The pace and rhythm of his life away from work were equally beyond his control. He was more than financially dependent on his boss. Work in close proximity to the entrepreneur and continued pride in craftsmanship encouraged his adopting the values upheld by the entrepreneur, particularly in France where the battle to free industry from constraints was never quite won. The artisan aped middle-class values: 'self-help', 'self-improvement', and 'robust individualism'. His values and loyalties clearly contradicted his immediate economic needs. Yet in the workshop culture the questions he asked were limited to the universe of craftsmanship, a dream of the old guilds and organizations and were never more than the respectable and meticulously anti-political trade unions 'working through proper channels' and upholding law and order. His idea of liberation was not to take over society but to be integrated into society.

But in France there was no valid law and order to uphold. The artisan became the foot-soldier in the early middle-class battles for economic and political enfranchisement. Whereas the wish for social integration in England led to his appending himself to middle-class reform movements, in France he was forced to be a revolutionary first in the name of the middle class and then, through the logic of the battle, in his own name. In 1848 and 1871 chaos forced a revolution upon the artisan. Early French trade unionism reflected these paradoxes. Its tone was revolutionary but its intent conservative. It was radical in action but surprisingly limited in the demands it put forward. When the workshop culture was challenged by mechanization the artisan combined with his entrepreneur to defend its values. When we think of the immense social atomization in French society we see it has occurred because this group has not disappeared. In his narrowly defined world which dreamt of a past and not of a future the artisan evolved towards the Right. A class that was moderate in its demands in Britain was forced into a bizarre revolutionary-cum-reactionary stance in France. The May events only hardened its reactionary tendencies.

The mechanical phase or the division of labour

The mechanical phase started in the late nineteenth century and continued well into the twentieth in most European countries. Again it was marked by a complete transformation of institutions and values in those countries like Britain and Germany where it occurred rapidly or most profoundly. It was marked by the division of labour resulting from the introduction of mass production and assembly lines, a great increase in the size of the plant, an expansion and concentration of the money market and a new organization of work in the plant. It led to increased intervention by the State to buttress financial markets and in some instances to guide investment and run certain basic industries as general services. Its hallmark was specialization and the need to organize human resources by ranking and grading them according to 'skills'. A national system of education which both transmitted these skills without upsetting the social balance and inculcated pupils with the need to maintain the new society spread quickly from one European country to another. But in France the new industrial system was introduced relatively late and never achieved the pre-eminence characteristic of Germany and Britain. France was still agrarian by the 1930s and the new industrial system made little headway against the older craftsman and workshop tradition.

The middle class was made up of entrepreneurs, managers, civil servants and the professional groups dependent upon them. Whereas the smaller entrepreneur stressed localism and the *laissez-faire* State, the new industrial class was imbued with nationalism and attacked Catholicism. The State, a highly polished machine, guaranteeing their economic system, their foreign markets, their colonies and charged with inculcating their values was deified. To read the prose of the *Radicaux* at the turn of the century lauding the State and attacking the bastions of religion in the name of Reason and Science indicates the power of these feelings. In France the intensity was all the greater because the new industrialists were isolated, without a hope of obtaining power in their own right. Where mechanization was most widespread, as in the United States, it bred a society which could widely distribute its goods. Where it penetrated deepest, as in Britain, it opened the way for compromise between the workshop and industrial middle classes. But outside a few urban areas, France never reached this stage.

The industrial middle-class view of the world was much less restricted than that held by the early entrepreneurs. It was still largely based on the idea of individual initiative, competence and private capital accumulation – what one might call the small shopkeeper mentality. But a more complex industrial set-up laced its views with the idea of a strictly defined hierarchy and a tolerance of unionism so long as trade unions controlled their members. As their investments were in the primary sector, they were hostile to State 'intervention', and in more recent times, to nationalization of such basic industries as metals, transport and public utilities. They believed in State intervention so long as it contributed towards easing their burden. It ought to provide the education necessary to perpetuate an elite – hence the small university – the education necessary to perpetuate their values and the provision of those social services which industry could not afford or would not provide. Hard pressed by the small entrepreneur and faced with a need to compromise their principles to obtain a modicum of power, the French industrialists reacted more violently towards trade unionism than their British counterparts, were more adamant about restricting the power of the State and ready to go to almost any ends to prevent compromise. The CNPF (French Confederation of Industry) has remained their spokesman, refusing to negotiate with trade unions and refusing to entertain the idea that trade-union meetings could be held on factory premises. Their attitude not only made a genuine liberal government impossible but as soon as a Left-wing Government came to power the industrialists went scurrying for protection to the small entrepreneur and rural France. Together with the small entrepreneurs they form the backbone of the French middle class whose frustrations and intolerance have guaranteed the instability of almost every

French Government. Reform is equated to Communism and violent revolution is seen at every corner. To them the May events were the classic chamber of horrors, the demon working class was unleashed by traitors to their own class encouraged by the absurd Gaullist reforms. Incorporated against their will into the Gaullist movement, they are now campaigning vigorously to speed the repression and go back on the wage rises and other concessions won by the trade unionists during May. Jean-Pierre Vigier shows how this anomalous middle class is shaking the Gaullist movement to its foundations, willing to defend its Liberal values to the last drop of its opponent's blood.

The manual working class was very different socially, culturally and politically from the artisan. Where the artisan totally manufactured his goods in a small workshop, the manual worker produced a component, with the aid of a machine, in an enlarged factory and was judged not by the product but by how well he adjusted to the machinery he operated or which controlled his labour. He had contact neither with the entrepreneur nor with those who used the component he produced in some later stage of production. The divorce between his labour and his creativity was complete. In that sense work was usually drained of interest. His interest centred on getting away from work. To escape from its discipline which robbed half his waking hours of purpose there were two possible routes. First, by escaping into leisure, second by finding satisfaction and gratification through buying and possessing goods and such labour-saving devices which, in fact, either allowed women to join the work force or were a compensation for the fatigue of work. His idea of liberation was through amassing what his society thought was valuable – namely goods. Unable to see his society from its factory floors to the councils of state and cultural values as a whole, he never understood the relation between work and non-work. His sole concern was escape from the discipline of the machine and the factory which perpetually defined him as a child and divested him of the elementary right to decide what he wanted to do and how it could be done.

Because of the way he viewed the world, his social demands were limited to increasing his buying power, his leisure time and to seeking improvements in working conditions in the factory. The idea of taking over the factory or replacing factory discipline by collective decision never came from within the manual working class, only from outside and/or through an economic collapse. But even his limited *quantitative* demands called for a far-reaching organization and direct intervention in politics. These demands went beyond what a factory or large company was willing to offer. They went beyond what pressure through progressive middle-class organizations could offer. Day-to-day concerns, like security of work, shorter hours, better working conditions, and the right to bargain for these demands required national organizations.

In the first instance large craft federations and later, in some cases, industry-wide trade unions were organized. In most countries they eventually organized the majority of the manual working class. At the same time, the working-class political party emerged. But aside from putting forward quantitative claims and defending trade-union rights, they never departed from the political rules of the game. The idea of organizing groups of revolutionary activists had no support at all. The idea that the party should be democratically organized ran up against the need to work efficiently. To work efficiently within the terms of the system required a hierarchical organization. The idea of Revolution was raised only during the early years of the movement's growth and was only resurrected in times of political or structural collapse.

In France the vast majority of the working class fit into this category. Their trade unions are the CGT, closely affiliated to the Communist party and the CGT-FO, a much smaller federation traditionally close to the Socialist movement. Although they never departed from the ideology mentioned above they have acted somewhat differently. Because they have remained small, because the manual working class never accounted for more than 30 per cent of the population, they were never able to obtain the rights and recognition of British trade unionism. Even though their claims were no more than quantitative claims the spirit of revolt was kept alive because they had never been able to secure the most minimal demands.

31

Surrounded by enemies on all sides, French trade unionism never accepted middle-class norms to the extent they were accepted in Britain. It formed its own cultural values and remained stubbornly independent, critical and totally un-deferential. André Barjonet and other contributors to this volume stress the fact that in normal times the political organizations representing the manual working class were reformist. Indeed, the PCF was satisfied with an advisory role in the Popular Front Government of 1936 and a minor role in the 1945 Government. When it came to a choice between supporting striking workers and remaining in the Government, the party tried to maintain its ministerial positions. In both 1936 and 1947 the party attempted to stifle the strike movements. Its rationale was that one could not be aggressive to the extent that one endangered the party. But the problem they never solved, and indeed, never spelled out, was that if one did not risk the party organization then one did not fundamentally challenge the capitalist regime. In opposition the PCF plays an unconstructive negative role. Not only does it not draw up a strategy comprised of revolutionary demands, it stifles these demands, for the reason that demands like those for democratic planning proposed by the CGT in the 1950s would upset the balance of power between the party and the trade union, or those like workers' control would mean reorganizing the party.

The PCF is governed by a number of conflicting purposes. It is supposed to be a revolutionary party, the representative of the manual working class. But the manual working class, as we have seen, is not revolutionary in a permanent sense. It is supposed to put forward their immediate demands and has organized itself in a hierarchical and ponderously bureaucratic fashion to do this efficiently. Yet this form of organization defies its revolutionary vocation. Its position is complicated by another factor. Since the time when the Socialist movement split in 1920 into the present-day PCF and the SFIO, both organizations have been engaged in a 'battle for the delivery of the goods'. After some preliminary skirmishes, the SFIO emerged to take a moderate line and the PCF an exaggerated hard line to emphasize its differences from the SFIO. Why did these differences persist?

Firstly because the PCF attracted unskilled workers and the SFIO highly-skilled workers, and secondly because the SFIO slowly became more attached to a parliamentary role than one as a spokesman of the traditional working class.

Hence the answer to the question why the PCF opposed the May movement is clear: because of the structure of its clientele and the way they looked at the world, the party could not be revolutionary unless it played an educative role channelling every day-to-day demand into a demand that challenged the basis of capitalist society. This meant that it had to be more than a normal political party. But it never faced up to this problem. It was never more than an organization to defend the working class. Indeed, it never organized offensive actions because its structure was only suited to the defence of existing interests. Every offensive action of the working class from the sit-in occupations of 1936 to the strikes of 1947, 1966 and 1968 occurred outside and despite the PCF. Finally, the PCF reacted with extreme hostility in May because what was being challenged was the party organization itself.

But the groups the party represented were potentially revolutionary. If the way were opened for them, if the perspective were made clear, if a spark came from outside, and if they were thrust into a position where they were forced to act, the native receptivity of a genuinely revolutionary working-class culture was there. As we will see these circumstances were present during May and the PCF could not change gear.

The continuous-process or automatic phase

Most advanced industrial countries are now experiencing what technologists call the continuous-process revolution. In France it was introduced quite soon after the War and to an extent probably greater than in any other European country. As one might expect, the social and political repercussions have also been greater than elsewhere.

Continuous-process means automatic production with very little human intervention. Although this is now normal in some industries it probably cannot be universalized. But it is one of the many indications of a veritable social revolution. We are now seeing the general introduction of advanced scientific techniques into industry, not only in production itself, but more importantly in marketing, planning, distribution and organization. It is a very complex streamlining of chains of command, research, design, educative, productive and consumptive processes. Planning that we referred to above is the means of regulating, controlling and tying the bundle together. This phase requires highly-skilled producers – technicians, draughtsmen, engineers, researchers, managers, teachers, and highly 'skilled' consumers to absorb many of its latest products designed to 'fill in' leisure time: the car for travel, the television to forget about work or learn acceptable ideas, books and other cultural activities. This new stratum is well-paid because industry can now afford higher wages, and because it requires a greater distribution of goods if production is to be maintained. In that sense, a movement is under way from a society where basic needs are unfilled towards a society where some needs are over-catered for even to the point of ruining cities and polluting the air that one breathes. Not only does this new stratum respond by assuming that items once regarded as luxuries are now necessities but it is actively encouraged to do so by mass media, communications and the hard and soft sell that dominates the cityscape with neon lights, the newspapers and even the image of the good itself. As this sector has existed in France longer than most other European countries, has been consciously developed, and is, according to estimates, twice as large as a similar group in Britain, one would expect that it would play an important role. I have maintained that this sector sparked off the May revolt. If, as I have just pointed out, they achieved the dream of the manual working class, how can they be described as revolutionaries?

The worker no longer produces a product or a part of a product, but works in a team that presides over machines which do all the work. In some cases he trains people. In that case, it is a human product. Or he is planning a process where again he comes directly up against the human element. In the earlier phases the question 'for whom am I producing?' was not asked.

In the continuous-process phase the question is inescapable. What makes it positively acute is the fact that the worker is highly trained. He is taught to relate things which at first glance appear to be unrelateable. Studies show that strain at work is not physical. Greater idleness, the shorter working week, more time on one's hands is no longer 'an escape to freedom'. In his work the worker asks: what are these techniques for? Why am I planning this city when I know from what I have seen that it will soon be congested or will provide no improvement? Why the television? Why the car when it just gets me to work because there is no public transport? Why a holiday when I return and nothing will be changed? Why teach when what I am teaching is respect for authority or cramming and not knowledge which is useful? What occurs is that the worker no longer sees one segment but the entire society. First, the worker sees the entire social system as a whole, and he cannot be integrated by its commodity fetish. Secondly, his immediate demands are met and he asks what rules determine what we produce, hence his basic demands are those that society cannot answer. Meaning must be restored to human activity by activity being rehumanized and subject to human decision, and that decision must be made directly by those involved, not by obscure and distant bureaucracies. The search is for the means to escape the laws of a consumer society to reappropriate work, what José Pierre calls the 'rediscovery of creativity'.

These demands have been slow in the making. Their first echo was found in surrealism by painters suddenly aware of the commercialization of art, the fact that the artist was being turned from a person who produced what he wanted or in response to a social need into the glorified salver of the conscience of an unbeautiful world. The engineer, the white-collar worker, the draughtsmen affiliated to the CFDT (once a Catholic union whose Catholicism was a symbol of middle-class status) evolved after the war towards an extremely radical social critique which rejected the idea that wages could satisfy discontent, that trade unionism alone was enough to reform society, and that any existing political movement had the power to make needed changes. This led to the CFDT dropping its confessional status and beginning a vigorous campaign for workers' control and turning the trade-union movement into a new kind of movement that went beyond traditional trade unionism and political parties. André Jeanson's articles indicate how far the CFDT has moved and why the CGT is hostile to its position. Not only has the CFDT outflanked the CGT on its Left, but during May it detached many of its most militant sections. Throughout May it was denounced as 'nihilistic', 'anarchistic', 'middle-class rowdies', and its demands for a new society as 'vacuous' and 'empty'.

Such a change in attitude as a result of a change in social position and incorporation into the productive process can be seen in the development of the student movement. By the 1960s UNEF, the national union of students, began moving from a programme calling for reform within the university to a programme which claimed that university reform was impossible without social reform and a new political movement which contained not only trade unionists but students, young people and the mass of unorganized white-collar workers. As Edgar Morin points out, the movement had been long in the making and the May events marked its waking up to political realities and its final severance of its bonds with traditional middle-class values. Again the SNESup (National Union of Higher Education) travelled the same road. As Edgar Morin points out, the contradiction between learning techniques and critical learning led from asking 'why', to proposing alternatives and finding, if one attempted to put them in operation, that the full weight of the State was against one.

As this phase is new so are these groups, their critique and what they propose to do. But it is clear that none of the institutions of French society are capable of replying to these demands. The PCF and the SFIO have accepted the consumer's society as have the CGT and the CGT-FO. Until the Russian détente the CGT could hide its true orientation under a mask of rhetoric. But when its domestic policy finally coincided with the Soviet Union's wish for a détente at all costs, it was free to abandon its verbal critique of a capitalist society. When its social and economic planning committees drew up reports criticizing quantitative demands, they were rejected with undue haste. The people who drew up these plans, Pierre Le Brun and André Barjonet, were slowly forced out of the CGT. When the engineering section of the CGT called upon the trade-union central committee to take a political stand during the Algerian War, it was excluded from the party. When shop stewards took up contacts with CFDT shop stewards or pushed for greater freedom of decision on the shop floor, they, too, were excluded. In many areas the CGT not only took steps to keep 'dangerous young workers' out of the trade union but forged a violent racist policy against Algerian, Turkish and Portuguese immigrants. When some of the radical clubs affiliated to the SFIO and the FGDS produced radical programmes calling for structural reform, they were quietly shoved aside. These organizations cannot but oppose these demands. It was clear from the beginning of May. Their slogan might be 'Treat reality as desire' to which the reply would come back 'Treat your desires as reality'.

Hence the new forms of opposition were only just emerging. The notion of a possible community of interest between students and these new workers, first mooted during the Algerian War, was still treated with suspicion if not outright hostility. There was no organization to unite them; only the knowledge that something had to be done. They could not work through the opposition because the opposition had ceased to be an opposition. Yet they were a small minority, less than 10 per cent, faced with incomprehension whipped into hostility by the PCF, the small peasants and agricultural labourers who should have been their allies.

I have tried to show the divisions in French society and how an alliance of the discontented was impossible. The artisans were not revolutionary. The manual workers were potentially revolutionary but their consciousness precluded their acting outside and against the system unless they were motivated from without and their organizations fought those groups that might activate them. But the political system was equally insecure. It was based on an alliance of frustration and embittered cynicism. Gaullism by 1968 had stretched its resources to the limit to maintain that alliance. But its greatest power was the inability of the opposition to unite on a programme which challenged the consumer's society and the traditional middle-class savage hostility towards change. Such a regime is viable in a divided country but should the country become more homogeneous, as France was becoming, it could not be maintained. By 1968 the political ramifications of these changes were becoming increasingly clear.

By the late 1960s something was in the air. Once France had to abandon her planning system on entering the Common Market, the economic boom came to an end. 1966 in particular saw a wave of strikes in private industry led, for the most part, by technicians and engineers. The student movement, weakened by internal fighting, appeared to be rediscovering its militancy in a campaign against the Vietnam War. But there was no reason to believe that, as in the past, the Gaullist regime could not manipulate one group against another and ride out the storm.

Firstly, the students were in the cockpit of the new changes and adjustments. The uncertainty of the university, of the staff, and the battle between liberal and technocratic values being acted out before their eyes gave their restiveness a focal point. Adult society whose first claim had been its ability to take decisions calmly, to override 'mere' differences of opinion with fact and reason underneath its technocratic and liberal window dressing, was found to be hypocritical. Any control of student activity from the banning of political discussion in universities to the segregation of sexes in lodgings was seen as a means to condition the student to hierarchical control. Knowledge in such a society is only the knowledge of techniques and 'know-how' and never the knowledge 'why' and 'for what purpose'. But for the student the list of whys became endless. Why do we study 'deviants', they asked and why not compulsive adjusters like the man who never protests, the banker and the politician? Why study the insane and not the businessman who remains calm in the face of inhuman working conditions and degrading jobs? Why not study the stockbroker who thinks of wars in terms of share prices and not those killed? Why study the habits of the poor and not the practices of the very rich? Why assume a model man and not take people as they are? Why ask questions of people rather than search for solutions with them? Why study molecules and build rockets rather than use the resources we have at hand? Each question leads to 'who decides' and 'who is excluded from deciding'. Where do decisions come from? Why should some people be excluded? What right has someone to decide who is a deviant, what is intelligence and what is a problem when these decisions and these problems must belong to society as a whole? Must we put someone in a pigeonhole merely because we have such complex economies that he must fit in somewhere? Are the number of punches on a computer card going to decide the number of possibilities open to us? From small beginnings the tension grew and exploded at what might appear to be otherwise mundane issues: an opaque announcement by a Dean, a new swimming pool at Nanterre, a new regulation or a postponed examination. The struggle that started was one that authority could not understand because it could not see the turmoil below the surface. 'When the wise man points at the moon', said a poster at the School of Oriental Studies in Paris, 'the fool looks at the finger.'

A great wave of strikes swept advanced industry in 1966. The strikes took an unprecedented form. At the Rhodiacéta plant in Besançon the engineers and technicians organized a sit-in strike, the first seen since 1936. They attempted to bring the manual workers into the movement and spent their time discussing factory organization, the relationship between their plant and the economy, consumer society and self-management. A similar movement took place at Thomson-Houston. For the first time a movement managed to override trade-union differences and the CGT hierarchy. For the first time the entire work force was involved. But the 1966 movement was soon forgotten, but only *outside* the trade-union movement and the political organizations long campaigning for workers' control. For the *cadres* it opened new perspectives.

The stop cycle, characteristic of most modern economies, was upon France at the end of 1967. The manual workers, without a strong trade-union organization, were the first to suffer. In the power struggle between the technocrats and the traditionalists, the victory was temporarily with the traditionalists, and deflation-ary measures through decrees emasculating the social security system and a wage freeze were initiated. The trade union's answer was equally traditional. They responded with no more than a twenty-four-hour strike. Significantly demonstrations, like those in Le Mans and Caen, were taken over by young workers and rapidly escalated into violent street battles. Clearly the militancy of the rank-and-file was in advance of the trade unions.

The first to suffer from these measures were young workers. Unemployment was much higher amongst the young than amongst the old. Young people not only matured biologically more quickly than their parents but in the consumer society they were considered old enough to be fully-fledged consumers. Advertisements, products, cinema and theatre were designed for them. But they were denied what were supposedly the rights that went along with these, responsibility and the possibility of choice. Youth culture put an accent on the free youth, youth running the world, youth deciding, but for the consumer society youth was an apprenticeship in how to adjust to hierarchical control whether in the factory, the lycée, or the university. By defining youth as a privileged social group, French society only indicated its lack of privilege. The flashy youth culture it purveyed evoked an ironic response. The cowboy underwent a metamorphosis from the lone hero to the very real Vietnamese guerrilla and Che Guevara. Youth's normal propensity to reject parental values grew into a rejection of parental society with its ideas of hierarchy masking as democracy. Interestingly the 'deviants', the street gangs evolved from 'loners' to dandies to para-political organizations, that is, from outsiders to political groups. These groups of *barjots* and *blousons noirs* played the role of the restless '*classes laborieuses, classes dangereuses*' of the 1790s on the barricades of May.

Class differences were not only overridden by dress but by the loud and clear echo with which working-class youth answered the student call. The institutions designed by their own class provided no answer. The C G T spoke haughtily in church-like tones to its minions praising the discipline of Communist heroes of the past, rejecting the Cubans, refusing to take a stand in favour of the Vietcong, policing its youth organizations and telling young workers that they must follow the example of their elders unquestioningly. The urban community basking in the sham equality of amusement and the new permissiveness were no answer. Permissiveness, too, was a commodity of an adult society. Here, too, youth culture as soon as it became commercial was taken over by business enterprises. The contradiction between promise and act, between what was said and what was done was all too clear to them. Society made little sense and when it did what it said was illogical. The stages of the movement amongst urban youth are clear. First they retreated into the metaphysical introspection of the pop world highlighted by the narcissism of youth culture. This was the initial step to the next phase, to an onslaught on all that existed.

The movement also engulfed the very young even those who one would normally think of as a privileged minority. 'Look at us and what do you see', said a lycée banner, 'a tin of sardines.' The lycée is designed to prepare people for university and to pass the extremely difficult *baccalauréat*. The *baccalauréat* is such a difficult barrier that the lycées have become crammers, at best slightly humanized. The teaching staff, affiliated to the SNES and the SGEN, have little freedom to decide curriculum and little say in running the school. They are at the beck and call of the lycée inspectors, many of whom draw an added benefit from their exalted positions by not only designing the curriculum but also writing the textbooks used. And what textbooks! Mathematics and sciences are taught by emphasizing existing cultural values reinforcing the image that time is for work and man is made to consume, spend and accumulate. You disagree, say the inspectors, but it is what is wanted. But have you presented them with an alternative, came the reply. History ends with the First World War. The contemporary world is banned from the lycée because it is contentious. One might begin to find that adults disagree. History before 1914, of course, is no longer contentious. There are few people alive to say what they experienced and if there are, the past has been glamourized as such a beautiful spectacle that they too believe the colour magazines. So history is relegated to the slagheap of experience which we call facts. Discipline is strictly maintained by a corps of inspectors. Activities are forbidden not because they are dangerous in themselves but because one must learn that certain things must always be forbidden. Alphonse Daudet once commented: 'Why are children so promising and adults so stupid? It's because of education.'

I have said that these students, pupils and young workers were in the cockpit of change because they most clearly understood the transition that France was going through. For the first time in a hundred years, France's population was growing younger. Demographers and nationalists clapped their hands in utter delight. We are a young country, they say, therefore we must work hard to prepare a good future for our children. The propaganda was rammed home in every conceivable way. What future did youth see? Unemployment, discipline, bankrupt standards and a meaningless culture. The process of discovery, as José Pierre points out, vanished. In its place was a lengthy series of do's and don'ts never explained. To explain in full means opening a debate, perhaps even a general assembly, and there cannot be a debate because the hierarchy of control would be called into question as soon as the first problem was raised. What is, is because it is, said society. We know what it is to live. We know what responsibility is (said the Right). We know what the Resistance was (said the Socialists). We know when to make a Revolution (said the Communists). You must adjust to these truths. In a world where all institutions from the Government to the established Left spoke with the same voice how could they not seem to be one and the same to those who questioned what their elders called 'the past glories of France'? 'The past is the future turned upside down,' they said, 'let us put it on its feet.'

Let us not forget that France is still a large agricultural country. Although she has been urbanizing rapidly, fifteen per cent of the active population still work on the land. But they are very different from the rustic French peasant. Factory farming has been driving the small farmer off his land and depressing the income of those areas like Brittany and the Southwest where it is impossible to leave the land. The militancy of the peasant has grown over the last few years to the point where he has been discussing cooperative farming, nationalization of the land, dispossessing the large combines and forming an alliance with the industrial trade unions. From being a bulwark of conservative France, the farmer was becoming one of its chief opponents.

What happened in May? The student movement struck a responsive chord in all these sectors. Each was already prepared for some kind of action. The student movement not only hastened their response and spurred them to take action in forms they never intended but more significantly invented the very forms of action they were to take. What would normally have been a one-day strike in one sector, an isolated street demonstration in another and a riot in a third were subsumed by one large movement. As Edgar Morin points out, by engaging the police in battle the students not only won the active sympathy but also the participation of the working class. As André Jeanson states, the working class knew what it was to fight the CRS and could not but help those who not only stood up to the riot squads but dared to hold their ground. The barricades of 1968 aroused the memories of earlier barricades and of battles that might have been won, they thought, with a bit more courage. For the young, Che Guevara and the Vietnamese guerrilla were now in their midst. Guerrilla combat took place in front of the very neon signs that beckoned youth to invest its energy in the palliatives built by adult society.

Secondly, the students occupied their 'places of work', the Sorbonne-factory, built for a few thousand and housing many times that number, and Nanterre, raising its bleak towers next to poverty-encrusted council housing, competing for space with rubbish tips and the hovels of Algerian workers. The occupations became general meetings, sub-committees, planning committees, committees to contact factories, committees to distribute provisions, committees to control traffic combining into plenary sessions to raise questions about what the student should learn, how to open the universities, and how to organize a society where one form of knowledge is not privileged above all others. This was the action that moulded the response of all other sectors. This action not only catalysed discontent but gave birth to a new opposition. All the traditional demands were momentarily combined to challenge the entire society.

Why did this happen? From what I have said, each of the groups that we have examined constructed a view of reality from its daily experiences. The conditions in which they existed allowed them to see the world in different ways and elicited certain actions from them. That is, they built a structure of reality and tried to act in accordance with what they saw. For example, in the case of the manual workers it set limits on what kinds of actions they could take. But we also saw that each of these views was internally inconsistent. The fact that the manual worker seemed to be content with the consumer society did not take account of an underlying discontent of which he was not aware. He sought to overcome his discontent through accumulating goods. He reasoned: if I am deprived of the fruit of my labour, I will make up for it by buying those things of which I have been deprived: mechanical gadgets, those products which were symbolic of an easy life, those cultural frills which on the surface make one forget about the problems of work. The other way this was expressed was through what people called 'deviant' behaviour, attacks on private property, like shoplifting etc. Making wage claims was also supposed to be a panacea. But none of these actions satisfied, because the object of satisfaction was unknown. This is why the manual working class was no more than a potentially revolutionary class. But once the structure of the manual worker's world was shattered by the movement, the world he had defined for himself lost meaning. This world became 'irrational'. His desire was unleashed, unchained by its former landmarks, much in the same way that the patient under psychoanalysis, if we take up Maud Mannoni's theme, gives up the way he looks at the world and searches for a new world and a new structure for his ideas. The students and the technicians provided the formulae, explanations and actions which developed a new structure for those desires. Hence to the manual worker the idea of factory occupations became the rational thing to do. The idea of general assemblies and of political action became logical. The idea of a workers' State, of taking power into one's own hands became a necessity. What

Maud Mannoni says about the student also became true for the worker: 'The question which became paramount was that of the relationship of the subject to knowledge and truth, a question which no one can solve for anyone else, which is why the student is asking for the freedom to solve it by himself.' For a few days in May the barriers were down, and in that sense, a new political movement outside existing institutions, which ignored existing society and posited ideas about a new and better social order, took root and flourished. This is why May, far from being a brief utopia, was a revolutionary situation in the process of becoming a revolution.

In advancing towards its apotheosis the May movement confirmed several socialist theories about strategy. Lenin maintained that the theory which drives a revolution forward comes from outside the traditional movement. During May the ideology was developed by the students, technicians, etc., and adopted by the manual working class who at last had a theory which not only explained their own situation to themselves but opened new perspectives. As Lenin observed about the 1905 Revolution in Russia, the so-called spontaneity of the working class in May grew from this awareness and crystallized into the factory councils that began to spring up after 14 May. The processes of catalysis and coalescence, spelt out by Che Guevara, were also present. The movement not only united all the potential opposition but the act of unity gave birth to a new spirit and new demands. Gramsci's theory of cultural hegemony was also confirmed. Those who experienced the society's contradictions most harshly opened the way for the oppressed class who in their state of oppression were unable to see past their traditional role and demands.

The movement spread not because of the absolute numerical strength of any one particular group or faction nor because of their ability to infiltrate into the university and factories but because it responded to needs and because of the effectiveness of a chain of catalysts:

1. The students and lycée pupils who occupied their faculties and schools after the demonstration of the 13th and established the first action committees;

2. The technicians and *cadres* in the advanced industries who saw the action committees as a way of extending the movement begun in 1966 and as a means of moving towards a new form of social organization which was both industrially efficient and which was also genuinely democratic;

3. Those in the professions, law, psychology and medicine, who suddenly saw a way to harness their energy towards a social purpose rather than defending private property and adjusting people to society – like architects who with their students began to work on urban planning which was not just an excuse for lucrative property development, and planners who for years were not able to question why a certain development was necessary began to think in terms of providing adequate housing rather than a few exclusive blocks of flats which would remain empty;

4. The barren faceless dormitory communities which have mushroomed on the outskirts of Paris, comprising twenty-storey buildings where neighbours are unknown to each other, took over the idea of action committees and began to discuss problems of community culture, urbanism;

5. The Government-sponsored cultural centres designed to bring classics to the masses threw their doors open to these discussions and tried to devise theatrical and cinematographic forms in terms of people rather than trying to mould people to an art form;

6. The traditional working-class communities were forced to think in terms they never had before. With one blow the social barriers, the hierarchical barriers, that divided one culture from another collapsed and with them the time-honoured institutions and institutional procedures.

Through the action committees, as Jean Pierre Vigier points out, French society discovered a form of political organization that overrode traditional demarcations. Through the process of constant criticism and self-discovery, the new organizational forms were emerging. The process went furthest in the Loire-Atlantique and through bodies like the *22 Mars* which made all traditional political allegiances redundant. 'The difficult takes some time, the impossible just a bit longer,' said a slogan on a wall outside the Renault plant. Indeed, the secret of the movement was the way in which it constantly radicalized itself, the way each of its critiques implied 'something new' in its place and that this 'something new' could only come from such a collective return to a combination of the Greek marketplace, the psychodrama, and what psychologists, as Lourau and Mannoni point out, called *acting out* – discovering through doing or working together with others.

May was a collective drama, an experiment in human creativity, the first discovery of how to use the modern urban environment. It said that we who have discovered so much, who have invented so many techniques do not know how to use them. In the past these techniques were derived for the pleasure of the few. Now they are used to pacify. The time has come to find out how to use them and the mistakes that we will make are much more excusable, and indeed educative, than not trying. In this atmosphere of a world turned upside down on its feet, an idea was implanted that cannot be described. Its essence was not only that something was wrong but we now know how we should begin to change it. Its glimmer is irremovable.

Why did the movement fail? Why did it appear to fizzle out almost as soon as de Gaulle spoke at the end of the month? There are three reasons: firstly, the movement was halted by the PCF and the CGT; secondly, the movement was forcefully repressed by the Gaullists; and thirdly, the movement consumed itself.

The Communist party was unable to understand what was happening. In the past it had only to denounce the 'infantile Leftists' for them to miraculously disappear. But this time their following appeared to be deserting in droves. When Georges Séguy of the CGT concluded what he thought was a generous agreement, he was booed at the Renault works. But because the CGT and the PCF did not join the movement, and because they turned their trusty legions against the movement, it began to lose its impetus. The movement pushed ahead without protecting its flanks and once its impetus was lost, there was nowhere for the workers to retreat but back into the safety of the CGT's organization.

The resistance of the Communists and the hesitations of the

CGT heartened the Gaullists. By 26 May a large portion of the middle class appeared to be reconciled to a Left-wing government. At least it would be able to restore order. At that moment, it appeared that Gaullism was disintegrating and only the movement appeared to be a viable alternative. But once the Communists took a hard line against the students and strikers, the counter-revolution emerged through the CDRs (Committees for the Defence of the Republic) organized by the Right-wing Gaullists, the supporters of the old French Algeria movement and the traditional middle class. As their forays into students' bastions in Paris and the provinces, their raids on trade-union headquarters and strike-breaking activities met with success, the cry for blood increased in geometrical proportions. Old France rediscovered her feet, and guilty at her temporary lapse from sanity, called for vengeance against those who had led her astray.

But the main reason why the movement faltered was because the next step forward was not clear and lacked an organization. With only one or two exceptions the factory occupations did not evolve into factory management committees. The action committees, for all their enthusiasm, were unable to spread fast enough. The CFDT was far too weak to keep up the pressure for escalating demands within the factories. Something more than an action epitomized by the ORTF strikers circling the ORTF building in 'Operation Jericho' was needed. If the organizations of the opposition were insufficient, new ones should have emerged to take their place.

Part of the impetus behind the May movement was its rejection of the traditional notion of organization. But its attack against the idea of hierarchy and the remoteness of bureaucracies made it difficult for it to outline a new form of coordination, called by some the 'non-organizational organization', within the space of a few days. The essence of the movement's critique of contemporary society implied that a new form of decision-making was needed if their efforts were not to be dispelled like those of the Russian revolutionaries after 1923. The time was too short. The material was not available and the pressure was too great. Once the momentum was lost each of the groups that had momentarily linked its demands to the other groups that made up the movement retreated back into the parochialism of its own demands: students to demands about the university and trade unionists to wage claims. For trade unionists the situation was particularly difficult. True, the movement opened new perspectives that their organizations had never envisaged but against the counter-attack only the traditional organizations could defend them. Yet even here they resisted trade-union pressure until well into June.

A movement unsure of its aims, a movement which acts against itself and a movement which consumes itself because its forward thrust was lost is far from unique. Its first actions are uncharted and bound to be mistake-ridden. Similar mistake-ridden movements abound in history: the *sans-culottes* of 1793, the insurgents of Lyons in 1831 and the Paris commune of 1871. In all cases they represented the first battle of a new class and heralded the form the battle was to take in the future.

Hence the idea that the May movement is over and was a failure confuses the apparent with the real. Like Lyons in 1831 and Paris in 1871 May displayed the first active critique of a society and like all first critiques it was uneven, crude and even contradictory. This phenomenon of identifying an absurd world through a tentative and contradictory critique is what some historians have called primitive consciousness. Indeed, this is why André Glucksmann uses the image of Diderot's *Rameau's Nephew*. Rameau represents morbid consciousness able to discern the absurdity and irrelevancy of the pre-1789 social order. In fact, he perceives it so clearly that he can hardly understand the relevancy of his long soliloquies. His every motion is an agitated gesture, a magnification of the ills of his society whipped into hysteria. He has withdrawn first by a negation of himself and then by a negation of an intolerable world. As Rameau stripped away the idiocy of pre-Revolutionary France, so the May movement not only magnified the contradictions of twentieth-century France but went further and began to hack away at its moorings. Diderot wrote the preface to a Revolution and so the surrealists and situationists have written the preface to a new Revolution. Rameau's painful soliloquies found their equivalent in the action committee meetings, a new language and a new consciousness fighting to comprehend its own meaning and to create a world where it could exist. Once one has gone so far, there is no turning back.

What then are the lessons of the May events?

In the first place, the May movement rediscovered the essence of Revolution. For many years no one in a Western society would dare to use the term. It was erased from our vocabulary or debased by a consumer society talking about 'revolutionary new toothpaste' etc. Our social sciences assured us that Revolution was impossible. A Revolution they said was madness. Indeed, a Revolution must be collective madness because in their terms sanity means accepting things as they are. A Revolution can only be madness in the eyes of a social hierarchy which believes first and foremost in its own sanity and righteousness. When the first workers laid down their tools at Renault, the foreman said incredulously, 'You are mad.' So they were; in turning the world topsy-turvy; in refusing to accept the ordinary and in acting out the extraordinary where the drama and the play became reality and the old reality retreated back into the shadows; when the poems of Prévert long sung by children became descriptions of what they did. As their symbol they chose Jacques Roux, one of the leaders of the *sans-culottes* in 1793 and the name of his movement, the *enragés*. The students and young workers were possessed by this kind of madness, drenched in the commodity culture. They rediscovered that a Revolution changes people, creates and they must fight.

The Revolution changes people and then moulds institutions. It first propagates its Rameaus like so many seers who reverse the social order. In May the reversal was started. The commodity system which estranges man from himself and others, they said, was attacked. The pattern of hierarchy instilled through respect for age was turned upside down. As Maud Mannoni notes, youth led its elders. The movement began to replace a set of imposed values with a culture that grew directly from people's experience. To that extent, as a section of the French Psychoanalytical Association noted, the revolution was therapy. It discovered a new form of education called self-education or collective learning It spoke a new language composed of words painfully trying to catch up and reflect action.

A Revolution changes every facet of a society. Each succeeding change and critique conditions another and stimulates a new action. May attempted to capture this process and make it permanent. It was a new model Revolution because it was the first to deal with the sum and total of human relations, the first to relate problems of quantity to problems of quality and to consciously avoid the mistakes of the past.

It showed that there are no eternal values. Values are human creations. It showed that the question of how and what people decide, the relation between man and the manner in which he acts upon his environment, is the crucial question. It was a Revolution that questioned an entire culture. It showed that it was possible to make these changes in Western societies. It demonstrated that a Revolution is not only destructive but also creative. Once and for all it made the violence *implicit* in the consumer society *explicit*. It created, as Glucksmann notes, a new kind of strategy. This new strategy is its greatest contribution. Like the May Commune of 1871, it has set the mould for the new form of politics of the next generation.

Le joli mai 1871 ended in a massacre when 'petals fell like drops of blood'. In 1968 we have more subtle techniques in 'civilized' countries than killing people. We turn on the screws more efficiently and make them repress themselves.

But *le joli mai* 1968 like May 1871 is the cipher to a mysterious code known previously only as a few scattered symbols. May-the-cipher filled in the gaps and revealed the answers. Its general assemblies and action committees were not debating forums, but like their predecessors in 1793, places where people thought collectively, where they discovered themselves through others, stripped away the mask of roles and gave meaning to those mysteries of democracy, self-determination and understanding, once exhortation and marching orders whose secrets were the property of the few: the great man, the philosopher, the statesman and the scientist. May restored the notion of creativity

51

to human action. May is the new encyclopedia that Diderot could never write.

In Britain, as elsewhere, many groups have climbed on to the May band-wagon. The events of May, they claim, justify their doctrines. There are those who literally wish to create the May events from the 'red bastions' in British redbrick to the Ho Chi Minh demonstration dance. But Britain is not France and a tactic out of context is little more than a ritual. The differences between Britain and France are enormous. For example, the British working class was strong enough partially to prevent the authoritarian organization of the factory. The trade-union movement has been given the illusion of sharing power. Together with a deference to established cultural values this has nurtured the opposite of the revolutionary heritage that one finds in France. One can see this clearly in the reaction to the duplication of the red-bastioned universities. Again the advanced sector in Britain is much smaller and the *cadres* and technicians much less active. Britain also has a government which has neutralized the trade unions. Although the Labour party's original intention to build a technocratic society by an alliance between the 'new sectors' and its traditional working-class supporters has not been fulfilled, it reinforces the illusion.

The message of May is different. Certainly the British are attempting to travel the same road towards a technocratic society that the French embarked on over a decade ago, but if the basic pattern is similar – universities becoming State-managed hot-houses, the niceties of life being turned into commodities – the situation is very different and calls for a very different strategy, one which lays bare the contradictions and makes the kind of unity that one saw in France last May possible.

But what of the future in France? There are several possible outcomes. The days of traditional Gaullism are marked because of the thirst for revenge reverberating on the Right. The fragile balance between the technocrat and the traditionalist has shifted dramatically in favour of the latter and, given an unfavourable economic prognosis, no successor to de Gaulle can replaster the cracks. For many years the press has hailed the Gaullist machine for its political acumen. Will the movement not be swallowed up by the troops de Gaulle marshalled to defend the regime? Will its Quisling emerge from within? Indeed, the spark may be trivial in itself: expansion versus maintenance of the exchange rate of the franc or using the carrot or the whiplash in schools or factories. But by the end of 1969 the traditional Right may have wreaked its vengeance on its erstwhile allies. Despite elections and referenda, will we not see a new government led by the heroes of yesteryear and the most creditable spokesman of middle-class law and order, Giscard d'Estaing, backed up by the might of Massu and his paratroopers? Or will the Gaullist movement work its old magic trick and the technocrats emerge from the shadows not only to throw the Left into disarray but finally to deal a decisive blow to old France?

If the former, then those voices of Reason, strangely absent during May, will turn their pointed finger at the children of the Revolution, Rameau's nephews and nieces and, like the forsaken schoolmaster, say, look what you have done to us! Don't try to change the world, it can only get worse. Do what we did in 1958 and work for reform.

If the latter, then the whole 'incident' will have been good fun, a make-believe revolution, real living theatre and positive proof that an advanced industrial society can tolerate and contain even the largest general strike Europe has seen. The Revolution will be seen as a jolly good spectacle and perhaps we may even return to calling our youth 'delinquents'. After all, the costs will be lower.

The May–June movement ends in a question mark and the prospects, if we try to find historical precedents (a game no more useful than star-gazing), are not encouraging. The spiritual ancestors of the students and workers, the *enragés*, set out to destroy feudalism and build a cooperative society. They destroyed feudalism but only to replace it with capitalism. The *enragés* of 1968 set out to destroy capitalism and prevent the victory of a technocracy. Will they succeed in nothing more than sending one of those idols tumbling and replacing it by the gallant knights of the technocratic State? Will the destruction of the *sans culottes* be compressed into less than one year? Or will those *enfants du paradis* who carried the banner understood hitherto only by those few who read Hegel, 'We are the negation of all that is', live to solve the oldest philosophical problem of all: How to span the gap between what *is* and what *ought to be*?

August 1968

2. Chronology

The following chronology of events should be used with care. It is only a guide to help the reader visualize the events referred to by the authors in relation to other events and to show how people's view of what was possible and what was necessary grew from the mounting crescendo of activities in which they participated.

But a word of caution is necessary for another reason as well. A chronology can never be a substitute for a more rigorous analysis, especially when one is dealing with human experience and action. A chronology can be no more than a very selective list of events, in all probability abstracted from their socio–historical context. Many chronologies of the May events have already appeared. Most suffer from a peripheral account of the events. They concentrate on what is obvious to the outsider – the street demonstrations and the public speeches – rather than what the events meant to those who were involved. A chronology tends to give equal weight to all events. It deals in discreet historical time-sequences while history is experienced and constantly reinvented by the actor.

We have tried to soften these distortions in two ways. First, we have tried to steer clear of an endless list of demonstrations. A demonstration, whilst in the tradition of the accepted definition of action or of revolutionary activity, has a purpose. It is not merely a question of numbers or of violence. By concentrating on those events indicative of reforms, participation, self-management, culture, the action committees and the new forms of trade-union activities, we have tried to show the qualitative aspects of the May events, in what way they were different from other revolutions and rebellions and in what way they are indicative of the form social conflict is likely to take in other advanced industrial countries.

Secondly, for the sake of clarity, we have divided the following account into four phases: phase 1, the catalysts which led to the general strike, a survey of the immediate origins of the student and trade-union movement; phase 2, the corporative or economic struggle; phase 3, the political struggle; and phase 4, the future, the new forms of action and political organization to look out for.

For these reasons, we have omitted a precise account of the manoeuvres within the established administrative system. More importantly, a precise chronicle of what happened outside Paris is absent. All indications are that in both the universities and the factories, many of the provincial movements were as highly developed if not more highly developed than those in Paris. As much of the regional press did not function during most of May, information about these events is hard to come by. Whereas previous revolts and revolutions tended to be centred in Paris, the May events were much more decentralized. Future historians and social scientists will, no doubt, avail themselves of the information so far denied us and by doing so will probably change the picture we have of the May Revolution beyond recognition.

Prelude

Spring 1967

After the general elections in which the parties of the Left make some important gains, France is gripped by a wave of strikes in both the public and private sectors. Advanced industry, electronics, refining, etc., is particularly affected. Unofficial strikes break out at Berliet (lorry manufacturers) and Rhodiacéta (textile manufacturers) over the rest of the year. The strikes take a new form. Engineers, technicians and many white-collar workers (cadres) participate in large numbers. Founding of the

CVL (Vietnam committees in the lycées) – the first political organizations to secure membership in grammar schools. Increase in the recruiting activity of the JCR (Revolutionary Communist Youth) founded in 1966 to oppose the Communist party's 'lack of militancy'.

Summer 1967

The Government introduces a series of decrees dismantling the existing social security system and its element of participatory democracy and increases direct charges. It lowers benefits and curtails the power of consultative bodies. When asked whether these laws will be debated in Parliament, Georges Pompidou, the Prime Minister, declares: 'We will see in the spring.'

Autumn 1967

The Communist party scores some notable gains in local elections. The university term begins in absolute confusion; 1. new government reforms, theoretically in operation, are still not public; 2. the university faculties are grossly overcrowded. Paris alone has 30,000 students too many. University numbers, which increased little between 1949 and 1960 (from 135,000 to 220,000), skyrocketed to over 520,000 in 1967. The university system is divided archaically into three sections: 1. the *grandes écoles* with a restricted system of admissions, preparing the administrative and managerial elite; 2. the faculties, supposedly providing a broad and liberal education and preparing students for teaching and research (in 1967 180,000 students read arts subjects, 150,000 science, 111,000 law and social sciences, 60,000 medicine and 20,000 pharmacy). As research needs have grown, the faculties have had to assume this added burden. But given the Malthusianism of the hierarchical structure and Government restrictions on grants, they have expanded far beyond their teaching capacity; 3. the research institutes: the *Collège de France*, the *École Pratique des Hautes Études* and the CNRS (National Research Council), all financed inadequately and hierarchically governed.

The Government supports the idea of 'selection' on the British model, thus nullifying the original purpose of the *baccalauréat* giving access to the university. Staff and students protest at this proposal. Its main proponent, Marc Zamansky, Dean of the Faculty of Science in Paris, is blockaded in his office, and for the first time in modern history the police are called into the university.

At the new Arts Faculty of the University of Paris, established in 1964 at Nanterre, amid slums and waste disposal tips, as part of a plan to decentralize the university, students protest against disciplinary procedures, the concept of *in loco parentis*, courses and the lack of consultation in their subjects.

Winter 1967

A twenty-four hour strike called by the CGT (Communist-controlled trade-union federation, largely representing manual workers, organizing about 50 per cent of all unionized workers) and the CFDT (formerly a Catholic trade union, largely representing workers in advanced industries, particularly technicians and *cadres*, organizing about 25 per cent of unionized workers) is joined by students of eight Parisian lycées (grammar schools).

The Government introduces more regressive taxes whilst refusing to give compensatory rises to workers in nationalized industries.

January 1968

About 500,000 are unemployed, a large proportion of whom are young workers. An exceptionally large proportion of the unemployed are highly qualified workers: those in white-collar jobs and *cadres*. Over 3 million earn less than £50 a month for which they work an average of forty-eight hours per week. The difference between the top and bottom salaries has increased by over 40 per cent in ten years. The top 10 per cent of the population earn over seventy-five times more than the lowest tenth. The average class in a lycée numbers forty, the average class in a university between forty and fifty. Government expenditure on the nuclear deterrent is much greater than the educational budget.

A strike at the Condorcet lycée in Paris in protest against the dismissal of a student for political activities leads to the founding of a committee to defend lycée students, the CAL. The CAL establishes links with lycée teachers campaigning for educational reforms.

At Nanterre a men's residential block is occupied by women. Police are called and a riot follows. Students protest against the drawing up of a 'black list' of politically active students. *Le Monde* identifies one of the student leaders as an 'anarchist' called Daniel Cohn-Bendit.

In Caen and Le Mans violent street fighting when police attempt to break up demonstrations against unemployment. Commentators are surprised by the vehemence of young workers.

February 1968

Increasingly outflanked on its Left, its influence amongst youth declining, the Communist party adopts a more militant line on the Vietnam War to win back support in the factories, lycées, and the university. The Government intervenes in the administration of the *Cinemathèque* (the National Film Theatre) and tries to dismiss its director, Henri Langlois. The almost unanimous fury of French producers and directors against André Malraux's (the Minister of Culture) decision is successful. It leads to intense discussion about the role of culture in society.

André Philip (former Socialist minister) resigns from the presidency of the *Maisons de Jeunes* (cultural youth organizations) as a result of a dispute over the participation of young people in running the organization.

March 1968

In the university

2 March Demonstrations in Rennes and Besançon over student residential rights.

9 March Demonstrations in Nancy calling for modernization of curriculum and reduction in size of classes.

10 March UNEF (The National Union of French Students), the largest student organization with over 80,000 members, wins the right to represent Parisian students but loses a similar election in Lille. UNEF is in the midst of a double crisis, its grant from the Government cut because of its politicization of the question of university reform, and without a 'cause', like the Algerian War, it has lost its impetus and appeal. It is paralysed by factionalism and unable to take decisive action. Its main plank, that university reform can only be achieved through changing society by means of an alliance with the working class, remains a pipe dream. UNEF has lost support in Paris to apolitical groups (at the Faculties of Law, Medicine and the National Institute of Political Science) and to a right-wing organization, the FNEF (National Federation of French Students) in many places in the south.

15 March Meetings and demonstrations in Paris, Saint-Étienne, Clermont-Ferrand, Dijon and Bordeaux calling for university reform. The demonstration in Bordeaux is particularly violent.

21 March Demonstrations and meetings in Nantes to protest against police interrogating students active in the university reform movement.

22 March After the arrest of CNV leaders (National Committee for Vietnam) in Paris, an amphitheatre at the Nanterre faculty and then the administrative block is occupied by 142 students, who discuss new means to change society. They are first called the Committee of 142. Soon they will adopt the name *Mouvement du 22 Mars* (22 March Movement).

23 March The administrative block at Dijon University is

occupied in protest against disciplining of students for political activity.

26 March A meeting of the Deans of Science Faculties from many universities supports the Zamansky (Dean of the Faculty of Science in Paris) proposals for restricted entry to the university on the grounds that in financial terms it must be selective and cannot be a right.

28 March Meeting of protest at the Faculty of Science in Paris against the Zamansky proposals. Calls for a re-appraisal of the role of the university in society and rejection of the university as the training ground for technicians.

29 March The first meeting of the Movement for Action in the University, (MAU), founded by groups disturbed by UNEF's inertia, is banned by the rector of the Sorbonne, Jean Roche.

In the lycées

22 March The arrest of student anti-Vietnam war leaders arouses the protests of many Parisian lycée organizations and gives an impetus to the CALs.

23 March Student demonstration in Nice calling for freedom of political expression in the lycée

In the factories

2 March The CGT and the CFDT reject the Government's incomes policy for the public sector, claiming that the wage increases granted are less than the rise in the cost of living.

9 March A demonstration against unemployment in Nancy.

13 March Street battles in Redon (in Brittany) between police and striking workers joined, as in many recent demonstrations in the West, by peasant organizations

29 March Strike in the shipyards of Rouen.

In the communities

12 March The independent residents' association in the Government-sponsored mixed housing project at Sarcelles, near

Paris, decisively defeats the Gaullist association in the elections for a consultative assembly. Their campaign is based on communal self-government, rather than Gaullist 'participation'. Their influence spreads to Bagneux.

April 1968

In the university

19 April A student demonstration in solidarity with Rudi Dutschke, wounded by a gunman, gathers several thousand in the Latin Quarter of Paris. Other demonstrations are held around the country. But the theme is university reform.

21 April At the General Assembly of UNEF no one group is able to get its programme accepted. A motion calling for students to take the leadership in the coming confrontation between the Government and the working class is beaten. Jacques Sauvageot, from Dijon, a member of the PSU (Left-wing Socialist party) becomes acting president until problems can be resolved.

22 April Teaching staff at the Faculty of Medicine in Paris strike over working conditions and curriculum.

A demonstration organized by the UEC (Union of Communist Students) fails to attract more than 3,000.

23 April At the Nanterre faculty, dispute over the UNEF conference. The Left organizations grouped around the *22 Mars* claim that UNEF is a stale bureaucracy and that the student movement must be recast upon more immediate demands and a more rigorous social critique.

24 April A strike over lodging restrictions at the *Cité Universitaire* (University City) in Paris.

25 April Uproar at the Nanterre faculty during series of debates on the function of a university. Pierre Juquin, Communist deputy and spokesman on education, is forced to flee from meeting after not having answered questions to students' satisfaction. Laurent Schwartz, Nobel prize winner is allowed to speak only after intervention of Cohn-Bendit. He advocates the idea of university selection and rejects notion of politicizing the battle for redistribution of national resources. Only André Gorz, an editor of the *Temps Modernes*, is given a full hearing.

UNEF calls on its constituent members to consider boycotting examinations in order to secure negotiating, representational rights and university reorganization.

Nanterre students speak at Toulouse. A battle between Right- and Left-wing students. For the first time the CRS (riot police) are called in.

26 April Demonstrations against discipline and courses at Nanterre and Strasbourg. Cohn-Bendit is arrested on complaint of an FNEF leader.

In the factories

3 April Benoît Frachon, the president of the CGT, joins in the general Communist offensive against movements to the Left of the party by denouncing the CFDT as a 'pseudo-revolutionary organization'.

16 April Strike at the Berliet lorry works in Lyons joined by technicians and cadres.

24 April Large demonstration against unemployment in Toulon, part of the CGT–CFDT joint action agreements.

The textile trade-union federation calls for a strike for higher pay.

The beginning of a series of strikes in the post office for higher pay.

25 April Many strikes over the country against unemployment.

In the parties

7 April Waldeck-Rochet, the secretary of the PCF, denounces the 'adventurism' of student groups and the PSU (widely supported by students and leaders of the CFDT).

24 April Failure of a motion of censure in the National Assembly against the Government's intention to introduce commercial radio and television without first consulting Parliament.

The Catalyst

Wednesday 1 May: A Remembrance of Times Past

Traditional May Day demonstrations throughout France. For the first time in many years the Communist party is permitted to stage its traditional march across Paris. Commentators note the lack of enthusiasm.

Thursday 2 May: The Die is Cast

In the university

At Nanterre the criticism of teaching methods, course content, and university organization is intensified during the two days of the Anti-Imperialism Campaign organized by the *22 Mars*, which has by now transcended the traditional divisions between the contending groups on the Left.

Daniel Cohn-Bendit and five other students appear before the Paris law courts charged with 'verbally attacking' a UNEF leader.

In 'an unprecedented act' (*France-Soir*), Pierre Grappin, the Dean of the Nanterre faculty, closes the campus indefinitely. In his words: 'There is a strange climate in the faculty ... a very real war psychosis.'

The *22 Mars* condemns the closure, claiming that Grappin has consistently refused the dialogue offered by students and staff, and calls for a demonstration in the Sorbonne to protest at the illegal arrest of the six students.

The Rector of the Sorbonne, Jean Roche, forbids UNEF to distribute tracts calling for a boycott of examinations.

An extreme Right-wing organization, *Occident*, attacks and sets fire to the FGEL (students' union) offices in the Sorbonne.

The Communist leader, Georges Marchais, denounces the Nanterre movement: 'The pseudo-revolutionaries at Nanterre and anywhere else labour in vain, they will change nothing of historical reality.'

Humanité (Communist daily) launches a virulent press campaign against the Nanterre students whom it labels a *groupuscule* (minigroup).

At Aix, a battle between Left- and Right-wing students. At Montpellier theology students strike over curriculum.

The departmental council of Loire-Atlantique (in the west) cancels its subsidy to the UNEF branch at Nantes university because of the students' political activities and their 'meddling in affairs that do not concern them'.

Friday 3 May: The Gaullist Reflex

In the university

At Nanterre 500 CRS surround the campus blocking all roads. They search all cars and students for weapons.

At the Sorbonne, whilst Professors Henri Lefebvre, Guy Michaud and Alain Touraine plead the case of the six Nanterre students, a large meeting protesting against the closure of Nanterre takes place peacefully in the courtyard. The UEC denounce the assembled as a *groupuscule*. The gendarmerie, apparently summoned by Rector Roche, suddenly arrive to 'avoid incidents'. As the students quietly file out of the courtyard, according to *Le Monde*, they are attacked by the police with tear gas bombs. Other students arrive to defend the attacked. By the evening over 596 have been arrested. In an unprecedented move the Sorbonne and the Science Faculty are both closed.

The SNESup (National Union of University Teachers) calls a strike. UNEF calls for demonstrations for 6 May. Professor Touraine comments that 'a nonsensical university can only engender nonsensical movements'. He calls for the establishment of a critical and creative university.

Saturday 4 May: The New Politics

In a long statement the *22 Mars* denounces the Communist party for trying to separate progressive forces in the country from each other and in particular for separating the student critique of the university and society from the working-class movement. In a modern society, they claim, change can only be secured by a new political movement with a new form of political action and organization.

Sunday 5 May: Failure of the Government

The response of Alain Peyrefitte, the Minister of Education, is to call the SNESup strike 'illegal'. The result is to anger many professors not attached to SNESup. The strike spreads to the new Science faculty at Orsay where twenty professors sign a call to strike action.

With undue and unprecedented haste the courts meet on Sunday to fine and imprison seven students for their role in Friday's demonstrations.

M. Paul Delouvier, the prefect for the Paris region, bans all demonstrations.

Student demands that negotiations begin at once are not answered.

Monday 6 May: The Government and the PCF
decide upon Oppression

Due to the intervention of the CRS the demonstrations called by the students take a violent turn and escalate the call for immediate reforms into the first occupations of university centres.

In the university

Strikes and demonstrations are organized by many groups, including UNEF and SNESup, throughout the country. In Paris many thousands assemble at the Châtelet in the afternoon. To prevent them from reaching the Sorbonne, their dispersal point, the Government calls in the CRS. As the 60,000 demonstrators, made up of students, professors and some young workers, reach the Latin Quarter they are attacked by the CRS. Scores are arrested, 739 go to hospital in the most violent demonstrations seen for many years. To protect themselves the students erect the first barricades seen in Paris since 1944. Many students from the lycées join the demonstration. Many are accompanied by their parents.

The science faculties of Montpellier, Marseilles, Dijon and Grenoble join the strike. Large demonstrations take place in Grenoble, Clermont-Ferrand, Strasbourg, Rouen, Toulouse and Nantes, where a general strike is called, and in Aix.

A letter from Michel Leiris, Colette Audry etc., call upon the rector of the Sorbonne to resign.

The Minister of Education claims that the disorder was caused by 'students playing at revolution'. *Humanité* echoes his statement claiming that the students are playing into the Government's hands.

The *22 Mars* comments: 'Because students now use the methods of the most active sectors of the working class, by demystifying the authoritative structure of the university, they are radicalizing their own struggle.'

In the lycées

Michelet and Condorcet, two Parisian lycées, call meetings and strikes, as do the lycées at Montreuil and Ivry until a total of fifteen lycées in the Paris area are on strike.

In the factories

Strike at the Sud-Aviation plant in Nantes against unemployment.

The CFDT supports the student claims whilst the CGT refuses to support them.

Tuesday 7 May: Escalation in the university

In the university

The demonstrations in Paris continue into Tuesday morning. *Massacre in the Latin Quarter* headlines the newspapers. *Le Monde* blames all on the opaqueness of Roche, the Rector, and Peyrefitte, the Minister of Education, and their unwillingness to negotiate. 'Few organizations could have endured waiting so long and still maintain their equanimity,' comments Alain Geismar, the secretary of the SNESup, on staff and student demands. UNEF and SNESup draw up a joint list of demands: until imprisoned students are released, the police are pulled out of the Latin Quarter, and the faculties of Paris and Nanterre are reopened, they will remain on strike. The 25 April movement in Toulouse, founded to guarantee the right of open political discussion, battles with the police. Demonstrations in Bordeaux, Lille, Rennes and strikes in Lyons.

The *grandes écoles* in Paris go on strike in support of student demands. Many young workers join demonstrating students in Strasbourg.

In the lycées

Lycée professors (SGEN, SNES) call a strike. CAL spreads the lycée strikes in Paris to Buffon, Antony, Rodin, Turgot, St Germain-en-Laye, La Bruyère de Versailles, Pantin and Meaux until seventeen lycées in the Paris area are on strike.

In the factories

Technicians at the Sud-Aviation plant in Cannes call a strike over wages.

The post office workers strike for higher wages until Thursday.

The CFDT declares its total support for the 'just claims' of the students.

The first student appeals for support from factory workers are issued.

In the parties

After advice by François Ortoli, Jacques Foccart and Jacques Chirac, the leaders of the technocratic wing of the UNR (Gaullist party), de Gaulle tries to use the occasion as a means for achieving a technocratic reform of the university.

The PCF denounces the demonstrations as the 'acts of pampered adventurists'.

Wednesday 8 May: Towards the Alliance

In the university

20,000 demonstrate in Paris at invitation of UNEF whilst the rector discusses how to reopen the university with the Deans of its various faculties. Debates and discussions organized in various faculties led by Professors Touraine, Monod, Kastler with Sauvageot (UNEF), Geismar (SNESup) and Cohn-Bendit (*22 Mars*) participating. At the Faculty of Law in Paris, the students demand the creation of a staff–student joint committee (*comité paritaire*). The faculty decides that its only course of action is to cooperate with the students in building a new university.

A student demonstration in Marseilles is supported by workers in large numbers. The demonstrators are cheered in the streets. UNEF declares: '. . . where there are no police present there is no disorder.' Other demonstrations in Grenoble (supported by the progressive city council), Lille, Rouen, Besançon, Caen and Nantes. Jean-Paul Sartre and others declare their full support for the student movement.

In the factories

Under the theme '*L'ouest veut vivre*' ('The West wants to live'), large demonstrations are organized in the nine Western *départements* by the CGT and the CFDT. Many demonstrations in Rennes, Lorient, Brest, Le Mans, St-Brieuc and Nantes are joined by both workers and students. In Nantes discussions on how to combine student and working-class protests.

The CGT asks the Government to reopen the universities. The CFDT announces its full support of UNEF.

In the parties

The Government decides that no action is required at the moment; the situation must be allowed to 'ripen'. In a debate on social policy in the National Assembly the student question is hardly alluded to.

The UJCF (Union of Communist Youth) warns the students that they are courting disaster.

'The question of reopening the faculties of Nanterre and the Sorbonne were not even raised at today's Cabinet meeting', specifies the Minister of Information, Georges Gorse.

The first *comités d'action* (action committees) are formed. Their aim is to establish grassroots democracy outside the existing political structure and to serve as counter-institutions.

Thursday 9 May: Politicization of the Student Movement

In the university

The Rector and the deans finally decide to reopen the university. '*Official: the Faculties Reopen*', headlines *France-Soir* early in the afternoon. In expectation students begin to mill around the

Sorbonne but are informed that Peyrefitte, the Minister of Education, has vetoed Roche's decision. UNEF and the SNESup announce that the strike will go on and call for the students to occupy the Latin Quarter themselves.

At Clermont-Ferrand the students hold a meeting with trade unions to explain their actions and demands. In Lyons a joint demonstration of students and young CFDT workers takes place. In Dijon a demonstration of students is supported by the local CGT, CFDT, CGT-FO (Socialist trade union federation), the PCF, FGDS and the PSU. The Dean at Besançon withdraws charges against students active in the recent demonstrations. Several faculties are occupied in Strasbourg, Nantes and Rennes whilst demonstrations take place in Reims, Metz and Aix.

In the lycées

Many *lycéens* attend a meeting organized at the *Mutualité* in Paris where Ernest Mandel declares: 'The struggle must lead to a general struggle by the working class for a socialist revolution.' Lycées in the provinces begin to join the movement, notably in Rouen.

Cultural activities

Television technicians at the ORTF (French equivalent of the BBC) protest that the ORTF has ignored the demonstrations and that the administration is biased.

Cohn-Bendit debates with the Communist poet Louis Aragon in company with *22 Mars* militants on the nature of a cultural revolution.

Friday 10 May: University vs. Government

Refusing a dialogue, immobilized by its own indecisiveness, the Government has no option but to fall back upon the use of the CRS.

In the university and the lycées

In the morning the Nanterre faculty is reopened but is disrupted. Only administrative staff are admitted to the Sorbonne or its annexe, the Censier. In the afternoon the largest lycée demonstration ever seen gathers 5,000. They refuse to allow representatives of political parties to address them. A debate is held in open assembly about what to do. Now joined by many others they decide to debate educational reform, then march through working-class and immigrant districts to the ORTF, to the hospitals and to the Santé prison, where demonstrators are imprisoned, and finally to the Latin Quarter to occupy the Sorbonne. By late afternoon the demonstration has grown to several tens of thousands. By evening the Latin Quarter is occupied. Roche says he will negotiate with the leaders but is frustrated by the Government's attitude, the unwillingness of Louis Joxe (Minister in charge of law and order), Jacques Foccart (de Gaulle's chief adviser), and Christian Fouchet (Minister of Justice) to come to a compromise. When Peyrefitte hears Roche has been negotiating with Cohn-Bendit he goes to the Sorbonne to tell him personally not to give way to the 'rabble'. Later he confides to a former schoolmate that he had no choice in the matter, the orders came 'from the very highest quarters'. Meanwhile the demonstrators have protected themselves by building over sixty barricades. Professors Schwartz and Monod attempt to intervene, but whilst the Rector broadcasts a plea to the students, the order is given to the CRS to attack. By Saturday morning Paris has lived through the worst street fighting of the century. The CRS uses extremely noxious tear gas used in Vietnam, hundreds are wounded, hundreds arrested, at least 180 cars destroyed. The Government refuses to halt the police. Over 300 professors refuse to mark examinations in protest. Laurent Schwartz and Maurice Clavel resign from the university.

Twenty out of the thirty lycées in Paris are now on strike. 354 lycées are occupied in the rest of the country.

Nantes and Bordeaux universities are occupied. Students organize a joint meeting with the CGT and the CFDT in

Bordeaux. Demonstrations in Tours, Lille, Lyons. All lycées in Grenoble on strike.

In the factories

To protest against Government oppression the Left-wing parties, the CGT, the CFDT and the FEN (National Federation of Education) call a general strike for Monday.

Cultural activities

The ORTF is not allowed to televise the demonstrations. Radio Luxembourg (RTL) an independent radio station, is interpellated and threatened by the Government. Its reporters are harassed by the police.

Saturday 11 May: Halfway Measures

In the universities

The demonstrations at their most violent on Saturday morning. Toxic grenades are used by the CRS. People torn from their cars and from cafés and beaten. According to witnesses before a UNEF/SNESup tribunal several women raped by police in the streets. Georges Pompidou, the then Prime Minister, declares: 'I ask everyone, and in particular those who are leaders of representative student organizations, to reject the provocations of a few professional agitators and to cooperate . . . for my part, I am ready for peace . . .'

At 11 p.m. Pompidou overrules Joxe, Foccart, Peyrefitte and Fouchet, declaring that the Sorbonne will be open from Monday, the police will be withdrawn and the arrests 'looked into'. This fails to meet the minimum demands of the students and their professors.

The Faculty of law and economics in Paris establishes the first independent staff-student joint committees (*comités paritaires*) on reform and the social role of the University. In its view the hierarchical university no longer exists. In Nantes students occupy railway lines with young workers and the Faculty of science is taken over. At Clermont-Ferrand the local Federation of the Left (FGDS) and the PSU declare their support of the student movement.

In the lycées

A demonstration followed by a strike in the Nantes lycées.

In the factories

A demonstration against unemployment in Lille turns into a demonstration supporting student demands. Over 20,000 attend.

In the parties

The Gaullist deputy for the Latin Quarter, René Capitant, declares: 'It's daft to turn thousands of CRS troops loose on lycée children in Paris. Every passing day sees the movement expanding.' Alain Peyrefitte tenders his resignation but it is refused. The technocratic wing of the Gaullist party is determined to use the students to achieve their aim of destroying the Liberal university.

Sunday 12 May: The Government wishes May away

The Government intends to ignore the general strike, thinking that, as in times past, it will not lead to new activity and it will be easily forgotten. ORTF technicians announce that they will join the strike. Many are disturbed by the fact that television and radio had almost no coverage of the street fighting on Friday and Saturday.

The Economic Revolution

Monday 13 May: The Day of the Occupations

The general strike called by all the major trade-union organizations, including the students, teachers and *lycéens* is an enormous success, particularly outside Paris, much to the amazement of many trade-union leaders. The demonstrations are particularly large: in Nantes, 20,000; Marseilles, 50,000; Toulouse, 40,000. Attempts by the CGT to separate student and trade-union contingents in Paris fails. Between 3 p.m. and 8 p.m. between 600,000 and 1,000,000 people (depending on estimates) march across Paris. The ORTF claims only 171,000 marched in Paris. The demonstrations are violent in Clermont-Ferrand and Le Mans. Many towns which have not witnessed demonstrations since the Liberation are the scene of marches.

In the university

In Paris, the new Faculty of Medicine is occupied by students. The Faculty of Science demands complete university autonomy. The deans of all the Arts Faculties in the country demand an end to centralized education and Government interference by threatening to resign. Fifty-eight professors at Nanterre state that the university system is dead and they no longer recognize the educational system.

In the morning the CRS troops are withdrawn from the Sorbonne. It is immediately occupied by students streaming in with red flags. From this time the Sorbonne is established as the shop window of the Revolution. It houses many of the committees set up by the general assembly of students, which meets nightly in the courtyard to take decisions. Permanent teach-ins, discussions and entertainment are organized.

More important, the Censier Annexe is occupied. Here the *comités d'action* are located. They coordinate demonstrations, organizations and demands and begin to make contact with workers' organizations. Contact is immediately established with other universities, the Renault plants, Citroën, Air-France, Rhône-Poulenc and the RATP (Parisian underground) and many local action committees.

In the evening the students open the Sorbonne to the people, declaring that it has ceased to be a hierarchical institution and is henceforth a popular university. 'Labourers and workers are invited to come and discuss their common problems with the university students.'

After demonstrations the Arts Faculty in Strasbourg is occupied and debates are held. Other faculties at Clermont-Ferrand, Rennes and Nantes, where the occupation of the office of the prefect results in the restoration of the grant to the students' union, are occupied.

In the factories

Trade unions note that the demonstrations are the largest since the War, and the one-day general strike one of the most successful. In Le Mans and Nantes the offices of the prefects are besieged. There are street battles with police in Clermont-Ferrand. The workers at Rhodiacéta near Besançon prepare for a long strike, claiming that the token one-day strikes are meaningless.

In the communities

Many local action committees are set up in Paris and Nantes to discuss problems of local self-determination and self-government. These committees quickly spread, particularly in the Parisian 'red-belt', much to the consternation of the PCF which regarded these areas as its bailiwicks.

Tuesday 14 May: A new kind of strike

In the universities

The Nanterre faculty declares itself an autonomous university. Grenoble declares its present administration dissolved. Clermont-Ferrand postpones examinations and calls for a national assembly to discuss university reorganization, Caen demands staff–student co-management of the university.

The *École Nationale des Beaux-Arts* is occupied in Paris, and the Faculty of Law goes on strike.

The action committees of the University of Paris are organized. Their aim is an open university and the social reforms necessary for the establishment of that new university. The minimum demands of the Sorbonne general assembly are now lengthened to include the resignations of Peyrefitte and Grimaud, the chief of the Paris police.

The strike at the Faculty of Medicine in Paris spreads to hospitals. A permanent liaison committee is set up in Paris and an organization committee to contact hospitals and clinics in the provinces is founded.

By the end of the day almost all universities in the country are occupied or on strike. The National Conservatory of Dramatic Art is occupied.

In the lycées

Every lycée in Nantes is now on strike, the teachers join the students. The minimum demands are for complete reorganization of curriculum and student participation. In Lille over 3,000 *lycéens* demonstrate and in Marseilles a strike is called to gain recognition of the CAL.

In the factories

The evening shift of workers at the Sud-Aviation plant in Nantes, led by young workers occupy their workshops and lock the director in his office. They immediately contact other branches of Sud-Aviation and the University of Nantes, calling for solidarity.

In Rouen and Elbeuf students and workers demonstrate together.

In the parties

General de Gaulle leaves in the morning for a state visit to Rumania. The National Assembly meets in the afternoon to debate the 'student problem'. The Mayor of Grenoble declares his support for the student movement and action committees.

Cultural activities

The ORTF finally transmits a programme on the student demonstrations. Workers and journalists set up a 'committee on objectivity'. They vote to hold the first total strike in ORTF history, their demands are that the ORTF should be used for educational purposes and that it should be free from Government interference.

Wednesday 15 May: Revolt of the young workers

In the factories

Strikes and occupations spread over the country. The workers at the Cléon plant of Renault in the Seine-Maritime follow the example of students in occupying their plant and immediately contact other Renault branches. By the late afternoon the shipyards at Bordeaux and the Sud-Aviation plant in Cannes have also been occupied.

CFDT leaders take part in a round-table discussion with students in the Sorbonne.

A large demonstration protesting against unemployment in Bordeaux is joined by students.

In the universities

Strikes and occupations spread to Clermont-Ferrand, the *Conservatoire Nationale de Musique*, Rennes, Dijon, Nancy, Amiens and Caen.

General assemblies of staff and students to discuss reorganization meet in the Faculty of Medicine in Paris where professors join the action committees, Toulouse where the 25 April Movement demands an end to the rectorate and calls for co-management, the Beaux-Arts in Toulouse where demands are for a critical and open university, Grenoble where a transitionary assembly is established, Strasbourg where the University is declared autonomous and the school of Dentistry secedes from the Medical Faculty, Poitiers, Rennes, Nancy, Montpellier, Amiens and Lyons.

In Paris teaching and examinations are abandoned in the Faculties of Law and Medicine pending reorganization. Marc Zamansky fails to reorganize his faculty without student participation.

The strike now spreads to the *Polytechniques* and the *grandes écoles* as well as technical schools, schools of social work and catering.

In the professions

The Saint-Antoine hospital in Paris declares itself autonomous and dissolves the all-powerful hierarchical council.

Cultural activities

The Odéon, the national theatre, is occupied in the evening by demonstrators who declare it open to the public for discussion on society and cultural expression and as a meeting place for students and workers and artists.

In the trade unions

Taken aback by the burgeoning movement the CGT tries to slow down the strike movement whilst conceding that a 'new spirit is developing'. The CFDT reaffirms its support of the student movement, and the CNJA (Union of Young Farmers) declares its support of the students in their endeavour to reform and open up the educational system.

Thursday 16 May: Each Sector Undertakes its own Revolution

Georges Pompidou, the Prime Minister declares: '. . . groups of *enragés* (madmen, the name used to describe the extreme Left during the French Revolution of 1789) are encouraging the spread of disorder with the aim of destroying society and the very bases of our free society . . .' The students and young workers respond by adopting the name *enragés* to describe themselves: '*Nous sommes de plus en plus enragés*' ('We are becoming angrier and angrier').

In the factories

Still without official trade-union encouragement and support, the wave of occupations continues to spread. By midday all of the Renault plants, Cléon, Flins, Le Mans, Boulogne-Billancourt, are occupied as is the Lockheed plant at Beauvais by its technicians, the UNUBEC plant at Orléans, and the *Nouvelles Messageries de Presse* (Newspaper distributors), where students help man the picket lines, Kléber-Colombes, Dresser-Dujardin, and the shipyards at Le Trait near Rouen. That evening a meeting between students and workers takes place at the Renault plant at Boulogne-Billancourt and at the Sud-Aviation plant in Nantes where future actions and workers' control are discussed. The metal-workers in Nantes join the strike movements, as do miners in Alsace and the Ardennes where the pits are occupied. Many small firms have their first strikes, particularly in the Gironde (the Bordeaux area), Lorraine and Seine-Maritime. Air traffic is disrupted.

In the universities

An important meeting takes place at Vierzon (Cher) of student leaders to coordinate activity nationally and work out ways of spreading the strike movement.

The students of the *École Polytechnique* in Paris call for co-management and those at the *grandes écoles* for an 'autonomous, pluralist and critical university'.

The following universities and faculties adopt staff–student co-management as the future means of organization: Brest, Tours, Strasbourg, Aix, Rennes, where the resignation of the Minister of Education (Peyrefitte) is demanded. Caen becomes an autonomous university. All the faculties at Toulouse are now under occupation, students form joint action committees with striking building workers in Besançon and Nantes. Teach-ins and round-the-clock discussions at Poitiers, Saint-Étienne, Bordeaux, Montpellier and Nancy. The medical faculties at Lyons and Nantes are on strike and embark on discussions on reorganization of the medical profession.

The School of Agronomy in Paris is occupied. Staff and students issue a statement announcing their refusal to become 'technocrats' and call for joint action committees of workers, students and peasants (CLEOP). CLEOP spreads to Roanne, Montpellier, Saint-Étienne, Angers and Rouen.

Most of the art faculties in the country are now on strike. The *atelier* set up by students and artists at the Beaux-Arts Faculty in Paris begins to produce posters to help the movement, artists form support committees, round-the-clock discussions on the role of art in the new society are launched.

In the lycées

The lycées in Lyons and Villeurbanne are on strike. The CALs call for a new form of assessment. In Paris they meet to discuss the future of the *baccalauréat*.

In the professions

Led by adherents of Jacques Lacan's (well-known psychiatrist) groups, the hospitals of Sainte-Anne, Pitié, and Cochin are occupied, management committees are overthrown and discussions start between students, doctors and patients.

Cultural activities

The ORTF finally broadcasts a debate on university problems with Cohn-Bendit, Sauvageot and Geismar. A general assembly of the ORTF staff calls for an extraordinary meeting of the entire ORTF staff. It passes motions calling for a general strike as the only way to 'obtain the ORTF's real independence from Government control, and demands the resignation of the administrative and general management councils'. Jean-Louis Barrault, director of the Odéon, announces that he agrees with the students who occupied the theatre.

In the trade unions

Confusion reigns in the CGT which appears to have lost control of its most loyal factories.

In the parties

The PSU tells its members to 'consider yourselves mobilized'. Tense discussion between the Left and Right-wing factions on the central committee of the PCF. Georges Marchais, one of the chief organizers, takes a very hard line against the students and strikers.

Friday 17 May: The Long March

In the factories

The Berliet and Rhodiacéta factories in the Rhône are occupied. All air traffic comes to a halt. The strike spreads to the shipyards in Saint-Nazaire and the Seine-Maritime. Rail traffic is snarled. An action committee is established in the RATP with student help. Most aeronautic firms are on strike. Many factories are opened by the workers to allow local residents to hold meetings and to provide entertainment for children. The Le Creusot works are occupied. The post office workers go on strike. The national bureau of statistics, the INSEE, declares its support of the strikes. Shipyards in Provence and Brittany and some of the mines in the North are occupied. In Lyons a large demonstration supporting the strikers takes place.

In the trade unions

In the afternoon Georges Séguy, the secretary of the CGT, holds a press conference, the Right-wing newspaper *Figaro* declares that: '... for the diatribes of the workmen of yesteryear M. Séguy substitutes the firm and cold language of the well-versed managing director.' The police trade union claims that a dangerous situation exists in its ranks and a strike may be imminent.

The CFDT calls for the spread of the strike movement. It declares that the movement is not a contagious disease but a *'prise de conscience'* (a new consciousness).

The FEN says that the Government alone must bear all the responsibility for what has happened.

In the countryside

The peasant trade unions, the FNSEA and the CNJA, call for a massive demonstration for 24 May.

The FNSEA, the spokesman of the larger farmers, warns its members to ignore the student and worker movement. But the Breton organization follows the example of the students and occupations of depots and farms spread throughout the West. The local FNSEA, led by Bernard Lambert, calls for immediate occupations of the land by agricultural labourers.

In the Loire-Atlantique distribution breaks down completely. A joint student–worker–peasant organization is established to assure all services, control prices, marketing facilities and govern the *département*.

In the universities

Ignoring the objections and threats of the CGT, the students start the 'Long March' across Paris to the Renault works at Boulogne-Billancourt, where workers and students, despite the efforts of the CGT to keep them apart, meet. Similar meetings occur throughout the country and in some places joint committees are established. The leaders of the student movements call for national action committees to coordinate all activity. UNEF issues its four-point programme: student power, autonomous universities, autonomy of communications, and a worker–student–peasant alliance.

In Paris the Law Faculty rejects the existing consumer society, the Science Pô (National Institute of Political Science) calls for co-management, the Faculty of Medicine calls for a reorganization of medical services which responds to social needs, and the Orsay and Sorbonne faculties demand complete university reorganization.

Rouen and Nantes are declared autonomous; Nice and Limoges are occupied, Grenoble is completely reorganized; there are strikes at Brest and Aix; a co-management system is established in Toulouse and discussions continue in Lyons. Dijon demands the resignation of Peyrefitte.

In the lycées

The CALs spread, the Minister of Education claims that the *baccalauréat* scheduled for June will take place, teachers and students at a lycée in Villeurbanne establish a co-management system.

In the professions

A battle in Paris between Left- and Right-wing lawyers over the reorganization of the legal profession.

The Broussais hospital is occupied and the director overthrown. New management committees are set in motion at Sainte-Anne, Saint-Antoine, and permanent liaison committees with medical students are established.

In the parties

The departmental council of the Haute-Garonne (Toulouse area) declares that the future of the University lies in social reform and workers' power.

Michel Rocard, secretary of the PSU, says that the struggle marks the beginning of a new form of politics.

Cultural activities

The States-General of the Cinema meets to discuss how to stop the Cannes film festival from taking place. Directors like Resnais, Lelouch and Forman withdraw their films. Many Paris theatres are occupied by actors who open them to the public to debate the role of culture. The *Théâtre de l'Est de Paris* stops its productions to engage in discussions with the students. The actors' trade union calls for a strike to forward the cause of the new society.

The ORTF calls a strike.

Saturday 18 May: L'enchaînement

General de Gaulle returns from Rumania. Pompidou presides at an emergency cabinet meeting. A poll shows that 55 per cent support the student claims, and 60 per cent want to see a new form of society, yet 50 per cent oppose the strikes.

In the factories

The SNCF (railways) is totally paralysed. The ground staff of Air-France occupy their places of work. Métro lines and bus stations are occupied. The postmen occupy post offices. The gas and electricity workers promise to maintain supplies even though they are on strike. The police intervene and seize several post offices. Many very small firms are now affected by the strike.

In the trade unions

The CFDT in a statement says that industry must be democratized just as the students are democratizing the university. The CGT and the CGT-FO refuse to follow their lead and propose only quantitative demands. But Robert Cottave from the CGT-FO technicians' federation declares: 'We must accept extraordinary proposals to escape from our present situation and study and start to build a new society where expression and participation are assured.'

In the parties

The official Left-wing parties find it difficult to keep up with the movement. The PCF and the Federation of the Left speak only of the need for further consultations. The PSU speaks of the need for workers' power and calls for the spread of the action committees.

A motion of censure against the way the Government has handled the crisis is to be debated in the National Assembly. René Capitant, Gaullist deputy for the Latin Quarter, announces he will vote against the Government.

The Gaullists begin to organize *Comités de défense de la République* (CDR) under the aegis of Roger Frey, Minister of the Interior, and Robert Galley, a Gaullist M.P. The extreme Right volunteers support in return for the release of General Raoul Salan imprisoned during the Algerian War, as do the *Anciens de la Division Leclerc* (an organization with a large following amongst army officers) and former supporters of Antoine Pinay. Galley starts to organize prospective Gaullist demonstrations to be timed for the crucial moment. The Government launches a petrol scare backed up by the strong-armed tactics of the CDRs. 2,000 demonstrators of the extreme Right-wing *Occident* demonstrate at the Étoile.

In the universities

Co-management has been accepted at Strasbourg, Mulhouse and Caen. Commissions are working in Angers and Rennes. Toulouse University is declared open to the public. The *grandes écoles* call for co-management.

The Beaux Arts call for a new curriculum based on cooperative study. The Union of Musicians joins the strike. The Science Faculty sets up a provisional co-management system.

In the professions

Interns in most hospitals join the movement. A white paper is issued calling for reforms and a medical system based on collective team work. More hospitals are occupied. A psychiatric action committee is set up at Sainte-Anne.

Cultural activities

The Opéra, the Opéra-Comique, the TNP, the TEP, the theatres at Saint-Denis, Satrouville and the cultural centres of Toulouse, Caen and Le Havre are occupied. Theatre takes to the streets and plays to the strikers in the factories.

The States-General of the Cinema meets to reorganize the film industry. The Cannes Film Festival is broken up.

Art students and artists march to the Museum of Modern Art, their theme being that museums are morgues and storage depots, not meeting places.

The actors' trade union demands the right for repertory companies to decide their own repertoires.

At the ORTF the radio journalists take control of news programmes and pledge that in the future the news will be both honest and objective.

Sunday 19 May: La Chienlit

De Gaulle meets his ministers. At the end of the meeting he declares; '*Les reformes, oui, la chienlit, non!*' to which the strikers replied '*Le chienlit c'est lui!*'

François Mitterand, the president of the Federation of the Left says a joint Federation-PCF programme must be worked out. Pierre Mendès-France says the Government must resign.

The strike now covers all transport, the nationalized industries, the metal industry, the banks, public services and some of the tertiary sector.

The Government pushes the organization of the CDRs.

The action committees are organized into a federation.

Roger Blin and Delphine Seyrig found the student–actor

action committee to take art into the streets. Pierre Tabard sets up a workshop in the Mouffetard quarter of Paris to blend art and revolution.

The ORTF trade unions now on strike meet to decide further action. Pompidou asserts that the Government must maintain its control over the ORTF, implying that censorship is a necessity because in modern times the State needs 'modern means of control' over the population.

Monday 20 May: The CGT Attempts to Exert its Authority

The Government announces that a referendum on the question of 'participation' will be held. It is almost ignored.

In the factories

The strike spreads to Michelin and Peugeot, which has never known a major strike. The strike in the mines and all major ports is now total. A strike spreads across the major department stores in Paris and provincial centre. The *Bibliothèque Nationale* (National Library) joins the strike as does the *Banque de France*. The previously non-unionized Citroën works are occupied. The workers at the Renault plant at Boulogne-Billancourt call for the overthrow of the regime. Only in Lorraine is the strike movement not completely effective.

In the trade unions

The CFDT holds a joint press conference with UNEF. Its president, André Jeanson, declares that workers and students are united in their demands for power and they are not mere 'bread-and-butter demands'. 'We are one with the students because we are involved in the same struggle against oppressive and overbearing institutions,' declares the CFDT's secretary, Eugène Descamps.

Georges Séguy, secretary of the CGT, declares that he is not concerned with such 'vacuous ideas as workers' control, reform of society and other inventions'. On Europe No. 1 radio station, he declares: 'Going the whole hog means a general rise in wages, guaranteed employment, an earlier retirement age, reduction in working hours without loss of pay, and the defence and extension of such trade union rights in the factory'.

But the CGT and CGT-FO technicians declare their support of the demands of the students' movement and the idea of workers' control.

In the parties

The PCF warns the 'ultra-Left' against provocative behaviour. The *Occident* raids the Science Pô, the Opéra and the Saint-Lazare station. The Federation of the CFDT and the CGT-FO hold a joint meeting. The PSU declares that the crisis has now become the crisis of capitalist society itself.

In the countryside

The FNSEA Federation of the Loire-Atlantique attacks the notion of an economy based on profit which crushes men and calls for an occupation of all large estates. It joins the students and workers in running the distributive systems of the *département*.

In the universities

The Dean of the Rouen faculty resigns in protest against the Government's actions but is promptly elected president of the recognized faculty by the co-management committee. The examination system is abandoned in Strasbourg and Nantes. The new co-management committees start to operate in Grenoble and Lille. Committees on reform are established at Reims, at the newly independent pharmacy faculty at Bordeaux and at the Catholic Institute in Paris. Only Nanterre experiences great difficulty in setting up co-management committees. The Dean of the Faculty of Medicine in Paris announces his support of the proposed reforms. Co-management is accepted at Mulhouse.

In the lycées

The lycée Henri IV in the Latin Quarter is occupied. Debates continue in the occupied lycées, many begin to organize their own classes and to reform their curriculum with the support of parent organizations.

Cultural activities

Led by Michel Butor, writers occupy the *Société des gens de lettres* and establish a committee with students and workers. An action group is formed to help the Beaux Arts students. The students of architecture in Paris occupy their workshops and with established architects begin to work out plans for a new Paris.

The Federation of Youth Centres accepts the principle of co-management.

In the communities

Encouraged by marauding bands of CDRs thousands and thousands of immigrant slum dwellers, terrorized by the resurgent Right-wing organizations, begin to flee the country. The total number will never be known because most entered the country illegally, but were encouraged in order to keep the wages pressure down.

Tuesday 21 May: Revolutionary Reforms

In the factories

About ten million are now on strike. In most factories there are occupations and discussion concerning the future management of industry and society in general. Despite the total paralysis in the public services, workers promise that essential services will be maintained. The entire atomic energy sector is strike-bound. The workers call for an end to nuclear experiments for war and destruction.

In the trade unions

Young technicians and engineers invade and occupy the head-quarters of the CGC (*Cadres* Organization) supported by the political organization *Technique et Démocratie*, and establish a group called C4 with its offices in the Sorbonne. The offices of the CNPF (French version of the CBI) are occupied for a time.

In the countryside

The FNSEA federations of Allier, Creuse and Brittany refuse to wait for a national strike and begin occupying depots and estates.

In the parties

The censure debate begins in the National Assembly. The Government sweetens the pill proposing an amnesty for all students and police, but since the question of reform is not mentioned, nor that of brutalities, the SNESup and UNEF decline the offer.

In the universities

Examinations are postponed or abandoned at Clermont-Ferrand, Marseilles, and Montpellier. Dijon is occupied. The Law Faculty in Paris accepts a co-management structure, revamping of teaching methods and courses.

In the lycées

Technical lycées now join the strike. In some areas primary schoolchildren join the strike. Turgot, in Paris, begins an experiment in co-management.

In the professions

Debates on role of medicine and psychiatry continue at Sainte-Anne, Saint-Antoine, Saint-Louis, Versailles and Cochin. The

Psychiatrists' Association declares that a fruitful questioning of society must be allowed. Mass resignation of interns in private hospitals.

Young magistrates begin to organize themselves into a trade union, discussing how to establish an independent judicial system. They call on Mendès-France to assume power.

Cultural activities

A writers–students committee is formed.

Occupation of cultural centres at Bourges, Grenoble, Aix and of Bourseiller's centre. They are opened to the public in solidarity with students and workers.

Wednesday 22 May: Discrediting the official opposition

The motion of censure is defeated, receiving only 223 votes. Capitant and Edgar Pisani, former Minister of Agriculture, resign from the National Assembly. The Government refuses to allow Daniel Cohn-Bendit back into the country.

In the universities

Reaction to the Government's banning of Cohn-Bendit is immediate. In less than two hours over 10,000 march on the Palais Bourbon at the call of UNEF and the SNESup. The CGT calls the demonstration a provocation and condemns its organizers.

The ENA (National School of Administration) calls for social reform. The demands of Science Pô students are supported by the staff. The faculty at Orléans is occupied. Examinations are abandoned at Limoges.

In the lycées

Students rename a Marseilles lycée, 'Lycée de la Commune de Paris'.

In the factories

The strike continues to spread. The FEN strikes. The police continue to oust strikers from post offices and occupy them.

In the trade unions

In a joint communiqué the CGT and the CFDT state their willingness to negotiate with the Government for an extension of trade-union rights. The CFDT announces that it supports the views expressed by the PSU. It calls for the end of capitalist society and upon the workers 'to master their work and their future'.

The CNJA calls for a 'real economic and social democracy' and calls a general strike of young farmers.

In the professions and cultural activities

The offices of the General Association of Footballers are occupied by supporters. The Union of Young Lawyers calls for 'humanization of justice'. The Broussais hospital establishes a collegial management system.

Thursday 23 May: Isolation of the students

In the universities

Students demonstrate to prevent police from entering the Latin Quarter. Over the last week the face of the quarter has been changed. With no police in sight traffic management and services have been taken over by students and workers. The police charge student barricades. Two hundred are arrested. Similar demonstrations take place in Lyons, Bordeaux and Caen. Whilst reaffirming its support of the student movement the CFDT refuses to take part in the demonstrations.

Meeting of the action committees in the Sorbonne. The

SNESup national conference approves the stand taken by its secretary, Alain Geismar.

Examinations are postponed or abandoned at Nancy, Bordeaux, Besançon, Lyons, Limoges, Rennes, Toulouse and Poitiers.

The CNRS discusses the reorganization and reorientation of research.

The *Institut de Pédagogie Nationale* is occupied and renamed the *Institut de Pédagogie Populaire*.

In the lycées

The Minister of Education admits that the *baccalauréat* in its traditional form cannot take place. Occupations and reorganization continue.

In the trade unions

The CFDT raises its minimum demands to a measure of control in each work place. The CGT refuses to follow suit. The chief economic spokesman of the CGT, André Barjonet, resigns as does Arthur Haneuse, in protest against the CGT's refusal to support the students and unwillingness to extend the movement. After a joint action meeting between the CFDT and the CGT to outline a common front in the forthcoming negotiations, the CFDT delegates, Descamps and Lucas, are severely criticized by members of the national executive for giving way to the CGT.

The CGC splits. A new organization called the *Nouveaux Cadres* is formed.

Cultural activities

The Minister of Posts withdraws the right of independent radio to use radio-telephones hence to give on-the-spot coverage of strikes, demonstrations and meetings. Radio Luxembourg is warned that unless it toes the Government line its office in Paris will be closed.

In the parties

The PCF is deeply split between those favouring the traditional demands and working within the existing society – Georges Marchais, Waldeck-Rochet (the secretary), those pushing for more audacious action – Louis Aragon, Roger Garaudy, Roland Leroy, and those preaching a return to Stalinism – Jacques Duclos and Jeanette Vermeersch-Thorez.

The Political Revolution

Friday 24 May: Catalysis

In a speech broadcast to the country over the radio, manned by Government-hired technicians barricaded on top of the Eiffel Tower, de Gaulle announces that a referendum on 'participation' will take place early next month and if he loses he will resign. Immediate reaction is disbelief (on the Right), hostility (the Centre) and derision (on the Left). The trade unions declare they can now achieve this end without his help. The CFDT calls upon its members to redouble their efforts. Mendès-France says that the people are not willing to wait.

After a CGT demonstration numbering 150,000, over 200,000 gather in the forecourt of the Gare de Lyon. The police, intent on sealing off the square, cause a great battle to begin. As soon as de Gaulle's speech is over the demonstrators march off in small groups all over Paris erecting barricades. Police stations are sacked, the Bourse is set aflame. The police attack passers-by, including Red Cross workers, indiscriminately. Several are killed and hundreds are wounded in Paris alone.

Other demonstrations gather at Boulogne-Billancourt, Aubervilliers, Ivry, Argenteuil and Saint-Ouen in the Paris area, and degenerate into street fighting. 'The street is ours!' cry the workers. In Lyons, Strasbourg, Bordeaux, Perigueux and particularly in Nantes workers, students and even peasants battle with the police. A police officer dies in Lyons and the strikers, in effect, take over Nantes.

After the poor reception of his speech, Right-wing leaders and representatives of the *Anciens de la division Leclerc*, with the trump card of the army in their hands, tell de Gaulle on what grounds they will support him. De Gaulle communicates with General Massu in Germany to work out terms for army support.

In the countryside

The peasant demonstrations are the largest France has ever seen. In Nantes together with workers and students the peasants seize the Place Royale which they rename Place du Peuple. Battles take place in Allier and Hautes-Vienne.

In the universities

Almost all medical faculties are now occupied and are busy working out new forms of organization. All the faculties of Aix are occupied.

Cultural activities

At RTL Jean Farran, the director, warns his reporters, 'Be careful not to cause a radio-riot. You know that Luxembourg can cut our antennae at will.'

Workers at *Paris libéré* refuse to print unless the editor changes false headlines indicating that work has been resumed. Workers at *Le Figaro* refuse to print articles by Raymond Aron (former Professor of Sociology at Paris University) unless he 'has more respect for facts'.

Saturday 25 May: The Cultural Revolution

The demonstrations continue late into Saturday morning. Five hundred are wounded and seven hundred and ninety-five arrested. The French Nobel prize winners together with Claude Lévi-Strauss point out that the Government is now threatening the students with complete annihilation. Pompidou warns that any further demonstrations 'will be dispersed with the greatest possible energy and dispatch'.

In the trade unions

The Government attempts to bring the 'troubles' to an end by calling for negotiations between the State, management and the trade unions. Pompidou, Jeanneney and Chirac meet with trade-union leaders. At 3 p.m. a general agreement is reached. Negotiations sector by sector are to be started later in the day.

Demonstrations continue in Brest, Reims, Clermont-Ferrand, Grenoble, Marseilles, Toulouse and Bordeaux, where over a hundred are wounded.

In the parties

François Mitterand calls for elections.

In the universities

UNEF declares that, judging by its actions and duplicity, the Government can no longer be regarded as a valid and legitimate negotiator. The University must take its affairs into its own hands. It calls for a demonstration for Monday.

The staff of the Sorbonne reject the idea of university reform emanating from the Government. Co-management is instituted in Montpellier.

Foundation of the *Comité de préparation à une réforme de l'enseignement artistique* (CPRECA) a staff–student–artist committee which proposes new forms of collective courses in art education by group and exchange teaching.

Cultural activities

The directors of thirty theatres and *Maisons de culture* (cultural centres) meet at Roger Planchon's *Théâtre de la Cité* at Ville-urbanne, amongst them Georges Wilson of the TNP and Francis Jeanson. They declare that culture which does not politicize is useless and a society where man can invent his own humanity is the only just society: 'We start with the assumption that culture must provide man with the means to break out of his isolation, to escape from his ghetto, and to place himself consciously in the actual social and historical context, liberating himself from the mystifications of a social order which turns him into the accomplice of those inhuman situations inflicted upon him.' Jean-Louis Barrault, not in attendance, signs the statement.

Meeting of the States-General of the Cinema which adopts a motion calling for the end to film distribution monopolies, abolition of the censor and the creation of co-management and integrated forms of teaching throughout the industry.

Sunday 26 May: Day of Waiting

In the local elections in Dijon the Left-wing parties make large gains.

The negotiations between the Government, the CNPF and the trade unions continue at the rue de Grenelle.

André Barjonet warns that the CGT cannot be trusted since it is being progressively integrated into the State.

Monday 27 May: Day of the pègre

In the trade unions

After twenty-five hours of negotiations, the Government, the CNPF and the trade unions reach the Grenelle agreements raising the minimum wage to 5s. an hour, and all wages by 10 per cent, allowing for a small reduction in working hours and a small extension of trade-union rights to be worked out between the trade unions and the CNPF. The CGT claims that a solution has been found, the CFDT is somewhat less happy and the CNPF emphasizes 'new and heavy costs'.

In the factories

Meetings quickly assemble in factories to debate the agreements. Almost everywhere they are rejected, particularly by young workers and technicians. 'We are no longer at that stage. We want the collapse of the regime.' Workers assembled at Renault,

Citroën and Berliet refuse to accept the agreements. At the Renault works, Séguy is booed. CGT federations in the Loire-Atlantique leave the federation announcing that the struggle is not economic but political. André Jeanson, of the CFDT, notes his pleasure with the decisions coming from the shop floor.

The strike spreads to the gas works at Lacq, Cadarache and to Philips. The workers at Sud-Aviation in Marseilles declare that the strike is part of the general movement to overthrow the Government and establish a socialist regime.

The CFDT finally refuses to sign the Grenelle agreements. All negotiations collapse. Civil planners join the strike declaring that urban development is a prisoner of the capitalist system of profit.

In the parties

The Government, mystified and frightened by its loss on control, launches a 1968 version of *The Great Fear*. Fouchet, Minister of Interior, declares that the movement is managed and manipulated by the *pègre* (scum) which have arms depots scattered over the country. The CDRs begin to distribute arms. The Government stops the distribution of petrol, blaming it on the strikes. The Government announces that the referendum will take place on 4 June.

The PCF dissociates itself from the students and Jean-Pierre Vigier, one of the leaders of the action committees, is excluded from the party.

The Federation of the Left refuses to consider setting up a joint government with the Communists (PCF).

Valéry Giscard d'Estaing, the leader of a Right-wing movement allied to the Gaullists, enters negotiations with other Right-wing organizations and launches a trial balloon that he will stand for President should elections be required.

The new politics

A large meeting gathering 50,000 is held at the Charléty stadium in Paris, its purpose to chart a new course in the deteriorating situation. It is supported by *22 Mars*, UNEF, SNESup, FEN, the CAL, the JCR, sections of the Federation of the Left, the PSU, the CFDT, and addressed by Rocard for the PSU, and Barjonet. Mendès-France attends. Barjonet declares: 'What the workers want is workers' power in the factories just as the students want students' power in the universities.'

The PSU declares that a transitional government must be set up.

Intense local meetings throughout the country. Many CGT sections, despite warnings from their leaders, join in the meetings and demonstrations. A coalition of students, workers, peasants, and *cadres* appears to be in the making in many areas, following the example of the Loire-Atlantique. Large demonstrations in Toulon and Nantes, where the strike committee alone is the effective government, Clermont-Ferrand, Marseilles and Besançon.

A Catholic group launches an appeal for a new society.

In the universities and lycées

The general assembly of the Medical Faculty in Paris calls for complete autonomy, co-management, the reform of medical training and medical services for the benefit of the working class.

Once again the *baccalauréat* is postponed.

Alain Geismar, secretary of the SNESup, resigns to devote himself to the action committees and political organization.

Cultural activities

The *Théâtres lyriques nationaux* propose a co-management structure. The action committee of footballers evacuates the Football Association's office.

Gallery owners announce their support of the movement, declaring that art is not marketable and must play a social role.

In the factories

Negotiations continue in certain economic sectors. In Brittany new strikes in small firms are reported. Caen is cut off by students and workers. In Grenoble meetings between students and workers on local autonomy continue. The CFDT calls for an intensification of the strike movement. The CFDT *cadres* call for complete workers' control.

In the action committees

An attempt to coordinate the various movements at the Charléty stadium is made by the *22 Mars*, JCR, Barjonet, Vigier, Geismar, UNEF, and Gilbert Mury (pro-Chinese Communists) fails. They only agree upon issuing a call to all their supporters to sabotage the referendum.

At the CSF (electrical) factory in Brest the workers begin transforming the strike committee into a management committee to run the factory. This was one of the few factories where this occurred. But the action is not followed up elsewhere.

In the parties

Peyrefitte, the Minister of Education, is finally allowed to resign.

The *Conseil d'État* (Council of State) declares the referendum unconstitutional. Pisani, a former Gaullist minister, calls for a transitional government. Waldeck-Rochet, PCF, says that no government would be valid without PCF ministers. Mitterand calls for a transitional government to be led by Mendès-France and announces his intention to stand for the Presidency. In meetings with the Federation of the Left, Waldeck-Rochet refuses their propositions, claiming that Mendès-France is too closely linked to the new movement. Hence the traditional political parties fail to come up with a solution. Their only action is to refuse to sit in the National Assembly so long as a debate on the Government's competence is not held.

Cultural activities

The news agency, *Agence France Presse*, and the publishing houses go on strike.

The theatre-in-the-streets movement spreads.

In the factories

The strike movement reaches its zenith. Strike leaders, in many cases previously non-unionized, and/or young workers wait for something to take them a step beyond factory occupations, the traditional means of *contestation* having been used to the limit of its effectiveness, but aside from large demonstrations in Grenoble, Nice, Caen, Saint-Étienne, Lyons, and particularly Marseilles, the spark is not forthcoming because:

In the trade unions

The CGT decides that the movement must be stopped. It attempts to reassert its control by channelling action into a traditional demonstration. 250,000 gather at the Bastille.

The CFDT, no longer finding the Government a meaningful negotiator, whilst calling for an intensification of the movement, does not have the means of pushing the movement forward and can do no more than propose a traditional political solution, bringing Mendès-France back to power. But this only has the effect of throwing the question back into the parties.

In the parties

In the afternoon several highly placed civil servants from major government ministries go to the Sorbonne to open negotiations on how to transfer power to the action committees, which in their view, will come to power within the next few days.

But in the official opposition negotiations between the parties of the Left are impossible because they cannot conceive of taking power without elections. Mendès-France declares that he is ready if needed but neither the CGT or the PCF nor ultimately the Federation are willing to accept him.

Despite the fact that Gaullist deputies, ridden with fear, sent emissaries to the Federation asking if they would be allowed to contest elections under the coming socialist Government and hint that they really admire Mendès-France, the parties on the Left remain immobilized.

The PCF faces a grave internal crisis. Thirty-six party intellectuals demand an internal debate on the role of the party and demand that the party's newspaper open its columns to criticism. They demand that Juquin and Marchais be dismissed and that the Renault workers march to the Sorbonne in solidarity with the students. Juquin comments, 'The party understood the events before they happened,' and suggests that the intellectuals meet with the party officials to discuss their grievances some time 'in the near future'.

Giscard d'Estaing, for the Right wing of the Gaullist movement, says the country needs elections and a new Government.

Amidst wild rumours that he will resign, de Gaulle leaves Paris to go to a carefully arranged meeting with General Massu where the agreements drawn up with the Right-wing organizations are ratified. Massu promises, in return for the release of Salan and other economic and political concessions, that the army will obey any legal government but could not openly intervene unless the PCF joined the revolutionaries.

In the universities and lycées

Co-management is adopted at Montpellier. Debates take place on reforms in the Orléans lycées. The CAL issues a text on lycée autonomy, communal organization and the need to reinvent the notion of 'education' under the auspices of a committee *Enseignement 70* showing the influence of the ideas of Célestin Freinet.

New organizational statutes are adopted by the dental, medical and pharmaceutical students. They call for the creation of consultative centres, integrated research, and co-management.

Cultural activities

The *Conservatoire national des arts et métiers* goes on strike. Musicians and actors announce a boycott of the ORTF.

In the professions

The Architects' Association calls for a new professional statute adapted to the needs of a socialist society.

Thursday 30 May: The great fear

After careful preparations the Gaullists launch their counter-measures, whilst the Left momentarily hesitates. In the evening a carefully arranged demonstration of about one million gather in the Place de la Concorde, having been given special petrol rations to get there, chanting slogans such as 'Cohn-Bendit to Dachau' and 'Students to the gas ovens'. In many cities the demonstrations are more violent; Gaullists in fast-moving cars attack factories, isolate workmen, and shoot at Left-wing demonstrators. The alliance with the OAS (extreme Right-wing former supporters of French Algeria) elements is apparent.

De Gaulle swiftly dissolves the National Assembly, announces new elections and names a new Government. The PCF's position is thus finessed. Only the PSU calls upon its adherents to 'paralyse the Government'. In a self-congratulatory mood the PCF thinks it will gain between 4 and 6 per cent in the coming elections. The PSU realizes that the gamble has failed: 'We have always said that Gaullism was extremely weak economically and socially but not institutionally; and in order to succeed one had to use other methods than those hitherto used by the traditional political groups.'

In the factories

With no follow-up possible and the Left in disarray, a return to 'order' is the only logical possibility. Negotiations start again in most sectors: gas, electricity, SNCF and RATP. Some building concerns start work again. But the civil servants in the Loire go on strike. In the textile industry an agreement based on higher wages and a slight extension in trade-union rights is signed.

Cultural activities

Workers insist that newspapers be more objective about the strike movement. The ORTF reiterates its call for reform. The actors' trade union calls for a popular and democratic Government.

Counter-revolution and the New Politics

Friday 31 May: The counter-revolution

In the factories

Negotiations are resumed everywhere. The CGT promises to respect the new agreements. In small enterprises, the post offices in the west and southwest and in the potash mines and the EDF (electricity board) work starts again.

But in many areas organization in the factories continues. A typical structure would include two committees: one dealing with the management of the strike and the other on coordination and study. Neither extend their spheres of interest but as a Renault worker declares: 'It seems to me that we came very close to something very new.'

Cadres protest against the hierarchization of wage structures. Séguy warns the CGT not to interfere with the elections.

In the parties

The new Government has the same complexion and shows the same contradictions as the old: between the fundamentally individualist old middle class and the technocratic Gaullists. The contradiction is heightened by relying upon the extreme Right-wing elements of the former group whilst simultaneously emphasizing the technocratic side by promoting Chirac and Tricot. This Government marks Gaullism's final incorporation of the Right in view of the coming elections to be held on 23 and 30 June.

Pro-Gaullist demonstrations in Besançon and counter-demonstrations in Brest, Clermont-Ferrand, Lyons, Nancy and Nantes.

Anti-Gaullist peasant demonstrations, particularly in the West.

In the universities

A modified *baccalauréat* in the form of an oral examination will be held. The *École polytechnique* calls for experimentation in teaching and courses. Co-management is accepted in Tours

In the professions and cultural activities

The works in the *Ponts et Chaussées* attack technocracy as do the *cadres* in the Historical Monuments department. The actors' strike continues.

And so *le joli mai* came to an end.

Saturday 1 June and after

Saturday marks the beginning of a bank holiday just as Whit weekend 1871 marked an end to a different series of events. By now all possible cards have been played and the effervescence is dissipating. The die is cast: the back-to-work movement is inevitable because the old-established structures prove too resistant to the movement, unable to give the final thrust forward. Yet the guidelines both for the defence of the regime and for a new form of opposition are laid down clearly. In that sense the events of June provide an anticlimax to May. The Government assumes that the overflow can be halted and politics returned to the old form of *contestation*; hence it assumes that elections, the final form of collective spectacle, will absorb all political energies. A vote for the UNR is also logical, even for the most hardened striker; it means a respite. Elections no longer have the slightest meaning in terms of what was experienced in May; they are part of the system and as such not part of the *contestation* of the system; such is the interpretation placed on the elections by some of the more independent members of the Federation like Charles Hernu.

Hence 1 June symbolizes the failure of all the old alliances: Mendès-France fails in his last attempt to reconcile the PSU and the Federation. The PCF is forced to discipline its own movement and shed its intellectual following.

The organization of the action committees goes ahead. By June there are 450 member groups in factories, communes, and faculties based on a refusal to accept any government not based on workers' control; the need for an extra-parliamentary movement; and the need for a new form of socio–political organization.

And so June becomes the month of the dialectic of repression/new departures. On the 7th de Gaulle spells out his idea of reform: participation but without changing the values of the consumer society and its political organization. The popular universities are created and the CRS occupies the Renault plant at Flins after a severe battle. On the 9th Georges Bidault, the former OAS leader, returns whilst many foreign students and workers are deported. On the 10th the election campaign opens to a flourish of Gaullist invective spreading the Great Fear. On the 11th a student is killed at Melun and two workers killed at the Peugeot plant at Sochaux; there is a violent demonstration in Paris marked by 72 barricades and over 1,500 arrests; violence and demonstrations occur in Nantes, Saint-Nazaire and Lyons. The Government bans several Left-wing organizations whilst refusing to ban Right-wing organizations. On the 14th the Government takes over the Odéon and on the 15th Raoul Salan is released from prison whilst a campaign for the arrest of Left-wing leaders begins. On the 16th the Sorbonne is occupied by the CRS. On the 17th Renault workers return to work, Peugeot workers on the 20th, and the first firings of trade-union leaders begin. On the 23rd over one million workers are still on strike and the Gaullists take a big lead in the first round of the elections. On the 30th a student is killed in Lille and the Gaullists complete their electoral victory. Michel Rocard of the PSU remarks that the electoral victory will prove Pyrrhic.

On 1 June a large demonstration assembles at the Gare Montparnasse and marches across Paris to the Gare d'Austerlitz knowing that for the moment the situation is returning to 'normal', the chant sounded by 50,000 is '*Ce n'est qu'un début, continuons le combat*'. ('This is just the beginning, we fight on.')

'The Actors'

3. The Student Commune

Edgar Morin

1. Origins

The student 'maelstrom' began as both a tidal wave and a ripple. Since the beginning of 1968 a great student rebellion has been sweeping across such dissimilar countries as Poland, Czechoslovakia, Germany, Italy, Spain, England and the United States. Though the ramifications in each case were different, the rebellion smacked of a kind of internationality. Meanwhile a handful of revolutionaries on the Nanterre-La Folie campus triggered off a chain-reaction which was to burgeon into the ebullience of a student commune between 6 and 13 May.

The present crisis has been explained in two different ways. The first interpretation, favoured in official university and government circles, argues that the semi-feudal and antiquated academic community, the university's failure to keep pace with contemporary needs, and the failure of curriculum to be both utilitarian and functional, was responsible for student unrest.

According to this view, what is wrong is that universities have failed to come to terms with the modern world. The remedy is to reform and adapt by abolishing the out-of-date, expanding teaching and plant resources and modernizing teaching methods. Hence the student would be offered an open, liberal and wholesome campus in keeping with modern morals and guaranteeing employment opportunities.

The second interpretation emphasizes the students' rejection of the shabbiness, mediocrity, oppressiveness and repressiveness of bourgeois society rather than their desire to modernize the university; their contempt of the technical and managerial functions which await them rather than their professional interests, and their wish to challenge an adult world they feel is fundamentally corrupt rather than become part of it. It is significant that highly 'functional' universities, like Berkeley and Columbia, have been the scenes of bitter revolt.

In the Paris-Nanterre cauldron, and notably amongst its social science students, the conjuncture of two contradictory factors proved to be the detonator: *an increasing number of qualified people have not been trained for existing opportunities, whilst the social sciences, and particularly sociology, have all too readily become the regime's hand-maiden.*

There are two kinds of students who study sociology. The first inherit a tradition, cut short about 1950 by the irruption of the questionnaire, leading to a sociology whose purpose is to master rather than serve society – to understand society in order to change it. These are the young revolutionaries seeking a method and insight rather than a career. The others are attracted to a 'with-it' subject, more alive than a philosophy which is too abstract and a history which is too old. Their disappointment is inevitable. To the revolutionaries the curriculum leads to the role of a bureaucrat-expert, the servant of authority. They want to escape from a system which turns them into questionnaire-hawkers or mere technicians of the 'human factor'. The others soon discover that there are no opportunities in sociology save those procured by luck, chance or patronage. Their despondency at finding themselves at a dead end leads to the embryo of a critique.

Rejection of a career and anxiety about a career, far from being self-cancelling, formed the two poles of an electrolytic reaction. Those who see themselves as redundant adopted the agitation and fermentation associated with redundancy. The turbulent sector was social studies and sociology. Students in sociology set out looking for a critical discipline and discovered revolutionary Marxism through the heterodox and sometimes re-orthodox (Althusser) versions of Marxism.

Politics marked the point of convergence between the critical schools of sociology and the dissident schools of Marxism. Sociology soon became the main source of politicization. Since the secularization and de-Stalinization of French Communism (1956–8), the key revolutionary ideas were provided by the *groupuscules* which took root and flourished in the fertile soil of the university. The two main schools of French Trotskyism rose from the depths, no longer evoking nausea and horror, whilst the Marxists–Leninists, enlightened by the thoughts of Chairman Mao, worked like beavers in the interest of 'theoretical productivity'. Anarchism now flavoured with libertarian Marxism was in vogue and was in the midst of an intellectual revival as was Situationism (despite its stormy and injurious history, it contributed some new insights into Surrealism). Christian youth organizations were also in ferment and becoming increasingly radical. All these schools interacted by fighting and ultimately enriching each other.

The Anarchists and Situationists tended to stress the need for liberation here and now and the necessity of revolt in and against the university. Committed to the 'Third World's' notion of revolution, the Trotskyists and Maoists looked further afield to China, Cuba, Latin America and Vietnam. In addition, the Maoists ostensibly proposed to turn their backs on the bourgeois university and offer their services to the large number of factory workers. However, in spite of, and by means of endless conflict between these *groupuscules*, the former's existential-libertarianism was permeated by the latter's international perspective and vice versa. Both maintained that the university was bourgeois society's strongest bastion because it educated its *cadres*, and also its weakest link because students were susceptible to the spirit of revolution and were a majority within the university. Whether one's aim was a direct onslaught upon this bourgeois citadel or its complete transformation, one had to act *in* and *against* the university.

The occupation of faculties in Italy, the Critical University of Berlin, and students' revolts in other countries all encouraged the revolutionary minority in their struggle to revolutionize the university. Whilst enlarging its audience, its real point of contact with the vast number of students was through university authorities obstinately clinging on to antiquated restrictions, such as separate lodgings for men and women and the notional ban on political activity on university premises. By combining grudging, partial and long overdue concessions with a Kerenskyesque[1] incapacity to understand how turbulence could not be caused by 'agitators' and disorder not created by 'trouble-makers', and their ill-conceived attempts to isolate, i.e., eliminate, the 'leaders', they enabled the *groupuscules* to win over hundreds of students and radicalize their critique of the university.

At the same time the international events in which the students were increasingly embroiled stimulated their struggle against the three- (then later four-) headed hydra of capitalism, imperialism, fascism, and Stalinism. Militant 'navigators' strove to transform the internationality of student revolts in the East and the West into internationalism. Demonstrations against the war in Vietnam were transformed progressively into demonstrations for the 'victory of the Vietnamese people'. The forays of the South Vietnamese commandos from the *Occident* group led to the organization of shock troops armed with clubs, protected by helmets and prepared for guerrilla combat.

The internal struggle and the external struggle first radicalized each other and finally coalesced. Hence we have the significance of the *22 Mars* movement, which led to unity of action between all the *groupuscules*, including the Maoists.

From that point radicalization in the university led to an attack on the sacrosanct examination system, which the most revolutionary students hesitated to challenge before. To question the examination system was to contest society's principles of hierarchy and selection. What is less clear, but of much greater importance, is that it amounted to a rejection of the main rite of initiation into modern society and into the corrupt world of the adult. By such a daring move, its proponents risked separ-

1. Kerensky headed the provisional Russian Government after 1917 and constantly under-emphasized the following of the Bolsheviks, whom he saw only as a handful of agitators.

ating themselves from the vast number of students for whom the desire for a career was still stronger than an impulse to reject. At this point the university authorities, fearing sabotage and political contamination, closed the Nanterre campus, propelling the student movement forward.

At Nanterre the very fear of 'revolutionization' provoked the first explosion, thereby leading to the 'revolutionization' it sought to prevent. At the Sorbonne, the fear that the situation would deteriorate into guerrilla warfare – an armed confrontation between members of *Occident* and the revolutionary movements – was the second and decisive spark. During the extraordinary week that followed, the arrest of student militants was marked by a wave of solidarity among students, then among young people.

The first act of repression put the finishing touches to that masterpiece of Kerenskyism which triggered off the student commune.

By his vacillations between would-be liberalism, and slow and excessively brutal repression, the Minister of Education did everything in his power to facilitate the revolt. By his actions, the student movement was encased in an ever thicker protective cocoon. Even those teachers repelled by the idea of university reform, not to speak of revolution, were driven to stand by their students. Middle-class parents of students and grammar-school pupils were more angered by the repression than by their children's recklessness. Baptism by truncheon and tear-gas gained the sympathy of the working class who had been initially hostile to 'Daddy's little darlings'. Finally the anti-Gaullist reflex of the Left-wing parties overcame the anti-Leftist reflex aroused by the Communist party.

The scene was favourably set for the six remarkable and unforgettable days that followed. Marked by heroism, euphoria, terror and finally studiousness, their hallmarks were the first battle in the Latin Quarter where the urchin guerrilla dared to reply to tear-gas grenades with cobble-stones, the eighteen-mile march across Paris, red flags surprisingly stopping beneath the Arc de Triomphe, whilst thousands of chests swelled with the 'Internationale', the barricades joyfully burgeoning forth followed by the savage confrontation of Friday and Saturday and finally two days and nights of uninterrupted discussion and inquiry in the Censier annexe, peacefully reoccupied on Saturday.

2. Youth and the People

Contrary to what one might suppose, the revolutionary minorities at the centre of student activity between November 1967 and April 1968 did not lead the movement during the 'six glorious days', but served as drivers and navigators. The revolt itself was a chain-reaction which stemmed from the brutal arrests in the courtyard of the Sorbonne. All important actions were spontaneous. Some, such as the Long March, the barricades and the occupation of the Censier were even opposed by the revolutionary organizations. The movement swelled spontaneously to include not only lycée pupils but young and sometimes unemployed workers. The revolutionaries' contribution was not solidarity, which was the essence of the movement from the beginning. On the contrary, they imbued the movement with a feeling of permanent fraternization between students and workers, Frenchmen and foreigners, the red flag and the 'Internationale', thus rooting it in the great revolutionary tradition moribund since 1935.

At the same time these *groupuscules* steered and channelled the movement without ever quelling its fire. They constantly coaxed and restrained: '*Les cocus au balcon!*' cried a group of youngsters on a march down the Champs Élysées; '*Mais non, camarades*,' a steward replied softly. '*Ah! bon.*' Others, like the Marxists–Leninists (Maoists) and the FER (Trotskyist–Lambertists, the old CLER), quickly withdrew from the movement though in the breach they reappeared. The navigators and drivers were a constellation of groups and individuals of which the most important were respectively the JCR and Cohn-Bendit. UNEF transmitted official communications whilst maintaining and coordinating the otherwise dispersed militants. The help provided by UNEF veterans of the campaign against the Algerian War and the disputes with the PCF was crucial as was all manner of support given by university lecturers caught up in a phenomenon which moved them from the first. This amalgam or collection of individuals and political factions reminds one of the Paris commune and, thanks to the work of the JCR, October 1917. Cohn-Bendit's combination of anarchism and bolshevism worked marvels. In the space of a few days he revealed gifts for strategy, prudence and daring which made of this 'German Jew' the most engaging French political personality of the moment. His thinking was more lucid at this time than that of the most eminent academic and political figures. Never a leader, always an agitator and defuser, never deserted by his admirable sense of mass democracy and respect for the ideas and beliefs of his brothers-in-arms, Cohn-Bendit was youth's symbol of anarchistic creativity. Most students and schoolchildren had no political education. Characteristically they had been unmoved by 'politicians'. But through their playful and equally extraordinarily serious experience of direct democracy, they unknowingly revived the Petrograd Soviets.

Play and seriousness

Any explanation which purports to do justice to this phenomenon must take into account both play and serious work. In this context, play does not mean 'larking about', something which disappeared very quickly, but *ritual festivity* – seen for example in the euphoric procession across Paris – or more familiarly, the playing-at-guerrillas or playing-at-history, where seriousness, a feature of all games, led to the barricades of the past and the guerrillas of Che Guevara. The game was, of course, masked by ideology. But a common remark was 'we've got off to a great start'. It was a game, in the strategic sense of the word, about coordination, terrain and offensives. It was a true game authenticated by real risks including death. For here the play dimension became its opposite. With absolute seriousness, faith in their unity and their action these young people fought and told the world of their struggle.

The transition from play to seriousness and thence to tragedy occurred on the evening and night of Friday, 10 May. In a moment of revelry barricades were erected. An entire generation yearned to reappropriate real, epic, and bloody history of which they had been deprived, the history of revolutions and just and heroic causes still burning in Vietnam and in Latin America.

In the primitive forest the ordeal of initiation consists in confronting terrifying and malevolent spirits. The fact that this role was played by the police defending the State ensured that it would be a real initiation into the adult world with all its bestiality and cruelty. For thousands the week marked their initiation into society – a true socialization. For most it marked political maturity, for even if they were drawn into the struggle by unsophisticated calls of solidarity they discovered that society was based on conflict and the need to separate political good from political evil. They had served their political apprenticeship.

For the individual the great festival of youthful solidarity was his entrance examination into society, clearly preferable and superior to academic examinations. For the group it marked their willingness to stand up against established society.

Sorbonne-Potemkin or Sorbonne-Aurora ?

By the time Pompidou returned and the Government sounded its Kutusovian[2] retreat, the phase ushered in by the occupation of the Censier was fully developed. The student commune had occupied the Sorbonne, Nanterre and many provincial universities. These were its 'battleships Potemkin'.

The Sorbonne housed its most radical, important and vigorous elements. Once in the Sorbonne the commune was divided, like Siamese twins, into a *university commune* and a *political commune*. The university commune transformed the savage creativity of the streets into seminar-meetings and mass committees of inquiry. Freed from hierarchy and constraint the students devoted themselves to a profound and unaffected debate that continued day and night (which shows how far an institution

2. Russian general who defeated Napoleon by retreating before Napoleon's armies until their communication lines were overextended, and then chose the moment to attack.

forces the best as well as the worst to hold their tongues). The number of committees freely multiplied. There were committees examining staff–student relations and the structure and administration of the university and subjects, starting quite naturally with sociology and going on to literature and sex. Unfortunately there were no tape recorders to take down the thousands of discussions which expressed and celebrated the vision of a university utopia where true knowledge, stripped of its 'class' content, could be interchanged freely.

At this point the staff reappeared. Their most 'academic' and official wing never stopped fretting for the punishment of the guilty with a fury worthy of Versailles. The more liberal staff protested against the repression. Out of indignation, shrewd reformism or fear of being left behind, many sided with the students. But now they were worried that the mechanisms through which reforms might be secured were going to be lost in the whirlwind. Finally, the most sympathetic members of staff warned the movement against the danger of 'nihilism', meaning, in effect, its libertarianism. Proposals for reform which sprung forth like so many mushrooms in the heads of liberal professors, sadly began to moulder. The trend was towards a concrete utopia highlighted by an open and free Sorbonne dedicated to the working people and devoted to festivity and music and trying to actualize that new and glorious slogan: 'Here imagination rules!'

When the movement settled in the university, the revolutionary minorities re-emerged. They developed into hardened battalions of between five and ten thousand militants ready to engage in the most heroic battles to liberate society. Leading positions had been occupied after 3 May by old student *cadres* – semi-rejects of the consumer society – who brought their experience, wits and daring to the movement. A great transformation was under way. The leaders of the student revolution began to see themselves as the initiators of the revolutionary movement destined to destroy the 'bourgeois State'. The Sorbonne became the throne of Macedon for these latter-day Alexanders. A movement originating in a few small and divided factions became the power behind a vast army once the private property of the Stalinists. A society which had carefully built its defences everywhere had been attacked under the belt in its sociological nursery. Was this not that chance in a thousand calling out for the daring of a Lenin or a Trotsky? Was it not their duty to transform the Sorbonne-Potemkin into a Sorbonne-Aurora to bring down the entire house of cards: Gaullism, the Stalinist Communist party, the official Left and bourgeois law and order?

At this point the rich and triumphant unity of the student commune began to break. The political commune not only distanced itself from but sometimes opposed the university commune. In the eyes of the political intelligentsia the transformation of the university was no longer simply a secondary issue. There was a danger it would become a diversion. It was time to abandon celebration and reorganize. The first problem was to turn the courtyard of the Sorbonne into the launching pad for a new assault.

But because the movement felt that the two faces of the commune – political and university – were the expression of one single struggle for emancipation, unity was maintained. Turning to the working class, far from dividing the movement, as some feared, it actually furnished an ideology to justify its cultural struggle for an open university and its political struggle for a workers' State.

Nevertheless university reform and social revolution have been separated. Today the conflict is centred on this issue because discussions have yet to go further. Curiously the most enlightened members of staff resemble those German Social Democrats whom the forces of reaction left in the front line against the Spartakists. They try to show how reasonable and profitable reforms can be by appealing, far from unconsciously, to the embryonic adult and bourgeois found in every student who is subject to the conflicting demands of personal success – qualifications and a career – and social revolution.

The outcome of this conflict depends on which of these two forms of consciousness achieves the upper hand. Careerism is favoured by the fact that the reforms to be initiated once the repression is over have been published already. The fact that the revolutionary leaders are already committed to the logic of permanent revolution, to action at any price and by any means, favours the revolutionary outcome. By turning itself into the revolutionary *avant-garde* of the entire society, the student movement has challenged society by appealing to the working class to revolt – through the occupation of factories – and by their own occupation of not only cultural centres but some key Bastilles of the modern world. Today we find two conflicting strategies: one which is institutional seeking to drain the revolutionary movement of its momentum by guiding its waverers back to their studies; the other which is revolutionary proposing a rapid onslaught on the nerve centres of society before reforms are initiated. We have reached a point where anything is possible from the extinction of the revolt without any further consequences outside the university to the overthrow of the regime or civil war. Is the least probable outcome a workers' State?

The working class is the key problem. Between November 1967 and the beginning of May 1968 the political *groupuscules* were isolated in their closed Nanterrian redoubt. Communication with the working class was patronizing and the dialogue, when established, an act of political ventriloquism. As such, Marxism was a means of rationalization, in the psychological sense, as much as an instrument of rationality. In the nihilistic void left by nationalism and bourgeois values it acted like Levi-Strauss's *pensée sauvage* separating the high from the low, the cooked from the raw and the rotten, applying rules of etiquette, adjudicating and consolidating.

Proletarian or young people's revolution?

But between 3 May and 13 May links were forged with the young workers in the streets. The great demonstration of 13 May and the students' ideological purification through the fire of combat gave a concrete meaning to the idea of a student–worker coalition. Marxism ceased to be purely verbal. It found living confirmation in the 'permanent revolution' and the strength of collective creativity. It became a guide to action and a tool with which to formulate strategy.

In the phase announced by the occupation of the Sorbonne,

the expression 'working class' became little more than stuffing to fill mental chasms – a magic word whisking away contradictions or, indeed, a litanical expression which consecrated them. The moving fraternal appeal to the working class had an enormous impact on workers under thirty, not yet *accustomed* to the stultification of their work and the smallness of their lives. It was strongly echoed in the more militant factories and even provoked the first occupations. But even if the occupations spread, would the official Left not retrieve the movement and use it as it saw fit? On the rocky road to power, the student *avant-garde* will run up against the trade unions and the large parties of the opposition who will do their best to absorb the movement, steer it towards reform, expel its most revolutionary element or even allow the revolutionary battalions to be butchered so that their memory, of course, can be commemorated in the future. Neither a week of bloodshed nor another June 1936, discrediting the Government and opening the door to the official Left, can be ruled out.

A good orthodox Marxist would ask if the revolutionary 'intelligentsia', whilst believing it has started the proletarian revolution of Marx and Lenin, is not really doing something quite different, namely marking the advent of youth and youthful ideas as a social and political force through their own version of 1789? Marxist concepts and forceps might be necessary to the operation to justify, enrich and guide its action and to give ideological coherence to an otherwise formless and nameless unrest.

It is clear that the student *avant-garde* is at present the 'intelligentsia' of a growing movement amongst young people. The main feature of the movement itself is that by means of a kind of spontaneous solidarity it is spreading to all classes of young people. In Paris and in many provincial towns, the lycée students have been actively challenging their headmasters, teachers and the disciplinary system in their 'barracks' schools since 3 May. Young workers and particularly young white-collar workers, exiles from the working class, and young *déclassés* have been active in the movement. Their agitation has won the support of young CGT members. Indeed, there was nearly a revolt of young Communist party *cadres* at the time of the secret central committee meeting on 11 May.

Given these conflicting elements, is the Sorbonne a 'Potemkin' heralding a new 1917 or is it a 'Bastille', a prelude to 1789? I would think it is something of a hybrid. By borrowing a revolutionary ideology it injects the need for social change into youth's need for renewal. Like all profound or traditional revolutions, it anticipates the future revolutionary needs of society.

3. The Days That Shook France . . .

May 1968 – June 1968

The working class has responded to the students' passionate call to revolt. Quite unexpectedly, a factory in Nantes was occupied by its workers. Within two days one factory after another was occupied throughout the country with the same spontaneity that accompanied the student occupations. Unlike the students, the working class was circumscribed by powerful trade unions. The CGT, the largest trade union, refused to accept an umbilical cord leading from the Sorbonne to the Renault factory. Symbolically they bolted the doors at the Billancourt plant against any would-be fraternizers.

Indeed, the issue of student–worker fraternization is an important aspect of a struggle to the death between two ideologies and conceptions of the world. Firstly, the rejuvenated 'Trotskyist' or 'Leftist' movements thirsting for revenge are pitted against a Stalinist machine which was first flabbergasted by the return of the 'Monte Cristo' it thought it had liquidated over thirty years ago and is now seething with a rage lessened only by the passage of time.

Secondly, the reformism practised by the Communist party corresponds to the material needs of a large section of the working class. Ideologically its revolutionary mythology satisfies some of the daily frustrations of working-class life. But young workers are not inured to the belief that wages, security, housing, holidays and children are all there is to life. Are

123

'workers' control' and 'revolution' the panacea which will destroy a system based on factory regimentation?

Awakened by the student movement, the fever of battle spread to the young workers who in turn stirred the half-forgotten dreams of their older workmates, long since invested in the USSR, spurring them to make militant claims. This is how the factory occupations spread.

The phenomenon may be no more than a flash-in-the-pan or a new 1936, the prelude to a Popular Front. We can only find out later.

For the first time in twentieth-century France a movement born in the university has spread, at an ever increasing rate, to the working class and particularly to salaried workers. Tentatively these events can be explained by the conjuncture of inter-generational conflict with the workers' struggle. The revolt of young people, not yet accustomed to the rhythms of techno-bureaucratic society, has merged with the traditional but weakening forms of working-class resistance to capitalist authority. By occupying the Sorbonne, the student commune imitated a workers' revolution. When the workers followed they did so with ease because they were renewing a working-class tradition. *In brief, the student* avant-garde *re-proletarianized the proletariat.*

Its repercussions may even be more extensive. By smashing the feudalistic university, the student commune aroused a libertarian, or at any rate a liberalizing, reflex against all forms of unconditional authority whether in the lycée, the ORTF, in provincial universities (where autonomy means decentralization), or in the factory.

The student movement became a national movement. Libertarian-revolutionary tendencies have come to the fore in the more exceptional cases and liberal-federalist ones in the more moderate cases. Amongst workers and intellectuals the libertarian school is seeking to reconcile itself with Marxism along the lines outlined a few years ago in the radical journal *Socialisme ou Barbarie*. In the provinces, federalism and decentralization, submerged for so long under Jacobin France, have re-emerged. In both cases the resurrection has been remarkable.

These events occurred because throughout the movement's development, youth and freedom have been contrasted with age and authority. The exceptional circumstances at the root of these events made such an identification possible. At the same time, the students' strategic mobility, their capacity to catch the public eye with spontaneous and imaginative acts – like the occupation of the Sorbonne, the challenge to the ORTF, fraternization marches – and their new modes of action not only succeeded in changing antagonism between university and factory into attraction but injected a dose of youthful libertarianism into the ageing body of France.

The student commune will probably not lead to a revolution but to a series of social reforms involving decentralization and rejuvenation. By battering the bureaucracies of the working-class parties and indicating new possibilities, they may have started the much heralded beginning of a new Left in France.

4. Metamorphosis

The fate of the student political commune is now sealed. The student movement has been weakened by its very act of destroying the feudal university and triggering off a semi-revolutionary upheaval. Once reforms are under way, the university commune becomes excess baggage. In one of those paradoxes so dear to history, the revolutionary explosion has been used to initiate, accelerate and extend a programme of reform. In the absence of a major social and political upheaval it is also likely that these reforms will be both 'technocratic' and democratizing. They will broaden the student intake and abolish all forms of professorial divine right.

The new dogma will be to interpret the crisis in terms of the failure of the university to adapt to modern society. This will open the way to a general rationalization of the university system and such things as time and motion studies. As a result larger and larger sections of the population will be integrated into the mechanism of a technological–managerial–industrial–bourgeois–consumer–leisure-society.

On the other hand, the fundamental crisis, that feeling of profound anguish or anger which model campuses, organizational seminars and open-minded disciplinarians will do nothing to reduce, will deepen. A new era has begun in which the student will be conscious, as he never was before, of adult society's radical inability to deal with its pernicious and techno–bureaucratic system of work, the petit-bourgeois ritualism imposed outside the work place as well as the poverty, sickness and human misery of the affluent society. This consciousness will be transmitted by the revolutionary minorities. They will also distort it by seeking immediately to put their ideas in practice. Despite their fixations and Manichaeism, they are the source of a global political consciousness as well as daring to break university taboos (though tending to create new taboos in their place). In society as in the university, the student detonator will have accelerated reform as well as the movement to contest the very basis of society.

By subsuming all the revolutions ever dreamed of and by genuinely challenging the established order, the student commune is almost a revolution in itself. Like all revolutions it is rich, foolish and good-humoured, a utopian explosion firmly rooted in space and time. It is historical ecstasy. It fosters communication between individuals and groups in a new spirit of comradeship and generosity. I am thinking here of those kids hopefully waiting that Friday for one thing only, that their unknown comrades, Frenchmen and foreigners, students and non-students would be set free, of the *agrégation* candidates who after so much hard work refused to sit their exams, and those militants who have dedicated their lives to the workers' cause.

The quasi- or peri-revolution is, of course, far from perfect. Even amongst the anarchists, libertarianism is not accompanied by that liberalism which experience of real dictatorship teaches, nor that capacity to distinguish words from deeds which comes with experience of a real Communist system, nor that really radical critique characteristic of the intellectual Renaissance in the East which dares to criticize orthodox Marxism.

A classical model

It is not clear if the outcome will be idyllic or tragic. *But whatever happens the student commune has contributed something new which would never have come out of evolution.* This something new has not yet crystallized. It grows from the encounter between a movement deeply rooted in youth with the helmsmen of small revolutionary sects. The prejudices of one and the ideologies of the other shroud the face of the advancing Sphinx.

Marx once said that the French Revolution was a classic revolution because it developed the characteristics upon which all succeeding bourgeois revolutions were modelled. Perhaps in a similar way, the Paris student commune will become the classic model for all future transformations in Western societies. The destruction of the University Bastille drew together all types of young people in much the same way as the destruction of that other Bastille united the Three Orders in 1789. The transformation of the Sorbonne into a forum-cum-festival-cum-laboratory of ideas created the image of an open society and an open university where imagination reigns in the place of a dismal bureaucracy, where education is available to all and where economic exploitation and domination have been eradicated. By reaching out to the extremities of society, the student commune foreshadows the crucial and vital role that the university will play in the future. Soon more than half the population of France will pass through the university. There the problem of transcending and creating something better than bourgeois humanity will first be encountered.

The historical role of the student commune will be all the more enhanced by its never having been anything but itself. Those who believe that its mission was to trigger a workers' revolution and those who feel that it should have restricted itself to university reform have misunderstood its role. Precisely because it has been utopian rather than constructive it has been able to envisage a future which embraces the entire society. Because it has refused immediate compromises it is already exemplary.

May 1968

4. The May Movement at the Lycée Pasteur, Neuilly

Y.L., teacher at the Lycée

'The majority is shit, but the minority – that's great.'
(Heraclitus, trans. Lycée Pasteur)

One teacher and eight sixth-formers from the Lycée Pasteur, a sample of those who were the most active in the strike and in the work of the commissions, came together at the end of June 1968 to attempt a brief analysis of the movement inside the Lycée. Clearly, this is only one particular example; in other places the movement takes different forms and is made up of different factors. We have tried to remain very close to the facts and to give each particular event and each particular person its due importance.

The pupils at the Lycée Pasteur come from the bourgeoisie: upper managerial classes, technocrats, liberal professions, high-ranking military personnel, etc. The sons of teachers and traders constitute, so to speak, the proletariat. In their discussion, therefore, the pupils start with the fact that the Lycée exists and that it is their natural milieu. Their fundamental questioning of it remains largely theoretical. They are not concerned with the problem of entry, of admission to the benefits of secondary education.

Nevertheless, although the problem in its social aspect is appreciated less here than elsewhere, the pupils are perhaps more conscious of its political implications.

One of the remarkable things about the movement is its distrust of existing political organizations and trade unions – the refusal of the majority of strikers to situate the movement *a priori* on a political level, in the existing political terms of reference. Besides, political consciousness was very low in the Lycée Pasteur before the events of May. On the other hand, the genuine process of politicization, not in terms of the political parties, but in the manner of approaching the relevant problems (problems of fundamental issues, of method and of tactics), has been overwhelming. In three weeks, unpoliticized youngsters were discussing questions of revolution and reformism, apathy, trade unionism, the relations between leaders and the masses, the quelling of a spontaneous revolutionary movement by the forces of reaction, movements designed specifically for 'social warfare', the conflict between the generations, the definition of culture, etc.

Y.L. (a teacher): Question. How was the CAL at Pasteur created?

ANDRÉ: It began when I was contacted by some guys from the National Vietnam Committee. There were about ten of them and they had some knowledge of politics. This Committee had only made contact with a few people. They didn't seem very interested in recruitment.

MARC: We never had any meetings inside the Lycée; there were a few inter-Lycée meetings and some debates on Vietnam.

ANDRÉ: Let me say something about the period before February. I was contacted at the beginning of February and people began to talk about the CALs. I attended a meeting on 27 February, the day after the strike of teachers and pupils. This meeting was very political. I got the impression that everybody, from the Communist party to the Right-wing extremists, had sent people along to take us under their wing, to try and get us to do something very political. Afterwards, this kind of thing was stopped; but we started discussing things at the Lycée between ourselves, and the members of the CAL came together again quite independently of the original politicized organizers.

MARC: Even so, the CAL really started because of a minor event – the Condorcet affair.[1] From there we got the idea of forming a pupils' union to defend pupils who were the object of sanctions of that kind.

FRANÇOIS: And to defend the freedom of political expression.

1. A student was excluded from the Condorcet Lycée on political grounds. This led to mass demonstrations in many Paris lycées.

MARTINE: I did not participate until certain significant events had taken place. The CAL was rather a closed shop. I had wanted to make contact, because some of the boys in my class were members, but I found it impossible.

ANDRÉ: That's true. At first, we were obliged to work in a certain secrecy so as not to arouse the authorities. There were only a few of us; it was like a little Mafia.

Y.L.: Question. Yes, wasn't there a certain fear of making contact with people who were not very committed?

MARC: Of course. And we also knew that as soon as T. or B. started speaking (I'm talking now just of people inside the lycée), the others would say 'Communist!' or 'Anarchist!' or something like that. And in fact at the beginning the CAL was very politicized, on the extreme Left. Comrades who already had a Marxist culture helped us to politicize ourselves.

FRANÇOIS: We must make the distinction between the CAL after the events in the Latin Quarter, when it grew enormously, and the CAL before. In fact, after the disturbances, we weren't very sure if there had been a CAL or to what extent we constituted one. Personally, I didn't know the CAL very well, although I knew it existed, since L. had told me about it in class. I didn't join, I don't really know why. Probably a lack of political maturity. During May, I realized that it was a useful means of getting things done, and I attended the meetings of the CAL at the Sorbonne. But we didn't know then whether it was merely an organ concerning itself with affairs inside the lycée, the *baccalauréat*, etc. – in which case anyone could join – or whether it was a revolutionary movement, in which case it was a question of the participation of a revolutionary minority.

ANDRÉ: The CAL had drawn up a sort of programme. A leaflet, which was handed out in the lycée on the day after the strike of 26 February, pointed out that 'life does not stop at the lycée doors', that 'the lycée's job is to promote understanding of life', and went on to claim the recognition of a pupils' union, the right to hold meetings, to communicate and to put up posters inside the lycée. It demanded pupil participation (in internal administration, in matters of discipline), the right of dissent and the right to make demands (supported, if necessary, by strike action), and it protested against the process of selection for entrance to university, which consists of the pupil being prematurely directed into one particular channel without being able to choose properly and without being fully conscious of what is happening to him.

MARC: And the first concrete action was the strike-call sent out by the CAL on 26 February. It fired the imagination of the pupils, and they began to think about uniting in order to give their action lasting effect.

Y.L.: Question. Was there any feeling of unrest in the lycée before the strike? If so, how did it manifest itself?

MARC: Yes, I was conscious of a certain unrest; I had drawn up some ideas on the teaching of history and Latin. When I spoke to other people about them, they were not particularly interested. They thought I had original ideas, which was not the case. And because I refused to learn the text books by heart and the notes which had been dictated to me, some of my friends thought I was an anarchist.

ANDRÉ: I think a lot of people were aware of it, but because they heard their parents say so, they thought that nothing could be done; that things being what they are, you have to make the best of them. Anybody who thought himself capable of changing something was seen as a kind of freak.

ALAIN: Many pupils were fed up with being robots; they were protesting against the destruction of their personality, against the predetermined path which leads nowhere.

MICHEL: Something must be said about the reaction against their background. There are many people who joined the movement as a reaction against their families and who were finally able to liberate their ideas.

ANDRÉ: There was even the ultimate reaction, against everything that existed. Everything merged into one.

MARC: There was reaction at all levels: on the Right as much as on the Left. Reaction within the family, but also among friends at the same lycée.

MICHEL: There was also reaction on a psychological level. The personalities of all the people I know have opened out spectacularly since then. It's fantastic.

ALAIN: They have become aware of the many problems facing society; they have begun to think about their own destiny, about the way they are integrated into their families, their background, the bourgeoisie, etc. And they have liberated themselves totally.

Y.L.: Question. How did the movement begin in Pasteur?

ALAIN: The strike began on 10 May, the day before the barricades. That morning there was a strike picket in front of the lycée. Only about twenty of us had been told about it the previous evening.

MARC: Yes, it was very strange the way the strike began. We got to school as usual with all our books, and then there were people telling us: 'No. No lessons this morning.'

MARTINE: There were twelve of us at half past seven. There were about a hundred who stayed outside, and then about two or three hundred came out again after the first lesson.

MICHEL: There is a bit of snobbery about the success of the strike that day. It didn't mean much, at least in those classes which I know. People stayed outside out of curiosity. The whole matter has been distorted. The strike would have taken place in any case on the following day, but on that particular day it had no chance of success.

ANDRÉ: Even so, there was a leaflet on the theme 'Free Our Comrades'. After the big demonstrations in the Latin Quarter we decided to organize demonstrations of lycée students in the suburbs: this, of course, implied a strike. And the novelty of the strike met with considerable success. After that, people read the papers and began to get better informed.

MARC: I think we must emphasize this. There was no snobbery or myth about the strike. Those who acted out of snobbery on the first day were never seen again. The others, those who stayed, did it for a reason.

Y.L.: Question. On the first day, there were about three hundred who stayed out. Active participation (that is to say, participation in the general meetings) never exceeded this figure. On average, if you count people who worked regularly in the commissions and who took part in the teaching experiments, the number of genuine active strikers was considerably less. In a lycée of 2,000 pupils, where there must be at least five hundred about to enter university, this is not much. How do you explain this?

MARTINE: First of all because we are in Neuilly; it's because of the area.

ANDRÉ: In the beginning, when it was a question of occupying the lycée, we had the majority of the sixth form with us. Then when we split up into working commissions many people, seeing that they were going to be required to work and to give of themselves, decided to stay at home, reading, taking a holiday, etc.

MICHEL: There is a remarkable non-participation in Neuilly, on the part of the young. I will give you another example – the *Maison des jeunes et de la culture*. It's very good, they organize a lot of very interesting activities, but attendance is very low. The young people have got all they want at home: comfort, radio, television, they go to the cinema whenever they like; they are not used to collective work which requires a certain amount of self-sacrifice.

Y.L.: It seems to me that Neuilly displays a sort of cultural or pseudo-cultural saturation. It is one of the places where integration into the consumer society has been the most complete. I detect a sort of apathy in the classes at the lycée.

ANDRÉ: Certainly. And in the classes people don't get to know one another, in contrast to many other lycées. Even the clubs have failed.

MARTINE: And it was the movement that brought people closer together. It changed everything completely.

Y.L.: It also brought the teachers closer together.

MARC: And teachers and pupils. But it was quite restrained. There were too many teachers who did not wish to participate in the commissions. There were at most six or seven who attended regularly. Out of one hundred and fifteen teachers at the lycée, it's a very small number.

ALAIN: And those who came were union members, of SNES or SGEN. On the whole we had confidence in them.

But they soon lost this confidence because of the attitude of the unions to the strike and to the problem of the *baccalauréat*. It is a question which we must deal with.

MARC: SNES has had a curious and a disappointing effect on the pupils. The union meetings which we attended were disappointing. We had the impression that when we attended meetings many things changed, we had considerable influence over the teachers and convinced them of many things.

MARTINE: There was one meeting, for example, where B. had begun to speak, and little by little he almost persuaded the teachers to denounce the *baccalauréat*. But it failed in the end.

MARC: There was another point on which we felt that we had been let down by the teachers. They said: 'Teaching experiments? – very good'; but, with one exception, they did not really participate. They failed to bring in people from outside, they took no great part in the large meetings; personally, I regretted this very much. I could not understand it.

MARTINE: I think that the teachers had agreed that all initiatives should come from the pupils.

MARC: That is true, but we found it odd that teachers, who sat on commissions at the beginning, never took charge of these commissions. There was a complete reversal of values.

MARTINE: They were frightened of the pupils!

Y.L.: As far as I am concerned, I purposely stayed in the background. I can give you the example of a work group to which two of us went. We found the group particularly silent, despite the fact that it had been in session for over an hour. We learnt later from the report to the general meeting, that the discussion had gone very well *up to the time of our arrival*. I think that both sides have certain habits which they must gradually get rid of.

MARC: When we created the commissions we invited the teachers to speak, to perform their normal functions and, if necessary, to direct the debate. They did not do so. We cannot understand why.

FRANÇOIS: Finding people willing to accept positions of responsibility on the commissions was very difficult.

ALAIN: We said we had to assume responsibilities and perhaps this was just what we did least. We said that the individual had to learn to speak and to be responsible, but it went no further than that.

MARC: The CAL people made a few mistakes, but it's all instructive.

Y.L.: There is a lack of practice. It reveals the deficiencies of the teaching.

FRANÇOIS: Yes, there were not many people who were really committed, who actively participated in the strike and not simply sat on commissions in a more or less passive manner.

The essence of the movement. Reform and revolution

MARC: You say 'committed'. Committed to what?

FRANÇOIS: To the direction of the movement. Look, I'll give you an example. I didn't go on strike on the Friday (10 May). I got to school, the strike began. I couldn't explain to myself why they were going on strike. So I went in and attended classes. After that, there was the night of the barricades and I came out on strike in solidarity with the students, against the repression. Later, I moved on to the stage of 'educational reform'.

ANDRÉ: That's it; that's very important. You go on strike first of all *against* something, and then *for* something. Two general meetings later, the commissions got moving. One must emphasize the way in which the problem of the *baccalauréat* catalysed the strike, just as the exams did for the students. Every meeting tended to revolve around the *baccalauréat*; we couldn't get away from it. It even slowed down the work.

MARC: Yes, but it was a matter of personal concern to everyone, much more so than when discussion was situated on a level that was too high.

MICHEL: The question of the *bac* gave a general direction to the discussions, as soon as it was posed in terms of its influence on selection and on orientation.

MARC: One might even say that the problem of the *bac* is a concrete political issue.

ALAIN: Certainly. There was a chain-reaction as soon as we attempted to define it, either as a terminal secondary exam, or as a university entrance qualification. People began to ask questions about the structure of secondary education and about the channels into which pupils tend to be forced.

MARC: Only a small minority grasped the fact that it was a political problem.

FRANÇOIS: Something extremely simple, which people took a long time to understand, was the fact that by trying to change the education system you automatically change society itself.

MARC: In this sense the *bac* is *our* weapon, our means of exerting pressure. This problem was posed right from the beginning. The teachers took a long time to react and so did SNES.

MICHEL: Some teachers went so far as to say that they did not want to hear anything more about the *bac*, that they wanted to put the thing on a political level, and that the union struggle was irrelevant in view of the added prospect of elections. So they gave up.

Y.L.: The elections meant depoliticizing the whole movement.

ALAIN: As far as the *bac* is concerned, it was a total failure. In the end the Government's plan has been put into effect.

MICHEL: Previously, nobody was particularly aware of the power of the Gaullist Government, of authority, of the Gaullist dictatorship. That came later.

ANDRÉ: In any case it is something which is much more international. Gaullism is only one aspect. It's here that the movement is especially interesting – in the way that it has attempted to disown the past and all the forms of authority which we have known: parents, teachers, the bureaucracy. It has suddenly become aware of the fact that the revolutionary movement can come only from the young.

MARC: We must examine the role played by the Right and Left during the strike. There was an explosion of consciousness which took place outside the current political terms of reference. I saw people from all shades of opinion, particularly from the extreme Right, marching with the movement, while others, let us call them Leftists, were afraid of the movement and have since become Gaullists (end of June). Everything is now reduced to the terms Gaullism and anti-Gaullism, whereas in the movement there was a complete change in political values.

ALAIN: Yes, they were all little reformists and revolutionaries. At Pasteur, it seems to me, they were mainly reformists and only a few revolutionaries. It was a question of a little bit of educational reform here and there. No social revolution was envisaged.

MARC: There was a meeting of pupils' parents where the parents said: 'Do you or do you not wish to transform society?' And the pupils replied: 'No, of course we don't want a *real* social revolution.' I felt like interrupting and saying: 'Of course we want a revolution and of course the movement is wholly political.' I refrained, simply because it was obvious that the majority of people at Pasteur were not in agreement. It was only true of a minority.

ALAIN: This was even more the case with the parents. They demanded a 'reform of the culture' and proceeded to go through the curriculum, emphasizing the need for the memory to be trained and the necessity for the formal lecture. Or else they said: 'What you're asking for was being asked for ten years ago.' They understood nothing.

MARC: The people who were the most active, the most politicized, at the beginning, were soon left behind. Because they were already well known, other people said: 'No, we want nothing to do with them; they'll only drag us into political movements'.

MICHEL: Even the teachers were against us at that time. And the teachers who wanted to organize some sort of action in the lycées were against politics. I know that in some schools teachers who were communists said: 'It is absolutely forbidden for you to come and stand outside the lycée without UNEF cards or to take part in any political agitation.'

MARC: The politicized people who founded the movement began in a very tactless way. They created an ambiguous atmosphere, bringing with them a sort of political folk-lore – 'Comrades' etc. It was only natural that they should do so, but it didn't work, and right from the start people tended to withdraw, to react against it.

Y.L.: Let us clarify this point. Do you think it was an 'apolitical' reaction, or a reaction of suspicion against existing political organizations?

ANDRÉ: I think it was a reaction of suspicion and not an 'apolitical' reaction.

MARC: It must be said that when you speak of 'politics' in a class, people immediately think of communism. This was very clear in our class; every time we spoke of politics, the reaction was: 'At our age politics has nothing to do with us.' It's important to remember this, because it means that whenever we undertake political action, people think that we are members of the Party.

ANDRÉ: So those who were the most politically-minded were persuaded to withdraw, making way for less politicized people, and by the end of the strike the main leaders were no longer those who had set the movement in motion; the initial nucleus had disappeared.

FRANÇOIS: Yes, I have often made one specific complaint to T. Whenever he wanted to talk politics, I said to him: 'I agree entirely, but first of all you must set up political information commissions. Most people who talk about politics do not know what a party is, what a trade union is. I often asked him to do this, but he never did.

MARC: When the strike began to break up, after the commissions had been working for two weeks, we decided to set up this political information commission. It seemed improbable to us that people should talk about communism without, for example, having read the Communist Party Manifesto. But the idea was advanced without sufficient preparation and it was badly received.

Y.L.: Question. Did any Right-wing elements participate in the movement?

ANDRÉ: The reaction of the Right was rather odd. There were a few when the commissions were set up, in particular the commission for joint control. One of them would interrupt at every opportunity, but he gradually settled down and had nothing more to say.

MICHEL: We never had any serious or positive opposition

from the three or four Right-wing people who sat on the commissions. They were always on our side.

ANDRÉ: Some have changed completely, even so far as to play important parts in the commissions. But on the whole we did not see much of them. They went into hiding, or studied hard for the exam, I don't know what they did. At first they said: 'It's a political movement; you do not understand. It's Communist subversion; don't get mixed up in it.' Then, strangely enough, a CDR appeared. So much for a non-political movement!

ALAIN: How can a young man be Right-wing anyway?

MARC: Influenced by relations and family. Just as there are some who are influenced by the Communist party.

ANDRÉ: On the other hand, there were fascists from *Occident* who were just looking for a fight. One day they raided the lycée. They gave us a lot of trouble, because they gave the authorities an excuse to limit the number of rooms available to us, to make us take down our posters, and to shut the lycée on Saturday afternoon when there were no lessons. A small minority, about thirty, wanted a total occupation of the lycée. But obviously, thirty people on their own are quite powerless. This limited the movement and contributes to the fact that the movement was not very progressive, that it was reformist and only slightly politicized.

VINCENT: There was also the attitude of certain Catholics. I was at a meeting organized by M. G. Sauge for young people, officers' sons, etc. The organizer told them to do their utmost for the revolution because existing society is abominable in the eyes of Christ. Naturally, society must not get into Communist hands, but it had to be changed and it was the duty of Christians to do all they could for the movement. It seems to me that the attitude of the Communist party was much more static.

ALAIN: Surely they were trying to use the movement for their own ends?

MICHEL: No, I think it was all quite sincere. For them the consumer society is something to be rejected. It seems to me that what is really against the movement is the conservative and retrogressive power of Gaullism.

MARTINE: After the strike there was a split in my class: on one side were the strikers; on the other were the non-strikers who wanted to continue classes in the traditional way – they annoyed the striking teachers and were all Gaullists.

ALAIN: There was a certain back-lash of parents and teachers who formed an 'autonomous' group.

MICHEL: There was the CDR, started not by pupils but by a teacher. Who joined? None of the guys on the Right that we knew.

ANDRÉ: At the time of the formation of the commissions, the teacher concerned set up another commission in his class. He gave his lessons in a manner which purported to be revolutionary. At first, even I was unable to see what he was getting at. He claimed to be apolitical. Then finally he gave out leaflets. The people in the CDR are basically the pupils of this teacher.

Y.L.: Question. Why did you organize elections to be held parallel to the elections of 23 June?

MARC: They were of no great importance. It was a vote indicative of the leanings of young people ineligible to vote in the elections.

Y.L.: That seems very equivocal to me. It is to enter into an exercise which should be rejected in principle, and to vote for parties whose problems are not your problems, and none of which really represent you.

FRANÇOIS: The vote reflected the division between strikers and non-strikers.

Y.L.: Question. What about next year?

FRANÇOIS: Whenever it's a question of prolonging the strike at Pasteur, there is one thing that disturbs me – the lack of people from the first-year sixth form. Their participation was very minor and distant.

MARC: It's regrettable, but understandable. In any case, they will have heard these ideas; they will think about them. Next year they will have the same problems; things will be carried on. They will not be unaware of what we have done. It's natural that in the second year you don't have the same preoccupations.

With you, it's different, you're going up to university, you're already much closer.

The work of the commissions

Several commissions operated for a fortnight, working on such subjects as educational reform, examinations, culture, student/worker liaison, the ethic of competition, etc. The commissions drew up reports, projects, draft programmes: reports on physical education, on music teaching, on art teaching, on modern language teaching. 'Proposals for Secondary Education' outline a system of secondary education based on a 'common stem' for all, aiming at the abolition of premature selection and of the irreversible chanelling process which takes place in the first and fourth years; they aim at removing all forms of segregation (for example, the distinction between 'short' and 'long' education). One project devised a comprehensive system of joint administration, bringing together the academic authorities, teachers, pupils and parents in the organization of education and in the internal workings of educational establishments.

The work at Pasteur also took a different form – that of the 'teaching experiments', already in operation at the Lycée Henri IV. The daily programme was as follows:

8.30–9.00	General meeting, in which the day's programme of group work is announced.
9.00–12.00	Group work. Groups of fifteen to twenty pupils meet freely every Monday to decide their work for the week. They ensure that at least one teacher is present, competent in the subject chosen.
12.00–12.30	General meeting, group reports.
Afternoon	Lectures, debates, films, sports.

These work groups were experimental; they represented an attempt to move from pure protest and theoretical discussion to practice, while avoiding all types of traditional 'lessons'.

The topics chosen for group work were very varied: reading and discussion of modern literature (Beckett's *Waiting for Godot*, Malraux's *La Condition Humaine*, Robbe-Grillet's *Les*

141

Gommes), debates on the Common Market and Europe, on Latin America, on the liberation struggles; talks on the application of statistics, on the study of biology; the study of a text by Heraclitus, during which one group produced the translation which has since become a watch-word at Pasteur: 'the majority is shit, but the minority – that's great'.

Lastly, the strike committee produced a news-sheet containing opinions, film reviews, poems, political commentary, etc. During the strike, many sketches, paintings and poems appeared on the walls, as well as several collective murals. Naturally, all this vanished with the return to 'order'. Similarly, with the return of the non-striking teachers and pupils, all the traditional patterns of authoritarianism/acceptance reappeared – active or passive refusal, competition, rowdyism. But no order lasts for ever. Only contradiction is eternal. In view of this, the prospect of next Autumn term must be regarded at least with interest.

June 1968

5. The CFDT and the May Crisis

André Jeanson

To give as clear and precise an account as possible of the sequence of events that marked the May/June crisis of 1968 and to analyse the many problems raised by these events, I propose to divide the period into three phases.

The first phase began when the Rector of the University of Paris, M. Roche, summoned the police to expel several hundred students gathered in the Sorbonne for a meeting on 3 May. This infringement of the Sorbonne's traditional extra-territoriality aroused the fury of even those students who had little to do with the small groups of extremists previously involved in clashes with the police.

From the 3rd up to the General Strike organized by the CGT, the CFDT, the CGT-FO and the FEN on 13 May the atmosphere was marked by expressions of working-class solidarity with the students as a result of police repression rather than as a result of working-class identity with student demands. Such expressions of sympathy were quite natural because the working class has long known what it is like to be confronted by the police.

At this time the CFDT looked behind the labels attributed to the revolt, whether systematic violence and intolerance or anarchism and negativity, and found that the students were clearly aware of the total paralysis of the French university system and their own total alienation from these institutions. Once stripped of its frills it is clear that the students' awareness of these conditions led to their formulating demands for the right to participate in the planning and organization of the methods and content of their education. For the CFDT such demands echoed its own theoretical preoccupations and the thoughts of its rank-and-file: that the workers should acquire the right to participate in every facet of their existence from the shop floor to the national economy.

This first phase achieved its apotheosis on 13 May, marked by the tremendous street demonstration joined that afternoon by several hundred thousand workers and students who with the greatest calm and discipline expressed their solidarity with the victims of the police repression.

For many of the organizers of the demonstration, it also marked the end of the events themselves. But the student movement had been launched by groups who were untainted by the influence of Communist organizations and it was only natural that they should continue to control something which was now mushrooming into a revolutionary movement. Not only did the PCF play no part in these events but it was severely challenged by them. For a political organization with the reputation of the only revolutionary power in France, they were thrust into an impossible position. But the workers' spontaneous solidarity with the victims of the Latin Quarter riots also meant that by broadening the struggle they could dissipate its energy and nip it in the bud. Clearly by the evening of 13 May the PCF and the CGT thought they had succeeded.

But events did not move according to the strategies of Place Kossuth or Rue Lafayette.[1] On 14 May a group of young workers at the Sud-Aviation plant at Nantes chose to follow the lead of their student comrades. Winning over other workers in the factory they struck, occupied their workshops and even imprisoned the works manager in his office. In the hours and days that followed, the strike movement, highlighted by factory occupations, spread up and down the country with extraordinary speed affecting the commercial and agricultural sectors as well as industrial enterprises and paralysing the nation's economic activity.

Many have asked if this sudden explosion had been foreseen or organized beforehand. First of all, the movement came as a

1. Headquarters respectively of the P C F and the C G T.

complete surprise. Secondly in their demands and daily activity whether in the workshop or industrial sector, the workers had run into a wall of incomprehension, refusal, managerial authority and hierarchy for many years. For the worker managerial authority was indistinguishable from political authority: the two were inseparable. In the space of a few days the students shattered this institutional setting whilst the seemingly invincible regime could do nothing to stop them. The workers instinctively understood that the time had come for them to confront authority, already vanquished in the Latin Quarter, and to directly attack the hierarchical walls already demolished in the University.

The speed with which the strike spread had much to do with modern communications, particularly the transistor. News of a strike and occupation at one plant was immediately transmitted to the rest of the country encouraging similar actions throughout France.

The CFDT was not particularly surprised by the events. For many years it had denounced the paralysis and inadaptability of the nation's political, economic and social institutions. Through its declarations and resolutions the CFDT pointed out that governmental, political and managerial authority were contrary to the legitimate interests of the working class and to the requirements of a viable modern democracy. Over these many years CFDT militants sometimes had the impression that they were preaching in the wilderness. They quickly saw years of hard work more than repaid during the first days of May.

For these reasons the CFDT was in complete harmony with the rank-and-file feelings which more or less explicitly propelled their occupation of their places of work. Just as the students gained control of their faculties and universities so the workers, by launching a generalized strike highlighted by factory occupations, could similarly become their own masters – if only for a few days.

On 16 May the national executive of the CFDT issued a statement which was to remain its philosophy throughout the crisis:

By their action the students did not merely intend to limit themselves to immediate material conditions or their own futures, but to re-examine fundamentally the ossifying and suffocating institutions of a class-bound society where they could not exercise their responsibility.

The student struggle to democratize the university and the workers' struggle to democratize industry are one and the same. The constraints and institutions against which the students are rebelling are paralleled by even more intolerable forms in factories, on work-sites, in offices and workshops.

Liberty in industrial enterprises corresponds to liberty in the university. Hence the student struggle is the same as the struggle in which the working class has been engaged since the birth of trade unionism.

Industrial and administrative monarchy must be replaced by democratic institutions based on self-management.

The extension of trade-union rights, the recognition of industrial trade unions, the guarantee of employment, the right of workers to participate in the running of the economy and of industry must be asserted with greater fervour than ever.

The CFDT's action is based on its view that the worker must be associated as fully as possible in all decisions which affect him. Hence it now calls upon workers and their trade-union organizations to discuss, organize and take action at their work to obtain respect for freedom and democracy.

Fully conscious of the extent and scope of the present crisis and loyal to the traditions of the French working-class movement, the CFDT declares its full support for all actions undertaken in order to build a democratic society.

This second phase of strikes, the beginning of the occupations of factories, offices, workshops, building sites, etc., has both romantic and political aspects. It was romantic because it was imbued with the revolutionary inspiration of the Sorbonne: where once one suffered daily the crushing burden of hierarchical structures and those who commanded, one was now immersed in the strike organizing life within the factory, the maintenance of equipment, property and sanitation in the workshops. Suddenly the worker had become the master.

It was political because the strike raised the basic problem of the form of the industrial enterprise and the relationship between those who command and those who are commanded. There can hardly be a more political problem.

Contiguously, an offensive against the Government in the form of a motion of censure was under way in the political arena. Indeed, at that time many thought that their movement could have political repercussions precipitating the fall of the Government.

When the Government managed to defeat the motion of censure in the National Assembly on 22 May, the second phase of the crisis drew to a close. From that point the hope of obtaining a quick political solution was, at least momentarily, extinguished and a new phase of action developed entailing a more classical form of trade-union action distinguished by advancing a number of social and economic demands leading to the equally classical form of settlement through negotiations.

Demands were certainly not invented to satisfy a specific cause. The demands raised through the generalized strike had been formulated quite some time before. Until the strike, trade unions had confronted a refusal on the part of both management and the Government to negotiate. But given the scope of the crisis, neither the State nor management could afford to turn a deaf ear. The idea of negotiations at the highest level quickly gained ground and on 25 May a conference was assembled at the Ministry of Labour, rue de Grenelle, bringing together the Prime Minister, M. Pompidou, representatives of employers' organizations and of trade-union organizations.

The conference lasted nearly forty-eight hours. On the 27th the workers had to decide on the results. As we will see, the concessions wrung from the Government after very difficult sessions were far from negligible – not only in terms of so-called bread-and-butter claims or quantitative claims like salaries, hours, retirement, etc., but also in terms of qualitative claims, that is, structural changes in the firm and the economy (for example, trade-union rights in the enterprise). But for the great majority of workers on strike the results did not measure up to the scope of their movement and did not seem to lead to sufficiently profound changes in the economic and social structure of the country.

It would be futile to claim that the workers were influenced in their decision by a particular school of thought or by any particular trade union or political tactic. They did not need outside influence to arrive at a negative conclusion which was then adopted by the executive committees of both the CGT and the CFDT.

At this point the crisis entered a new phase. Again the political character of the movement was accentuated. During the Grenelle conference the Government gave the impression that it was making the maximum possible concessions. Once these concessions were deemed insufficient by the workers, the Government, the established political authority, was called into question. Hence events took a political turn. Political authority itself began to disintegrate and, in fact, practically collapsed. It was already clear in the course of the Grenelle negotiations that the Prime Minister was defending the State's shekels with a certain uneasiness. It was symptomatic that the Minister of Economic Affairs, M. Debré, who hardly participated in the conference, was rumoured to be on the point of resignation.

The process of disintegration accelerated on 27, 28, and 29 May. The trade unions literally had no one they could see to process their demands. Hence negotiations at a national level ended on the 27th. With the Head of State's sudden departure from the Élysée Palace on 29 May leaving no indication as to when he would reappear the political void appeared almost complete.

In the absence of any organized political power the CGT arranged, on the afternoon of 29 May, a large demonstration which moved across Paris from the Bastille to the Saint-Lazare station. It was widely supported by a large number of workers and led by PCF leaders marching alongside the high command of the CGT carrying slogans calling for a 'popular Government', that is a government dominated by the Communists.

At this point the CFDT felt it its duty to call a press conference at which it declared that the social and economic crisis was now a political crisis and could only be solved by relying on the impetus given by the combined aspirations of students and workers. Neither a Government which was steadily losing its grip nor the newly established power in the streets led by Waldeck-Rochet were viable political solutions. Pierre Mendès-France alone amongst French statesmen had the prestige in both the university and the workshop to find the required political solution and to carry it through.

Authority's 'resurrection' marked by the return of the Head of State to the Élysée Palace and his radio broadcast of 30 May altered the course of events in a most spectacular way. He formulated a political solution, which though ridiculous in the eyes of many, for others constituted a way out of the crisis. It looked as though many democrats would try to make the solution work. But the strike movement once again found itself in the classical trade-union position whilst the political parties, strangely absent from all previous events during the crisis, found their feet and reverted to their characteristic methods and objectives to prepare for the general election. Hence the trade unions had to direct a return-to-work movement by intensifying their efforts through negotiations at the industrial and factory level to obtain results that would justify the return-to-work movement.

The return to work took several days and in many cases several weeks. According to the press the main reason was the energy and persistence with which CFDT militants in particular pursued their campaign for trade-union rights within the firm. The reason for the long delays was the obstinacy of management, in particular in the metal-based industries, and their total lack of understanding.

The situation was further dramatized by the Government calling on the police to intervene in order to speed up the return to work under the fallacious pretext of assuring the 'freedom to work'. Those responsible should have learnt some lessons from the history of the working-class movement and realized that police intervention always leads to a climate of anger and violence which can only delay any outcome. But the old pattern was repeated with the drama of three deaths.

By the time the June legislative elections took place, work had been resumed everywhere with the important exception of the ORTF. Workers and particularly ORTF journalists led an exemplary struggle to assure free and objective reporting.

So ended the social and economic crisis. The political crisis seemed to be resolved temporarily by the elections. The crisis in its scope and repercussions was the greatest the country had known for decades. Without a doubt it will be the subject of much thought especially when one considers that it arose under a regime which prided itself on re-establishing stable authority and a form of political continuity. However, such remarks are not the purpose of the present discussion. I would now like to draw up a balance sheet of the general strike, as it appeared only a few weeks after the events, and look specifically at the role of the CFDT.

It is clear that the workers made considerable progress in achieving many of the demands they put forward. But restricting ourselves to essentials, the Pompidou Government conceded a general rise of more than 30 per cent in the guaranteed minimum wage, the SMIG, accompanied by a general rise in wages of between 10 and 15 per cent for 1968. This clearly contradicted the Government's economic policy over the previous ten years. To be more precise, the Fifth Plan, originally imposed by Government *fiat* over the protests of the trade unions, was demolished. Here the trade-union victory was of signal importance.

In the struggle for higher wages, the CFDT demanded that the rise must be proportionately greater for workers at the bottom of the pay scale whilst other trade unions, the CGC and the CGT favoured a flat percentage increase across the entire pay spectrum. Speeding up measures to reduce working hours, increasing family benefits, old age pensions, and help for the physically handicapped went far beyond the intentions of the Fifth Plan.

Trade unions also scored notable victories in another area. Negotiations and contractual agreements between the State, management and trade unions are, almost alone amongst Western European countries, literally unknown in France. In that sense the mere act of negotiating at the highest level was in itself a considerable victory. Moreover, negotiations launched the re-opening of discussions between employers and trade unions at the branch level leading to signed agreements. Finally in the course of the Grenelle negotiations the employers gave an undertaking that they would meet with the trade unions in the autumn to discuss guarantees about unemployment.

Over these weeks of action, the CFDT concentrated its efforts on a campaign for trade-union rights. Apart from a number of laws concerning public services, no trade unions in France have rights inside firms. The employer can legally oppose the formation and growth of trade unionism within his company. The CFDT felt that legal recognition of trade unionism within the plant and the drawing up of trade-union laws were essential (the right to collect subscriptions, to sell trade-union newspapers, to allow meetings of trade-union members in the plant, facilities for the shop steward so he could fulfil his obligations) not only for trade unionism but to advance towards a more just and humane society.

The CFDT insisted on these objectives because they closely corresponded to the aims of students to run their universities and workers to run their factories. Hence the CFDT broached the question of workers' control without as yet defining it but nevertheless taking the first step in that direction by raising the issue of trade-union rights. Anything else would have been premature.

Here the CFDT seemed to have understood the general tenor of the events because its demands were favourably received and echoed in the university and in the workshop, in particular, by young workers and its own members. For these people the CFDT emerged as the trade union which had most clearly understood the implications of the university crisis and the attitude of the workers when they decided to strike and occupy their places of work.

The cardinal feature of the May/June crisis, as it was more or less explicitly stated, was the need to re-analyse the social, economic and political institutions of the country; the quest for new forms of democracy for the university, the enterprise and the economy was part of the immense harvest reaped from the preceding weeks of action. For many the CFDT had shown the way to exploit and further their aims. In many individual plants workers gained valuable experience in self-management. These experiments were led by both workers and technicians. The CFDT's aim was to encourage these experiments and pursuits as much as possible so that the revolutionary process far from ending with the return to work would continue to develop under the surface.

The CFDT's policies diverged from those of its main partner, the CGT. Both trade-union federations vigorously defended the struggle for higher wages. Whereas the CFDT avoided a demagogical approach, not always absent from the CGT's statements, on quantitative or bread-and-butter issues the two unions developed a united front.

The difference resided in the fact that the CGT would not support the revolutionary process unleashed by the students and workers because the movement did not develop under its auspices. The movement's proposals about social development, justice and democracy differed sharply from the PCF line. This is why the CGT tried to channel all claims and actions into quantitative issues like higher salaries and payment for working days lost through the strike, and tried to stop the movement as soon as minimal satisfaction had been attained. The CFDT's emphasizing of qualitative issues like democracy in the factory more nearly captured the imagination of the working class at that point.

Politically the CFDT was extremely critical of the form of politics initiated by the Fifth Republic. In contradistinction to the CGT, it felt that the struggle started by the students and broadened by the working class could find no tenable and valid solution unless it was imbued with the spirit of innovation and reform that motivated the movement. For this reason at the height of the political crisis the CFDT suggested the name of Pierre Mendès-France. Similarly it stressed the fact that elections would not be a political solution which would measure up to the problems raised during the crisis.

On the morrow of the general election if the French political Left was vanquished, the French trade-union movement could claim to have won one of the greatest victories in its history. The CFDT was conscious of having made considerable gains during the crisis not only in terms of a great increase in membership but in winning the confidence of the working class and making its views known to the nation.

August 1968

6. CGT 1968:

Subjectivism to the Rescue of the Status Quo

André Barjonet

About twelve years ago, in the days when Pierre Le Brun used to be responsible for the intra-union aspects of the CGT's Centre for Economic and Social Studies, I undertook a study of the power of our departmental sections using a set of sociological criteria.[1] The study, whose flaws I am now well aware of, intensely interested Le Brun, who immediately told Benoît Frachon (then secretary of the CGT) about it. A little later, Frachon asked to see me. Amazed and even angry, he tried in vain to guess the real purpose behind the study: 'What are you trying to do? What are you trying to get at?' Having rapidly quietened down, because he was fond of me, Frachon explained calmly that I was splitting hairs, that there was 'nothing' to analyse and that if some departmental sections functioned better than others it was simply because they were run by more active or more devoted comrades, that they were better organized, etc. . . .

Coming from a man like Benoît Frachon such a wilful and subjective attitude left me flabbergasted. But as the years went by I understood that although I had absolutely no reason to doubt Frachon's sincerity or that of any other leader, this way of looking at problems was one of the main traits of both the CGT and the PCF.

For example, the problem of the relatively low circulation of the trade-union press (*La Vie ouvrière*, *Antoinette*, *Le Peuple*

1. The departmental sections of the CGT are federations which group all the different CGT unions within one *département*. These federations are grouped together on a national level into the confederation, or central organization itself.

etc.) has been the subject of countless meetings over the years. Each time the problem was posed in terms of organization and propaganda. In the course of the last few years there has, indeed, been an effort to modernize the layout of *La Vie ouvrière* turning it into quite a pleasant-looking union magazine. But the national leadership has never asked itself whether the content of the paper should be changed, and still less whether one shouldn't also examine the very orientation of the CGT itself. But the CGT leaders, having 'modernized' the union press, emphasize the increasing circulation, whereas actually the number of copies printed declines inexplicably from month to month and from week to week.

This example – and there are many others – shows how difficult the work of the Centre for Economic and Social Studies was. Do not misunderstand me, I have always believed – and I still do – that it is up to the regular organizations of political leadership, and them alone, to take political decisions. There is a precision about political action which does not allow it to be reduced to its economic or technical aspects. In this context it was quite natural for the national executive not to subordinate its decisions to comments from the Centre for Economic Studies. On the other hand, the fact that important decisions were *always* taken before an economic or sociological analysis was quite unnatural. As far as the leaders of the CGT were concerned, the Centre's purpose was either to provide documentation on certain precise points (level of wages, movements in productivity, unemployment, etc.) or to *illustrate* already apparent tendencies. But by whose analyses? Those of the national executive! I must admit that for a long time Pierre Le Brun efficiently resisted this procedure. But his own political opinions became more and more distinct from those held by other executive members, whether on the subject of trade-union unity or the movement's programme. Somewhat discouraged, he partially abandoned economic problems to devote himself almost entirely to politics.

Thus for several years I had some freedom of action. I took advantage of this to start on the study of the new problems: the real meaning of automation, the structure of the working class as a function of the new industrial revolution, the modification of wage structures, etc.

It was precisely on the subject of the new wage structures (such as job evaluation) that I was able once again to observe the fundamental subjectivism of the confederal leadership. As we know, these wage structures were created using continuous-flow production, if not complete automation, as the objective basis of calculation. Its properties are a regular rhythm imposed by the machine, which means production does not depend on the worker increasing or diminishing his efforts. In this context it is clear that wage structures based on industrial output lose all significance and must be replaced by something new. Hence the idea of linking the variable part of the wage (i.e., bonuses for increased production) to the type of job itself came about quite naturally. Of course, this form of 'rating' of the above-mentioned characteristics (and their ulterior consideration) can lead to forms of discrimination encouraged by managerial arbitrariness – despite the pseudo-scientific jargon used by the experts. It was therefore both natural and essential for the CGT to denounce any managerial tendencies in this direction.

Despite all my efforts, no correctly-based attack was under-taken for years. For a long time the CGT (including those leaders of federations who, by definition, should have been closer to these working-class problems) obstinately considered job evaluation to be a Machiavellian and perverse 'invention' of management and therefore to be rejected *in toto*. But total rejection was, of necessity, impossible because the new method had come about of itself, given the objective trans-formation of productive processes. Under these conditions, the new method spread and the workers were not protected against some of its negative aspects. The real solution, the general introduction of monthly salaries in the place of weekly wages, was only considered belatedly and, in fact, incurred much suspicion at first.

Such examples of the 'subjectivism' of the confederal leaders are also true of the leaders of the PCF, of whom it can be said that they are not Marxists, or that they have never really under-stood what Marxism is about. For them Marx's contribution is essentially the discovery of the reality of social classes and of the class struggle, of capitalist exploitation and the fundamental law of surplus value. In so far as they recognize these principles the PCF leaders are, indeed, Marxist, and are at least theoretically different from most other 'Left-wingers'. Such a solid foundation has made it possible for both the PCF and the CGT to foil immediately any mystification about so-called 'participation, association between labour and capital, profit-sharing schemes', etc. For the same reasons the CGT and the PCF have always fought energetically against the 'sociological' lucubrations about the disappearance of the working class and about the convergence of the capitalist and socialist systems into a single industrial and consumer society. But here the Marxism of the Communist leaders comes to an abrupt halt: solid but incomplete. One is reminded of those concrete blocks one sometimes sees on vacant lots and whose remaining protruding iron leaves one dreaming of what could be built.

The missing element is dialectics. I mean real dialectics, of course, the dialectics of interaction and of cause and effect, and not the formal and verbal 'dialectics' of those congress speeches where everything is included in anything (and *vice versa*!) and which make one bitterly miss good old formal logic . . .

In concrete terms – and here we touch upon the events of May 1968 – this means that the CGT was completely unable to understand the problem of youth, whilst it nevertheless considered it to be an extremely important problem.

The CGT started from a correct analysis: youth is not, in the Marxist sense, a social class. There are young people who are exploited and young people who exploit. Therefore, for a young worker, a 'young boss' will be a class enemy in the same way as any old fuddy-duddy from the CNPF (the French equivalent of the CBI). Following this line of argument, the CGT then denounces generational conflict as a bourgeois invention to divert the young workers from the class struggle. Speaking on this subject at the thirty-sixth CGT Conference in June 1967, Georges Séguy said:

They [the young] are also pleased that the CGT is setting an example of harmony between working-class generations based on their common class interests as opposed to the lucubrations about generation antagonism – substituted for the class struggle – and that within the CGT the oldest and most experienced trade unionists, whose contribution to union activities is so well appreciated, are surrounded by respect and affection on all sides.

In this context, the claims of youth are restricted to certain, as it were, physiological aspects (sports grounds, swimming pools, camping sites, youth clubs, etc.) – supposedly the essence of being young – but neglect the deeper aspirations of youth, since by definition, the young workers cannot aspire to anything other than what according to the CGT their elders aspire to.

Therefore, if the number of young workers who are members of the union is small, it is because propaganda was insufficient, because local leaders did not 'go into' the question deeply enough, in short, because the organization is unsatisfactory.

Thus the PCF leaders substitute the projection of a wilful plan to which reality must be made to conform at any price for the analysis, simultaneously concrete and dialectical, which is the very nature of Marxism. The problem can be seen most clearly in the question of 'spontaneity'.

As we know, Lenin battled keenly against the theories and the cult of spontaneity. In *What Is To Be Done?* (1902), he explains in a clear and convincing manner how the workers cannot develop a socialist consciousness on their own, that 'it can only come from outside'. Left to itself, says Lenin, 'the working class can only attain a trade-unionist consciousness, which is to say the conviction that they must form unions, fight against management, ask the government for those laws necessary to workers, etc . . .' This does not exclude that 'the working class moves towards socialism spontaneously' because 'socialist theory locates the cause of working-class discontent more deeply and more precisely than any other; which is why the workers assimilate it so easily, *if* this theory does not capitulate in the face of spontaneity, *if* it applies this spontaneity to itself.'

All the above statements do not raise any problems, and to say that such an analysis is also common sense is far from belittling Lenin. And yet from Lenin's teachings the Communist leaders of the CGT have only retained the word 'spontaneity'. If one carefully reads through national documents and conference reports of the last twenty years, one notices that a merciless war has been waged against 'spontaneity'; but spontaneity is never considered in any other light than that of movements outside the control of the organization. Speaking about the strikes of 1890, Lenin said that despite their immense improvement over previous strikes, they were still basically spontaneous movements. He was not for one moment condemning either the movement or its spontaneity; he is merely warning us that the movement will not become socialist spontaneously.

On the other hand, the CGT – and here lies the difference – absolutely refuses to entertain anything which might even remotely resemble mass spontaneity in any guise. Upon reflection, its conception is fundamentally anti-Marxist. It falls into direct and complete contradiction with the teachings of Marx, according to which 'Men's consciousness does not determine their being; on the contrary, their social being determines their consciousness.'

No doubt, both the CGT and the PCF proclaim aloud that working-class consciousness is determined by social practice – that is, through the class struggle. In fact this is not the case, because this practice is in every instance previously imposed upon the masses by the 'consciousness' of leaders which is *not* determined by social practice but is a phenomenon in itself inseparable from the organization.

In other words, working-class consciousness resulting from social practice is only valid when it has received the national executive mark of approval, which is only granted if this consciousness coincides with the *a priori* consciousness of the leaders. When it does not, it is obviously a deviation.

The concrete results of this attitude are, as one might expect, catastrophic. Whilst fighting ceaselessly against the 'spontaneity' of the masses, the Communist leaders spend most of their time either trying to encourage movements which, right or wrong, the working class does not consider necessary, or curbing those actions which, right or wrong, the party refuses to support. Hence a wet blanket is always thrown over working-class activity. There are countless examples of this attitude. To cite one, about 1950 we saw an incredible number of stoppages and strikes in the metallurgical factories in the Paris area, on every imaginable subject of internal and external politics. In not one case did these actions stem from the rank-and-file. The result was a very long period of relative debility, lasting until an entirely different economic and socio-cultural conjuncture, as well as a change in generations, gave rise to the explosion of May 1968.

The explosion was not and could not be understood by the party because it was not expected and it could not have been expected because *it was not in the programme*.

Because of the ever-present, wilful subjectivism in which it is steeped, the national leadership never tries to foresee a situation according to a scientific analysis of present political, economic and social conditions,[2] but according to a rapid examination (essentially political) that determines the main points of its plans of action, which in turn becomes the measure of all things!

In more recent times the programme was as follows: put an end to a regime based on 'personal power' by uniting all democratic forces through a common programme and create a vast anti-monopolistic front.[3]

In other words, the programme implied, on the one hand, a reinforcement of the union's unity, a tightening of the contacts with the CFDT, the establishment of a minimum range of agreement with the FO; and, on the other, the establishment of a common programme between the FGDS and the PCF.

The CGT's resolute parliamentarianism was shaken by attempts to bring the CFDT and the GDS together and the possibility of an agreement between the FO and the CFDT. In other words the CGT and the PCF were threatened by a fairly serious attempt to unify the political and trade-union forces on the non-Communist Left.

The CFDT, however, could only undertake such an operation if it broke away decisively from Gaullism and adopted an

2. The concept of 'prospective planning' provokes sneers: it is considered to be a booby-trap, a bourgeois distraction (like econometrics and cybernetics in Stalin's time). As for the idea of using operational research in the workers' movement . . .

3. *La CGT et la lutte pour les libertés syndicales et démocratiques*, a brochure published by the Confederal Centre for the Education of the Workers (*série B*), 1967.

almost systematically 'hard' line of a very Left-wing character.

For fear of being outflanked on its Left, the CGT reacted, on the one hand, in a very classical way by taking up certain claims it had not itself initiated and, on the other, by denouncing with the utmost firmness, any proposition or attempted action which it did not agree with.

This otherwise frank and loyal attitude caused the CGT – already worried by the so-called Chinese peril – to oppose with a firm and sometimes tough and brutal hand, young workers whom it labelled 'Leftists'. Before the May events the *Courrier confédéral* directed union authorities to see that no 'dubious' element infiltrated the delegation to the Festival of Youth which was to take place in Paris on 18 May.

From this point neither analysis nor any attempt at explanation was possible: instead of seeing the true nature of the phenomenon of *contestation* in time, the CGT could only think in terms of '*groupuscules*' and '*provocateurs*'. In one of those sad ironies of history, it revived the hoary bourgeois theory about 'ring-leaders' . . .

Yet the CGT's attitude during the May revolution was, despite appearances, frighteningly logical: surprised and disconcerted by the vastness of the student revolt, the CGT reacted to the police savagery and (with the CFDT, the FEN and UNEF) sent out a call for demonstrations and the general strike of 13 May.

By means of its latest move it could simultaneously demonstrate its sincere disapproval of police brutality and its hostility towards the regime, whilst at the same time rehabilitating itself in the eyes of the students and absorbing the leadership of the movement.

But the unforeseen and spontaneous vastness of the events of 13 May suddenly made workers aware of their strength, which proved to be much greater than they themselves had thought. And two days later the first strikes and occupations of factories followed spontaneously. This phase, too, was unforeseen, and all the CGT could do was to follow the movement while trying to keep it within the bounds of the usual kind of wage claims. From that moment onwards the CGT and the PCF waged a war on two fronts: against management and against all 'Leftist' elements (students and young workers). As soon as the minimum concessions were wrenched from management, Georges Séguy hurried to sign the agreement. His speech to the workers at Renault proves beyond any doubt that he hoped there would be an immediate return to work. For the third time the forecasts of the CGT were foiled by the workers themselves. All that was left for the national leadership to do was to 'harden' its position – no change in attitude at all.

In this context my resignation on 23 May from my position as secretary to the Centre for Economic and Social Studies of the CGT was not only a gesture of protest against the organization's failure in its revolutionary vocation and against its inadmissible attitude towards the students, it was also due to my certainty that the Centre for Economic and Social Studies had no purpose whatsoever for the CGT.

Such is the paradox: the CGT of 1968 (whose main leaders are members of the PCF's national committee) claims to be Marxist, yet undertakes political actions whilst ignoring economics and sociology and showing no interest whatsoever in the changes in structure taking place in society in general and the working class in particular, and only paying attention in a distracted and absent-minded way to the discoveries which are turning the productive forces of society upside-down.

In this sense – and here is the last paradox – the structured and disciplined CGT of 1968 remains curiously faithful to its Proudhonian and Guesdian double origin, where politics has always had the upper hand over economics.[4]

But at least Proudhon and Guesde were revolutionaries ...

August 1968

4. Proudhon felt that trade unions fettered the otherwise free worker. Guesde, one of the founders of the French socialist movement, felt that trade unions had to be kept under the thumb of the socialist political party.

7. Inside the Prefecture

Paul Gillet

At the Ministry of the Interior, the events of May caused a shock that was all the greater as they occurred in a period of complete social calm.

A negotiating procedure exists (called the 'Toutée procedure', after its originator) whereby the relation of wages to the cost of living is annually regulated in consultation with the unions. During the eight years after it was introduced, each Toutée negotiation was followed by twenty-four- or forty-eight-hour strikes, as a proof of the workers' discontent with the results they had obtained. In the spring of 1968, however, for the first time there had been no strikes.

Nevertheless, those responsible for law and order had for some time been paying close attention to the development of various organizations on the extreme Left which lay outside the control of the classical extreme left, that is, the Communist party. They were particularly interested in the Revolutionary Communist Youth (JCR) and the (pro-Chinese) Marxist–Leninist Union of Communist Youth (UJC M-L). It had been suggested to various newspapers – like *Le Monde*, *Le Figaro* and *L'Express* – that they should investigate these organizations.

Three events had put the police on their guard throughout the preceding months: the Rhodiacéta factory; the Saviem car works at Caen-Blainville, and above all the Renault car works at Le Mans, where extreme Left-wing groups had moved into strike disputes in an attempt to radicalize the situation. At Le Mans the attempt to push the movement towards a direct confrontation in the streets had been particularly clear.

Nevertheless anxiety at the Ministry of the Interior was not particularly great. There were some, in fact, who joyfully awaited the friction that the activities of these groups would cause within the workers' movement, since the Communist party was violently opposed to them.

As far as the students were specifically concerned, the Ministry knew all about the various Left-wing groups, as well as the *22 Mars* movement. They knew how many young people belonged to these organizations, the exact composition of the leadership and the names of particular leaders. They derived this information in two ways: on the one hand, through police infiltration, traditional in anarchist groups and very large in Maoist groups, for reasons that emerge from the political context in which these groups were founded in France; on the other hand, by way of traditional 'journalistic'-type research, to which the specialists in the General Information Department devote themselves.[1]

If the Ministry's services were well informed about these groups, some of them were nonetheless misled by their weakness in numbers, although certain important functionaries were convinced that the number of young people susceptible to their arguments was larger than was at first apparent.

The size of the first demonstrations especially those on 6 May caught the Paris police on the wrong foot. The 6th was the hardest day, and yielded the highest number of wounded. That morning the police tried to limit the area of the demonstration, a tactic that had been perfectly successful since 1962. They had also decided to experiment with water cannons. Their intention was to disperse crowds from a distance to avoid a face-to-face confrontation.

The number of police brought in (4,000 active policemen) was, however, disproportionate to the number of demonstrators; and they were soon overrun. Starting in the afternoon the situation deteriorated in the face of a demonstration that was seen to be perfectly organized. Extremely violent scuffles broke out after

1. The General Information Department (Renseignements Généraux) is responsible for keeping watch on suspicious persons and groups, controlling means of transport and centralizing information concerning the country's 'state of mind'.

3.30 p.m. By the evening, casualties had reached frightening proportions.

From now on the secular arm of State power was engaged in a process that was to grow in extent from day to day, if not from hour to hour. How was it going to react?

In France, in contrast to what may sometimes occur in certain other countries, the police are not a pressure group with more or less autonomous motivations. The police force is entirely the instrument of political power. This does not mean that it is an apolitical milieu, nor that it does not come under other influences, as we shall see in the course of our brief study. But, apart from the fact that it is under perfect control, these influences have moulded it so that it is an effective instrument. In the same way, while the events of May brought them face to face with the misunderstandings and hesitations of those in power, they in turn resolved a crisis within the police force that passed almost unnoticed at the time, but which was extremely revealing.

On a higher level, 7 May confirmed the lessons of the previous day. A great 'snake' of students wound their way through Paris. The Ministry decided to let the student march continue, or rather, it decided to leave Grimaud, the Prefect of Police, with a free hand. Grimaud took a risk and did not interfere. In fact, everyone was nervous as the great procession crossed the Seine in front of the National Assembly and crossed the Place de la Concorde, skirting the American Embassy and passing close to the Élysée Palace. The demonstration, which was very mobile, could not really have been controlled. From that moment onwards, and particularly on the night of 10–11 May, Christian Fouchet and the Prefect of Police were both to adopt the call for rapid intervention, in order to stop events taking a turn that would then exclude the possibility of compromise. The Government's panic and indecision had the opposite effect. Prefect Grimaud, who in other respects was to act throughout these events like a man anxious to avoid developments that lead towards the 'point of no return', made the crucial decision, at 2 a.m. on 11 May, to remove the barricades. When later asked to explain this decision he emphasized that any further delay carried the risk of his being responsible for many deaths.

At the grass-roots level, the ordinary policeman no longer really understood what was going on. He found himself confronted by a type of demonstration that was completely different from those he had had to face before: barricades, a particularly effective student police force that acted as a distributor of information about the disposition of forces in the streets, a loose but nonetheless real coordination, the use of roofs and finally, the use of makeshift weapons – cobblestones, Molotov cocktails, Calor-gas bottles, and crude bombs made by Chemistry students. . .

The tactics imposed on the police increasingly took them by surprise. They allowed the barricades to be built, the street fighting to begin and did not intervene until later, after long hours of nerve-shattering waiting when conditions made action very difficult.

They took as an insult the growing press campaign against police brutality, brutality that reached paroxysm on the 'Night of the barricades' (the night of 10–11 May) reminding the whole population of the excesses committed against the Algerians during the late fifties and early sixties.

Lastly there is another element which only has significance for a policeman. For a long time there have been a certain number of professional-departmental demands outstanding which have been left unsettled, particularly with reference to wages. This had little bearing for the moment; it would become a more sensitive issue when the workers' strikes broke out later that month. Political confusion, however, was now superimposed on active professional discontent.

The floodgates opened when Prime Minister Georges Pompidou, on his return from an official visit to Afghanistan on 11 May, declared that the Sorbonne would be reopened and prisoners released, and reaffirmed his 'profound understanding of the students' case' and his 'confidence in their good sense'. Policemen understood the Prime Minister's declaration to be a disavowal of their actions. The crisis that had been smouldering among them now exploded.

The Interfederal Union of Police Unions, including the influential General Union of Employees of the Prefecture of Police (covering Paris and the Parisian *départements*) published a communiqué which noted that 'it considers the Prime Minister's declaration to be a recognition of the rights and privileges of students and a total disavowal of actions taken by the police forces by order of the Government'. Petitions circulated among the Paris police demanding that the General Secretary of the General Union of the Prefecture initiate a mass movement, declaring 'we shall no longer accept the role of clowns'. One police officer circulated on his own initiative a bitter and revealing document. 'The demands of those against whom we have been sent into action have been declared entirely justified; the authorities have here and now accepted the foreign flags that they fly now as the symbols of the French University' (he is referring to the red and black flag). The word spread among the police stations, calling upon policemen to stop work. In fact, well-executed preparations for strike were under way, and the Paris police came within an inch of open strike.

The movement was only held back by the police unions, who repeatedly argued the issues out with the Minister of the Interior, the general secretary for the police and the Prefect of Police. Only after a period of eight to ten days did things return to normal, and then only when certain salary demands were granted.

The secular arm had trembled. But that did not prevent it from lashing out, and lashing out with all the more violence and viciousness as the police were disoriented and afraid.

Much has been written about the violence of the police during May and June, emphasizing the harshness of the battle itself and of the weapons used (grenade throwers, poison gas grenades, etc.). Stress has also been laid on the state of mind of policemen who tear into demonstrators, beat up young people under arrest in the police stations, burst into cafés, restaurants or private houses, and dedicate themselves to a brutal manhunt.

In order to understand that state of mind, however, one needs to examine briefly the way in which the French police force works and the influences to which it is amenable.

Law and order in France is maintained by three bodies. First, the groups of urban police under the command of Public Security and, in Paris and the Parisian *départements*, of the Prefecture. Secondly, by the Republican Security Companies (Compagnies Républicaines de Securité – CRS), who are mobile units that constitute the reserve for the Security Police. And thirdly, by the squadrons of gendarmerie who belong to the army, though they work in the ranks of the general police forces under the jurisdiction of the Minister of the Interior and the Prefects. Urban police, CRS and gendarmerie were all in action during the repression of demonstrations in May and June.

In the public mind, responsibility for the violence has essentially fallen on the heads of the CRS; the short slogan 'CRS-SS' expressed the reputation that the CRS gained during the repression. Certainly they are not known for their tenderness; indeed they were wilfully and cold-bloodedly brutal.

After 1951, when Jean Baylot became Prefect of Police, the Prefecture became the protected centre for intense anti-Communist activity that flourished essentially in two areas. On the one hand, it flourished among the superintendents under the command of Chief Superintendent Dides, and on the other, in the groups of ex-policemen who had been convicted of collaboration during the German occupation and 'purged' at Liberation. They continued, nevertheless, to hover around the services, waiting for the day when they would be reincorporated. That group disposed of a 'parallel' service, set up by this same Superintendent Dides and by an absconder who had been convicted for his attitude during the Occupation. That service was responsible for gathering information – spying, that is – on the Communist party and the trade unions. It was nourished by the whole backlash created by the war in Indochina and the decolonization that was now under way; it provoked among the police a hatred of those who had 'sold out' the Empire, intellectuals and progressives, Communist and trade-union militants, all of whom were indiscriminately presented as enemies of the nation, manipulated by the 'hand of Moscow'. At the same time a virulent racialism was growing, directed at first against the Indochinese and later against the Algerians.

When in 1954 Baylot and Dides were fired by the Government of Mendès-France, certain functional elements of this structure disappeared; first of all the Delarue service and then, much later, Dides' own area of influence. The essential element, the atmosphere, remained however, and there was still an area open to extreme Right-wing, that is protofascist, influence.

The vicissitudes of the long Algerian War nourished a racialism that was to culminate in the bloody repression of Algerian demonstrations in Paris, and the 'rat hunts' (*ratonnades*) in the streets and the shanty towns on the outskirts of the city. No less violent was the behaviour of the Paris police towards those Frenchmen who wanted Algerian independence and fought for it. The repression of the anti-OAS demonstration on 8 February 1962 left eight dead at the Charonne Métro station.

Similarly, the practice of clandestine activities within the Prefecture of Police did not disappear. The Gaullist *coup d'état* of May 1958 was helped by the constitution of secret Committees, called the Committees for Public Safety, within the Prefecture itself. Later the men of the OAS were also to dispose of underground support there.

Clearly, a police force formed in this way provides an authoritarian regime with a formidable weapon. Although generations of policemen may themselves change and be renewed, the young men are sufficiently well 'put in the picture' to ensure the transmission of practices and attitudes from one generation to another.

This explains the significant role played by one organization in particular during the events of May. It reforged the links between the police and the Gaullist regime, which had been slightly weakened at one point as a result of the Government's attitude; and it thus reinforced the determination of the police in their encounters with the students and the strike movement. The organization is the Civic Action Service (SAC), created by the Gaullist party.

When events had begun to acquire some importance, members of the SAC had come to demand helmets and clubs in order to go into the attack against the barricades at the police's side. Others organized among the police themselves groups called the 'uncontrollables', who declared their readiness to act even outside the orders of their own police chiefs. It is to these groups that one can in the main attribute the majority of the excesses.

When the Committees for the Defence of the Republic (CDR) were created, after de Gaulle's speech of 30 May, and under the direction of ex-Minister of the Interior Roger Frey, the SAC distributed among the police and the CRS a tract calling upon them to join the SAC. In this way they recruited activists within the police force itself.

Those in power could draw two basic conclusions from the role played by the police in these events.

The first concerns what have been modestly called the excesses. They saw clearly that it was dangerous to allow a state of affairs to develop in which the police were cut off from public opinion. The violence had been widespread, and it had been so strongly disapproved of, that measures had to be taken. That is why Prefect of Police Maurice Grimaud addressed a letter to all policemen; it was intended to be a confidential letter, but it became generally known all the same despite the pressures exerted on newspapers not to print it. He wrote:

If we do not explain ourselves with the greatest clarity and frankness, we may win the battle in the streets, but we shall lose something much more precious which you as well as I hold dear; and that is our good name. I know from having spoken to many of you, that the majority of you condemn certain methods. I know as well as you do that things have occurred that no one finds acceptable ... I have the evidence that many of you also possess. I know how bitter you are at the unflattering remarks and the vituperation that have been directed at yourselves and your families. The only way to redress this deplorable state of mind among the public, however, is constantly to show yourselves in your true colours, and to wage pitiless war against those, admittedly few, among you, who, by their ill-considered actions have given credence to this uncomplimentary image that people are trying to impose upon us ...

The second conclusion concerned not the conduct of the police, but the fact that they had allowed themselves to be taken by surprise by the suddenness of events and the new aspects of their development. Doubtless, they had been engaged for too long in the repression of the movement for colonial liberation and of a workers' movement of the classical type. The forces of law and order had found themselves faced with enemies whose actions they had not been able to *predict*.

September 1968

8. Forbidden Freedoms

Claude Angeli

A few days before the first barricades appeared in Paris, a senior French civil servant remarked with a slight edge of spite in his voice that Prague Television and Radio had a much greater freedom of expression than the ORTF. Censorship was not only exerted over news and current affairs programmes but extended to the few cultural programmes that existed, as well as to light entertainment shows.

Often producers, directors and even journalists had to spend over half their time vainly justifying projects and proposals against the strongly entrenched ORTF bureaucracy. Radio and television were totally subservient to the State. This was how the ORTF was moulded by the Fourth Republic. The Fifth Republic firmly put her stamp on this arrangement by placing her own carefully chosen 'technocrats' in the ORTF hierarchy. Few had any knowledge of radio and television but all were highly trained administrators perpetually at the beck and call of the Gaullist machine. Far from being a sinecure, a position in the ORTF was one of the most sensitive in the Gaullist regime. The ORTF was charged with carefully conveying Gaullist propaganda so that it didn't look too much like propaganda whilst applying the authoritative methods of Gaullism to its 14,000 employees. A symbol of this submission, labelled *tutelage*, in the legal statutes, was a hot-line from the office of the Minister of Information to the offices of the directors of the ORTF. France is the only country in Western Europe to have a Minister of Information who is fully expected to intervene openly not only in the general management of radio and television but in deciding the content of particular programmes.

Over the last few years television gradually has become one of the chief means of political manipulation in France. With a captive audience numbering several millions at any given moment, it is the perfect vehicle for a constant stream of propaganda. The French public, initially much slower than the English to discover the soporific effects of the spectacle in their homes, gave way to pure fascination, whilst the Gaullists, bowled over by the way de Gaulle skilfully made use of the medium, quickly awoke to the possibilities of the ORTF and the corresponding need to make it docile and available at any given moment. Ministers scrambled for the limelight – anything from a brief appearance on television news, to television parlour games – and the ORTF directors and journalists were forced to acquiesce in their less ridiculous demands.

The ORTF was used to two ways: to ensure that the regime's propaganda was put across in an attractive manner, and to soothe and tranquillize the people with visual bread and games. During elections and crises the ORTF was taken over by the Gaullists; for example, when de Gaulle was engaged in his battle with the rebel generals in Algeria, the OAS or the Communists. During the lulls the aim of the television and radio was to ensure that nothing interrupted the stability of the status quo and that the values of the consumer society were dutifully transmitted. In this light we can understand the Government decision to allow advertisements on state-controlled radio and television. This surely was the logical conclusion of their policy.

As part of this policy the viewer did enjoy one privilege – excellent coverage of foreign news. To turn the viewer's attention from France, television newsreel cameras were often turned to the world outside – those infernal regions where there was no de Gaulle – in order to persuade the 20 to 25 million viewers that everything was going badly beyond the frontiers of France. The war in Vietnam was given very large coverage; street battles in the American ghettos supported de Gaulle's contention that the American alliance was wrong; fighting in the Middle East and the Congo showed the role that France could play, and film reports on Italy in a state of acute crisis and miniskirts getting shorter in London were meant to serve as a contrast to the health of Gaullist France. Saturated with the spectacle, the French, according to Gaullist theory, would be dissuaded from their traditional violence by catharsis. Curiously this brand of political McLuhanism did not work. For many the omission of home news was a greater spur to action than reporting the news would have been. The effect of stories of Vietnam and of Che Guevara in Bolivia appeared to be mimetic not cathartic.

Hence Gaullism relied on the ORTF as its main weapon to maintain its shaky alliance. This was why during the May/June crisis it was considered more important to guard the ORTF and keep it running than it was to hold the universities and factories.

But the barricades of May were to endanger the entire structure. The new circular ORTF building which was so strictly supervised and controlled and which appeared to be as invulnerable as the Fifth Republic itself almost failed to survive the crisis. To the surprise of the ENA-trained administrators, ordinary workers, directors, journalists, electricians and even typists united, refused to be bought off by wage rises and demanded that the misinformation enterprise that was the ORTF be changed from top to bottom and they be given a major voice in its management. The May message of autonomy, control and self-management entered the ORTF – the institution that could least tolerate such a message.

The process started late. As late as 10 May when there had already been six days of street fighting in the Latin Quarter and elsewhere throughout France, there had been not one television interview with a demonstrator. Reporting of the demonstrations was scanty. Only the Minister of Education, Alain Peyrefitte, formerly a Minister of Information, and a few trustworthy journalists who echoed his every view, had come forward to present the Government's version of the 'facts'. The demonstrators were so disgruntled by the strong bias in the news reporting that several ORTF vans were attacked whilst those belonging to Radio Luxembourg and Europe No 1 – the independent radio stations broadcasting from Luxembourg and the

Saar – which had made an effort to report the news were untouched. The barricades that night changed everything.

The following morning the revolt reached the ORTF. A group of directors and producers, responsible for the news and current affairs programmes called 'Cinq colonnes à la une', 'Zoom', and 'Caméra III' assembled in a studio, and when this was closed to them, in a nearby cafe.

'Television, like the university, has to be smashed and then completely rebuilt,' said one. Another added: 'We are shamed by the poor quality of the news reporting on television.' Perceptibly the mood was hard and the demands escalated quickly. Groups of employees began drawing up communiqués, plans for action, plans for the reorganization of the ORTF. Groups began to study and debate the use of mass communications in neo-capitalist society whilst others began to discuss problems of workers' control. Others began to make contact with the student groups: the JCR, the *22 Mars* and the Maoists offering them aid, information and advice. The Ministry retaliated with its usual threats but was met with unexpected resistance.

The general strike and demonstration of 13 May brought matters to a head. Whereas a conservative estimate put the number of demonstrators at between 600,000 and 800,000, the 8 p.m. television news broadcast the astonishingly precise figure of 171,000 issued by the prefecture of police.

Groups of producers, directors and journalists met again at the television studios in the rue Cognacq-Jay. Locked out of the building, they finally forced Pierre-Yves Ligen, the assistant director, and Édouard Sablier, the head of the news service, to come out and negotiate with them. Twenty-four hours later the administration was forced to screen a 'Zoom' reportage on the gathering storm. After an impassioned report from Marcel Ophüls, a discussion between the leading spirits of the movement – Jacques Sauvageot, Alain Geismar, Daniel Cohn-Bendit and Castro - together with Gaullist and Communist deputies was screened.

But even this concession was not enough, for the Government insisted on its prerogatives. For the first time the workers at the ORTF ignored differences of rank and trade-union affiliation, and an intra-trade-union committee was founded to attain their aim: a free information service. After chaotic gatherings and meetings followed by the intervention of the police a strike was called. It hit the regime where it hurt most: its monopoly of information.

At first the journalists continued to work. They attempted the impossible. Unsure of what kind of strike they had launched and filled with illusions about the possibility of their controlling the television news, they thought that the best tactic was to remain on the job and pressure the management. The Ministry would have none of it. They simply cancelled programmes and sent journalists into exile in the provinces. Equally stung by the criticism that to continue working led the French to believe that the news presented by the ORTF was objective, all but twenty-three journalists with civil-servant mentalities, rejoined the strike movement.

At this point the battle-lines were sharply drawn. The Government, after much consideration, staged a strategic retreat. The studios were abandoned to the strikers and for the rest of the crisis the ORTF for all intents and purposes was a small 'studio-bunker' atop the Eiffel Tower. Hiring an army of 'blacklegs' commandeering military technicians and surrounding its last redoubt with CRS and army troops, the Government prepared for the siege. To buy time, the entire ORTF hierarchy was replaced. Even the Minister of Information was changed. Every evening Yves Guéna, the new Minister, sought to ensure the continuity necessary so that 'France would once again become France': 'The French are sad. A bit of the news, then twenty minutes of anything – no matter what the quality – but even that's not enough. A film a day is what is needed.' But directors, producers, dramatists withdrew the right to show their works on the ORTF. So every night the French were treated to twenty minutes of political harangue by army broadcasters followed by the inevitable American musical or situation comedy.

Meanwhile Guéna let the negotiations drag on with the trade unions hoping that he could split the movement or that the journalists, who had never had the experience of a strike before, would be outfoxed by his promises and make a wrong move. The strategy was attrition – give them enough rope to hang themselves.

The journalists at France Inter, the state radio, managed to establish control over the news programmes. They elected a committee of five to be responsible for its editorial content and the day-to-day running of the news programmes. The results were surprisingly good. Without too much experience, France Inter began to report faithfully the news in an often exciting way. Reporters themselves became extremely heady. But what could one expect after ten years of servility?

At the private radio stations, Europe No 1 and Radio-Télé-Luxembourg the situation was different. The attitude of the two stations, which attract a large audience in northern France, was dependent upon the balance between inside and outside pressures. But the pressure brought to bear by their teams of journalists was never enough to counterbalance the pressure the Government brought to bear to silence news reporting of the strikes and any hint of criticism. To cite one case: on Saturday, 11 May, the day after the first night of the barricades, Jean-Pierre Hutin, speaking for Georges Gorse, the then Minister of Information, rang the head of Europe No 1 and, in effect, said: 'It is becoming increasingly difficult to put the case for the station to the Government. We must insist that Government statements be given more prominence and that you stop that fool Cohn-Bendit from talking.' Hutin's threat was a very real one. The Government could, at any time, cut off the radio's studios in Paris from their centres of transmission in the Saar. So Europe No 1 modified its policy with certain reservations. Government statements were given more time though at least one more interview with Cohn-Bendit was broadcast.

But the Government increased the pressure. The owners of the private radio stations were accused of collaborating with the enemies of the Republic. Yet Maurice Siegel and Jean Gorini at Europe No 1 and Jean Prouvost and Jean Ferran at Radio Luxembourg were far from enemies of the established order. Prouvost, in fact, is not only a major mill owner but has wide interests in the press: *Paris-Match*, *Télé 7 Jours*, *Marie-*

Claire, and *Le Figaro* are all known for their Right-wing if not antediluvian political opinions. Prouvost may never have been a thorough-going Gaullist but a challenge to a capitalist France is also a challenge to his interests and Prouvost was never a man to be mistaken about what was best for him.

Whilst brandishing the supreme threat of cutting their communication lines on 24 May the Government forbade mobile reporters to use their radio-telephones. The pretext was that all available frequencies had to be kept free for the police and fire brigades. The radio-telephone systems had supplied on-the-spot reporting of the street demonstrations and of the meetings assembled at Nanterre, the Censier, the Sorbonne and in the provinces. They made it possible for the movement to communicate and for demonstrators to know what was happening in the next *quartier* and the format of their reporting, the opening of the radio to ordinary people using ordinary speech played a tremendous role in demystifying the modern means of communication. Rather than being a voice which guided and led, a voice to which one could not reply, the radio crystallized ideas and allowed for a Levellers-type debate in which for the first time even the most lowly found a role in the creation of a new kind of society. For the State, the dialogue had to be stopped because it threatened its father-figure-like role. So permission was withdrawn.

Miraculously the reporters were allowed to use their radio-telephones again half an hour before the beginning of the big 'spontaneous' Gaullist demonstration of 30 May. Obviously new wave lengths had been created out of thin air just in time for the triumphant return of the Fifth Republic! On the 30th petrol again flowed from the pumps and on-the-spot reporting returned as if by divine intervention.

But the main battle was centred in the rue Cognacq-Jay, Avenue Kennedy and in all the ORTF studios. Meeting followed meeting. The strikers unanimously demanded the resignation of all the heads of radio and television. They demanded that the statutes of the ORTF be abrogated and that the ORTF be declared an autonomous service run by its workers. Demands for salary rises took second place. The

Government was amazed that when it offered wage rises all round, its offer was scornfully turned down. Pompidou, realizing that the carrot had failed, then tried the stick.

Just before the 6 o'clock news, after de Gaulle's speech on the 30th, the Director-General vainly tried to stop France Inter from broadcasting reaction to de Gaulle's proposals. Initially he was defeated, but at midnight he invaded the ORTF building and had the journalists expelled. The autonomy of the state radio came to an end: that of television never got off the ground.

The next day the police expelled the research services from the Issy-les-Moulineaux offices. Accompanied by Jacques-Bernard Dupont, the Director-General of the ORTF, they used the pretext of the right of work before bodily forcing the strikers out of the studios. The strikers retreated to the last redoubt of the movement, the main ORTF offices which were now surrounded by the police and the CRS.

On 2 June Guéna finally agreed to 'talks' with the representatives of the strikers. But the strike committee was never allowed to speak. Guéna said: 'Gentlemen, I have listened to you and you have listened to me. I will not allow any discussion to take place after I read the following statement. Then I will wait for your answer which I must have before midnight.'

Guéna's statement took two minutes and thirty-two seconds to read. It was a *ukase*. The Government would grant wage rises, improve working conditions, nominate a commission of 'famous personalities' to propose possible changes in the statutes of the ORTF but nothing more. Further, it was made almost impossible for the ORTF workers to meet to consider these proposals. For several hours the strike committee was refused admission by the police. The answer from the journalists and directors was clear. Their strike was a strike to guarantee 'a complete and impartial service' and nothing less than that.

François Bloch-Lainé, the vice-president of the administrative council of the ORTF, bitterly commented that the council had not been consulted nor had the Government bothered to present it with the necessary information which would have allowed it to play its role as a consultative body. Clearly the command was now coming directly from the Élysée Palace. The battle for radio and television was too important to be directed by the civil service.

The strategy of letting the strike consume itself paid off. Once the hopelessness of their position became clear and once a frightened France overwhelmingly voted for the Gaullists, the strikers started to trickle back to work. Particularly those who were newly politicized hoped to hold out. But the CGT, following the line laid down by Séguy and the PCF, demanded a return to work. Once the intra-trade-union cooperation was destroyed the strike collapsed. In vain Max Pol-Fouchet pleaded: 'The strike ought not to depend on political events. It must not be broken. We all should feel shame at the statements of Guéna-the-paratrooper. Our choice is between either giving in and dishonour or continuing the strike.' Once the strike was 'suspended' on 25 June the unions proved to be incapable of holding meetings to justify their decision.

Only the television journalists continued to hold out. But their position was hopeless. The Government had already decided the issue. Some were to be re-integrated. Others, particularly those engaged in production and direction presented problems. Some ministers wanted the ORTF to be taken firmly in hand whilst others cautioned leniency. Ministers like Malraux, Fauré and Schumann preached moderation but the largest group called for a reign of terror to revenge themselves. They even came up with a slogan to describe their programme; 'Clean up the ORTF.' Not very elegant, but certainly clear.

Sixty-six radio and television journalists were to be fired. Others, finding that their programmes had been dropped, found themselves redundant. But the Government had to give the impression that everything was as before – films, sports, games, etc. The soporific role of the ORTF had to be re-established as quickly as possible. The revolt had to be forgotten. People had to be made to think of the May events as a bad memory.

But perhaps they have been a bit premature. The crises in radio and television allowed a large portion of the French public to understand how the ORTF – and to a smaller extent the private radio stations – depended upon the ruling class. For many it was a revelation – but then not everyone grasps reality easily.

Perhaps just as important is that a great many Frenchmen who listen to the news when they return from work in the evening listen with a more critical ear. Because of the proliferation of newspapers, transistor radios and television, they are weighed down by a mass of information. But they retain or understand very little. It took the May events for people to see that this glut was an actual lack of information.

This has led to a new demand: the right for news. Up to now this right hasn't even been formulated. People merely criticized the controls placed on the ORTF. Of course, this demand in itself is far from a revolutionary demand – and it was never intended to be one – but it would be wrong to neglect its importance. To criticize the information one receives and the manner in which it is transmitted is a very important step.

It is also clear that this kind of democratic demand could never be accepted by any of the societies in which we live. It would mean opening the door to revolutionary ideas.

September 1968

The Strategy

9. Action [1]

André Glucksmann

If the movement set in motion in May had had to fight against only one adversary, the only problems for the future that it would now have to face would be those of decentralized popular organization in a socialist France, practising 'democracy to its ultimate degree'. The restraint exercised by the Communist leadership was, however, even more effective than governmental resistance. That leadership will never again allow the forces under its control to be unleashed at an unexpected moment. Yet methods of action were revealed in May that allow one to expect that the brake will be released.

1. The Contestation [2]

When it calls for the revolution against authority, and for the authority to make a revolution against those authorities who are not bringing it about, the movement comes up against three obstacles: apathy (which it kills at birth); fear, and mystification, which together give repression its force. A society that is ripe for revolution should, if it wants to give birth painlessly, forget that it is still a society at the moment when it sees that it is ready. When it does recognize itself as a society it should hide its readiness; the Right brandishes the spectre of

1. This essay is Chapter 5 of André Glucksmann's *Stratégie et révolution en France*, 1968 (Christian Bourgois Editeur, Paris, 1968).

2. We have left the awkward word contestation throughout the text as translation of the French *la contestation*. Since this is a key word and a complex one, no English word adequately expresses its meaning, for it means, a dispute, a contest, a challenge, a struggle; all these things are contained within the single French word. Translator.

anarchy, and the Communist leadership warns that its soundings reveal an 'unfavourable balance of forces'. This incestuous couple is prolific; the Left is afraid of the fear of the Right; the Right finds itself to the Left of its mirror image on the Left and the Centre notes that the opposition of the two is more apparent than real, while pretending to forget that the alliance is in fact sustained by the apparent opposition. A party of order that does not save society from 'totalitarianism' cannot save itself: a revolutionary party no longer marked by its revolutionary spirit is lost, both as a body and as a party. When the cards are dealt this way they lie untouched, for the rules of the game are not to play.

Hence the effectiveness of a contestation is that it seeks its opportunities in our society rather than looking for its principles in this or that book. It is satisfied with articulating what everyone is doing, and doing what everyone says he is doing in order not to have to carry it out. The 'balance of forces' is no more than a word play; since it is one which the forces of each 'camp' hold on to, and wear themselves out doing so, one need only treat words as words and strength as strength in order to undermine the whole fabric and provoke a surprise explosion. By bringing revolutionary action to fruition through the freedom to say everything, the 'movement' undermines counter-revolutionary action carried out in the name of 'freedom' of work and 'freedom' of speech. And it undermines revolutionary inactivity hidden behind the unliberated word. It is forbidden to forbid; thus the orders that faithfully share France out between them become unfaithful rivals: '... the alien god places himself humbly on the altar beside the local idol. Little by little he consolidates his position; and one fine day he gives his companion a shove with his elbow and down goes the idol with a bang.'[3]

General contestation accompanies every great revolution, undermining the whole social fabric, putting the last first and first last, and reversing the order of frivolous and serious; it makes it easier to bring the society down. It accompanied the 1917 upheaval, as it had, well before that, the 1789 revolution,

3. D. DIDEROT: *Rameau's Nephew*, Penguin Classics, London, 1966, p. 101.

when it was preceded by a subtle popular lack of respect that left its mark on the whole of the nineteenth century – surrealism 'in the service of Revolution' is one example. The daubed walls of the faculties speak a language as old as revolution itself, a language the working class has known for more than a century. The young workers have become the madmen of society, insane with renewed revolution. 'A really sensible person wouldn't have a jester. So anyone who has a jester is not sensible, and if he is not sensible he must be a jester and perhaps, if he is a king, his jester's jester.'[4] May belonged to Diderot's nephews rather than to Lenin's children.

Contestation does not become general by summing up the immediate demands of various sectors of the population. It attacks directly the State and the economy that impede any activities of this kind by producing and reproducing class divisions, as well as the divisions within them. It is only when the popular classes contest the bourgeois frame of reference in pursuit of a revolutionary perspective that they become *one*. The contestation is 'negative' insofar as it stands outside the divisions and disciplines of established society; at the same time it is prior to the construction of socialism (Marx had already left it to others to 'keep the pot of the future boiling'). The contestation is only strategically centralized, in order to coordinate its attack against the power of a centralized State. It is decentralized and corresponds to the decentralization of centres of popular decision in the future society: it has as many forms as the life of the country, and is as unified as its language. 'The Communist Revolution is the most radical rupture with traditional property relations; no wonder that its development involves the most radical rupture with traditional ideas.'[5]

Contestation does not attack an actual order in the name of a

4. D. DIDEROT: *Rameau's Nephew*, ibid. p. 83.

5. *The Communist Manifesto*, Foreign Languages Publishing House, Moscow, p. 82. Let those complacent 'intellectuals' who qualify their intellectual virginity as Marxist in order to put it on their card take their ease, when they discover that contesting 'everything' is too much for the theory they espouse. Instead of leafing through their histories of literature cutting out the label 'Romanticism', why don't they read Marx with a little intelligence? There they will discover that what is contested are the very relations of capitalist production, whose definition they will find in *Capital* or the *Critique of Political Economy*.

dream of disorder; it declares the reality of the disorder, and denounces the timidity with which it is hidden. The contestation is critique inasmuch as it makes a separation between two types of society; it is aggressive because that separation takes place within bourgeois society. It is the movement through which the forces of production form relations outside the relations of bourgeois production; and it does this not in order to abolish aesthetic, technical or scientific work, but to destroy those divisions and limitations through which work is adapted to the society in which we still live. Contestation is just a word; in this way those who will not see the movement of words and actions through which one epoch detaches itself from the past, glibly refute that movement. The key word and the regulating activity of the society that is now dying was 'accommodation' – the accommodation of the young to the old, of socialism to capitalism and vice versa, of human relations to the inhumanity of exploitation, etc. May stated clearly that accommodation was no longer to be manufactured, neither lineally nor cyclically, neither through evolution nor through participation. That process of accommodation is the first target of the contestation; of the two terms, one means nothing. Make your choice.

You do have to 'earn' your living in order to survive, to assuage your hunger; but you do not at the same time have to sing a hymn to accommodation. A society that rejects revolution converts its refusal into a religion; fear is its prophet and immobility its god. The contestation promises sacrilege.

It does this in two ways. As *critique*, it separates technical demands (productive forces) from the basic needs (relations of bourgeois production). Hence the protest of the workers, research workers and young *cadres*, who do not accept that investment in manual and intellectual work should be subject to the investment policy of powerful financial interests. As *revolt*, it brings together all the semi-pariahs of society; young people, foreign workers, etc. It destroys social barriers, the outer limits of the wisdom of nations where their vices flourish: racial and social segregation, sexual repressions, etc. Now the 'free' Sorbonne becomes a new 'ship of fools'; decent people see there all the perversions that haunt them.[6] Separately, these two strands of contestation lead to the stagnant waters of reformism on the one hand, and to literature on the other. Together they fuse cultural rebirth and revolution. When young workers and students are reworking language, action and politics, a new society is in the air. 'Good God, what you call the beggars' pantomime is what makes the world go round.'[7]

Contestation could not be neutralized as 'student folklore'; it shattered one of those important places where society takes itself seriously – the university. And it was heard and understood in a cultural framework – the revolutionary tradition – that is the object of ridicule for decent society. Forms of action and organizations to develop action can now be built upon the basis of that understanding.

2. The Movement: Workers and Students

The Sorbonne is not a factory; that is why the first red flag over the revolutionary Sorbonne provokes such activity within the factories. The students are 'strangers' to the workers, but they are not 'cut off' from them; they have acted upon them from outside and as outsiders.

Political class consciousness can only be brought to the workers *from the outside*; that is to say, from outside the economic struggle, from outside the sphere of relations between workers and employers. The sphere from which alone it is possible to obtain this knowledge is the sphere of relationships of *all* classes and strata to the state and the Government, the sphere of the inter-relations between *all* classes.[8]

The students are not the Bolshevik party; they did not bring (revolutionary) political consciousness to the workers. Yet they did introduce into that pre-existent consciousness elements which had previously been outside it. The simple fact of mass student activity shows the relations of State with all classes in a

6. The contestation is defined as 'irrationality' as against the adapted rationality of official society. Michel Foucault has noted the rise of a similar upheaval before the Revolution of 1789: *Histoire de la Folie*, vol. 3.

7. D. Diderot, *Rameau's Nephew*, op. cit., p. 122.

8. Lenin, 1902. V. I. Lenin: *What Is To Be Done?* 78–9. Foreign Languages Publishing House, Moscow, pp. 78–9.

new light; the new elements of extra-parliamentary action and student debate must now be included. Standing outside the relations of worker and employer, the student, through his action, and his words and countersigns in turn, both provides information and is an informant, revealing the revolutionary consciousness of the proletariat.

There is a barrier to communication between students and workers. This is less and less the result of the workers' secular suspicion or the students' initial clumsiness. It is more clearly due, as usual, to the very effective barriers raised whenever possible by the PCF and the CGT. The wall stood; yet contact was made. The Sorbonne became a revolutionary theatre, but the audience was not asked to applaud. The students invoked, their actions evoked, and the resurgent history of the workers' struggle provoked. The students acted on the basis of a lingering memory. They were far less 'conscious' than the professional Leninist revolutionaries; yet the 'spontaneity' of the French worker in 1968 is the result of long experience of the class struggle, an experience far more political than that of the Russian worker in 1900. Socialism still enters the worker–employer relation from the outside; the manner of entry, as well as the agents of transmission, varies according to the situation.

The work of introducing revolutionary consciousness from outside determined, for Lenin, the three theoretical, political and economic tasks of a Marxist party. Even without a party those tasks remain; for every revolutionary movement struggles on three fronts.

The students have occupied the advance positions for about fifteen years; they have organized a tough and uninterrupted struggle against the Algerian War, the OAS, and the American intervention in Vietnam. By setting violence against the violence of the fascists, they have won over the Latin Quarter. Although repeatedly condemned as 'Leftists' by the Communist party, they have created their own organizations (the *groupuscules*). What the students are introducing from outside is the condensed result of their struggles and their debates; and these are only closed to the complacent majority of average Frenchmen, be they pro- or anti-communist, who think that socialism is 'what is going on in Russia'. They do not see it as the coherent sum of ideas that has thrown the world into confusion for the last hundred years, and that is itself modified each time a new continent is discovered.

The experience of the students is only a specifically student experience insofar as the revolutionary movement elsewhere is weaker, if not non-existent. The struggle on three fronts and the hierarchization of those three fronts is a classic rule. If, on the one hand, the students did not climb the barricades simply to modify their methods of study and teacher–student relationships, they know, on the other hand, that without barricades university reform would stay a private affair in which governmental disorder could act as it wanted to.

The political struggle takes precedence over the economic struggle which is developed in its wake. 'The fact that economic interests play a decisive role *does not in the least imply* that the economic (i.e. trade-union) struggle is of primary importance; for the most essential, the "decisive" interests of classes can be satisfied *only* by radical *political* changes in general.'[9]

The theoretical ideas of the students remain divergent; there is, however, one idea that is common to anarchism, Marx, Lenin, Trotsky, Mao and Guevara. That idea defines politics as struggle and theory as a 'guide to action'; it judges the subordination of every political perspective to mere parliamentary activity to be an advanced form of cretinism. The streets of May crystallized a decade of political confrontations and theoretical discussions.

The student movement may be external to the workers, yet its experience has significance within the consciousness of the working class. It discovers in that experience the possibility of socialism and the elementary workings of a revolutionary movement; hence its explosive effect. The students have invoked the spectre that is haunting Europe, and it has appeared. It is now a question of revolution. Another phantom is in attendance – counter-revolution; it is a phantom born of every ineffective revolution.

9. Lenin, op. cit., p. 47 footnote.

The initial dialogue was not sufficient to exorcise it. Student action has taken over the position of workers' revolutionary organizations. But it is an empty and theatrical position, for it can never replace the workers' movement.

3. Forms of Action

Political life as we know it consists entirely in pushing *suggestions* up some hierarchical ladder until they reach a centre of decision – either central power or State representative. That centre in turn sends them back down another channel, which ends either in action or in nothing at all. The whole State apparatus stands between the man who speaks and the man who acts, between the word and the deed.

That apparatus is often repeated within the party bureaucracies – whether opposition parties or not – that imitate the State. If you haven't got the ear of your superior, you are reduced to the ballot paper, the wage slip and the television news. This depoliticization of society by the State seems so natural that any new initiative passes for 'mob violence' or demagogy. The May movement has forced the 'authorities' to confront the 'mob', and the mobs to dispense with an absent authority; it has brought the first opportunity for western societies to abandon the political desert where they are encamped.

Contestation is in itself constructive; it creates the conditions in which political life is possible. The many centres that emerge (action committees, strike committees, faculty commissions, student assemblies and the like) are political centres at the same time. They are not built as a result of a programme, but in order to decide on programmes; they do not spring from agreements between leaders, but from the right to hear the 'leaders' and to be heard by them. Every authentic democracy has had some sovereign places where all hierarchies are destroyed in the face of the equality of a discussion that undermines hierarchy.

The Sorbonne has become a public square, for, ever since Greece, the public square has been the birthplace of democracy.

The struggle for existence of these new centres of decision

defines the time, space and modes of action of the revolutionary movement.

Time

No revolution is made at one stroke. A revolutionary gives himself time to organize. The May strikes have engraved upon the reality of French society a classical political progression, one that was analysed by all the European Marxist parties after the Russian Revolution of 1905.[10] The progression was: strikes to general strike to political general strike to insurrectional strike to Revolution. It is a project for radical confrontation. Even if the two adversaries do not reach those extremes, they stand potentially on the horizons of their struggle. Each camp can invoke them, whether out of their movement's hope or its despair. 'Engagement is the only effective political activity ... even when it does not actually take place.'[11]

The May movement outlined one set of tactics: political strike to change of regime. This 'peaceful road' never depends on the good intentions of one of the adversaries. Both must recognize the possibility of a violent confrontation; and, in terms of its probable results, they must act *as if* that engagement had in fact taken place.

If the engagement in May had been real, the strikers would have gained the advantage. That is the paradox, for while it remained potential, the intimated threat reinforced the State. The two adversaries come face to face on one battlefield, but they are pursuing two objectives: the State restores order; the proletariat must either create a new order, or resume its place within the old.

The concurrence of these two orders can last for some time, producing what the Russian revolutionaries called a period of 'double power'. *If* the factories are occupied not only by the union *cadres* (as was most often the case), but by all the workers, the latter can control all negotiations *inside* the factory rather than from in front of the family television. Their representatives

10. By Kautsky, Rosa Luxemburg, Lenin.
11. Clausewitz, *On War*.

are then responsible to and revocable by the assembly of striking workers. The occupation then takes on its full significance, which is not only to close the factory to 'scabs' and *provocateurs*, but also to transform it into an autonomous and permanent centre of decision. Only direct horizontal coordination between these various centres and consolidation with other workers' groups (peasants, students, local committees) can ensure that the strike will last, by organizing the lives of those on strike (i.e. food, transport, town–country exchanges, resumption of work in self-governed factories to cater for strikers' needs and so on).

The second power ensures that the alternative of submission or chaos that the State brandishes during negotiations can be avoided. Ten million workers spread among their centres *constitute* a power that they do not *possess* in fact. It is the parties that dispose of that power; and while the Communist party demands the 'guarantee' of a programme acceptable to the whole of the Left before it acts, it pretends to forget that the only guarantee that the body of strikers can offer is their organization of the strike. And without that the rest is so many scraps of paper.

The road towards socialism passes through the organization of 'double power'. It will be 'peaceful' to the extent that the organized workers are able to intimidate the adversary and control the political stages of the movement (whether parliamentary or not), by consolidating their strength in coordinated centres of decision. When, between February and October 1917, Lenin glimpsed the possibility of a 'peaceful road' to socialism, it was based on the organization of workers into decision-making centres ('all power to the Soviets'), and not on the good intentions affected by any and everyone.

If time is not to escape the striking workers, there must be a massive and organized occupation. Wherever it took place, the strike held fast. As soon as the Communist leadership succeeded in creating a division between the unorganized masses and 'reliable' unionized workers (who are the only ones in occupation); as soon as they succeeded in cutting off each factory from its neighbours, the strike became fragile and lost its perspective. The transformation of each factory into a centre of decision; the acceptance by the workers themselves of the job of coordinating them (sometimes the faculties served as 'centrals'), determine the strike's power of resistance and its progress.

Time is the favourite theme of the powers that be. If the strike continues, examinations will not take place, the economy will suffer. Unless, that is, the strikers give themselves enough time to transform both examinations and economy. Time belongs to the masses exercising their power of decision.

Space

Meanwhile, each moment of the struggle is defined by a concrete relation of forces, in the space occupied by the struggle. The Latin Quarter is social space occupied by students; it is political space where the demonstrations of the extreme Left attract the mass of students, and the extreme Right may not bring to light its protection by the police. It is also geographical space, small in relation to Paris, minute in relation to France. The geographical occupation of the Latin Quarter depends upon the state of the rest of France; if everything is calm there, the police can invade it.

Just as action uses time to develop double power, it uses space for self-defence. The Revolution incubates within privileged centres – the factories as always, the schools, the universities and wherever the contestation is carried on. The forces of order may occupy a factory or faculty geographically; but they cannot occupy them economically or socially, they merely prevent their use.

No modern State can exist if its factories and universities are not working. The centres of contestation can no more be extinguished than the blast furnaces or the research institutes. Violent repression is necessarily limited, and the insidious pressure that is substituted for it is exerted in naturally hostile territory, in a society ripe for socialism.

Every police force in the world makes the mistake of confusing geographical space and social and political space. Repression sends the *groupuscules* 'underground'; that is to say, it makes their influence more profound. Every struggle on specific demands is joined by the struggle for the right to make those demands; police intervention itself gives a boost to action. The closure of Nanterre brings the debates to Paris; the entry of the police into the Sorbonne is followed by demonstrations and barricades; repression at the barricades brings on the strikes. The repression that threatens the whole movement (banning of demonstrations, persecution of *groupuscules*) welds the movement together. The will to freedom of expression takes precedence over the expression of divergences.

This retroactive mechanism does not function by moral virtue. The space hewn out under the repression creates in itself a revolutionary situation. It is revealed as the repression covers it. If the State defines itself by the monopoly of the 'legitimate' use of violence, the use of that violence can in turn define the State and rob it of its legitimacy.

Geographical space is not the determining factor until the final moment of struggle; so the movement is flexible and can choose its terrain without being pinned down. If night falls on the society glimpsed in May, the beacons of the contestation will reflect each other's signal, while shadows drift in the depths of the long-armed watches of the night.

The development of action

The rapid spread of the May movement was encouraged by a multitude of separate but contagious initiatives. An action speaks with three voices: it is carried forward *in pursuit of* specific objectives, *against* those who raise obstacles to it and with regard to the uncommitted spectators whom it wants to attract. The barricades of 10 May had a perfectly clear objective (to give us back the Sorbonne); they demonstrated the incoherent brutality of the powers that be; they rocked large sections of the population, particularly the working class.

Action extends in each of these three directions at the same time. The objective is necessarily limited, both in time and in social space (at the beginning of May the students were shouting, 'the Sorbonne to the students'); but it can expand progressively (for example, 'escalation' of demands). It is easier to generalize about the forms of action; the occupation of the Sorbonne emulates the occupation of the factories, and the student occupation is imitated in its turn in the factories. It is in general the forms of action that have the earliest repercussions; young workers, for example, join the students when the police attack. It is also, however, the forms of action that are most easily neutralized by the mass media (newspapers, radio, TV). The spectacle of repression is a shock at first; but as it is repeated the spectator can grow used to a 'little war' whose significance is as alien to him as the battles of cowboys and indians.

The effectiveness of action depends upon its content, its form and its power of communication. Mastery over these three aspects constitutes the essential problem of a tactic that must shock in order to attract attention and make people understand, if it is to gather support and ensure its growth. The exemplary and explosive content of action is not given once and for all.

The last barricades were used with the same triple objective in mind – by the other side. From Friday 24 May onwards, while the majority of students were demonstrating on the right bank (Bastille, Bourse, Opéra), the police closed off all the bridges across the Seine, except one – the Pont-Neuf. The students were made to cross it in order to get back to the Latin Quarter, and there the police carried out the repression – *in pursuit* of the restoration of order; *against* the 'rabble' of the Latin Quarter, and without regard to the uncommitted; that is, those made uneasy as much by the Government as by the Communist newspapers that took up its slogans. The object of the operation was to depoliticize the barricades; they were turned into the repetitive local folklore of the 'disturbances' in the Latin Quarter.

When the university crisis became a national crisis, the violent student struggle could only find significance and purpose by accelerating the national movement; and this it did. The student demonstration of Friday 24 May was more important than the CGT demonstration two hours earlier. Similarly the assembly at the Charléty stadium (on Monday the 27th) was joined by a significant number of young workers. In response, the

CGT organized its big demonstration on Wednesday, 29 May. The concurrence of several organizations temporarily reinforced the struggle.

This role of accelerator ceased as soon as the Communist leadership took advantage of the prospect of an election in order to abandon publicly the streets and bring the strikes to an end.

Since then the problem has become that of mastering the three elements of every action, and coordinating them not only in the Latin Quarter, but on a national scale.

July 1968

10. The Action Committees

Jean-Pierre Vigier

The most important political innovation of the May Revolution was the founding of the action committees (*Comités d'action*). These organizations sprang up spontaneously in the universities, the factories, urban and rural districts. As the socialist political party was once the revolutionary organization through which the working class challenged the early capitalist State, the action committees represent the new challenge to the modern capitalist State. Before we can discuss the development of the action committees and the theory behind them, it is useful to mention some facts about the social and political climate in which they developed. Effective political action always depends upon one's awareness of new developments and new contradictions in society. Without grasping the essential nature of these complex phenomena any political strategy is barren.

The Gaullist regime has been built upon a contradiction it has never been able to resolve. It has fostered what appears to be an extremely radical foreign policy based on an intensive attack on American imperialism. This policy is spearheaded by and for French industry trying to oust American imperialism from underdeveloped countries and replace it with French imperialism. But the effectiveness of such a policy has required a rapid modernization of French industry, and the political means to hasten such modernization which has paradoxically engendered those new social and political forces which threaten the regime. Hence a radical foreign policy has been underwritten by a distinctly illiberal policy at home. Radicalism abroad has been used to make illiberalism at home more palpable to much of the traditional French Left. Hence at those times when the Gaullist regime appeared to be socially vulnerable, in formal political terms it emerged as the most buoyant of forces.

De Gaulle, himself, thus represents two very powerful and not always homogeneous forces. He represents a challenge both to the American economic and political hegemony in Western Europe as well as to the French scientific revolution which has made France one of the most technologically advanced countries in the world.

But Gaullism has always walked a political tightrope. Its policy of non-participation in the Western alliance has been based upon a simultaneous alliance with the Left and the Right. Playing this complicated game has only magnified the social contradictions in its policies. They have always been potentially volatile and apt to explode. The May events were such an explosion and also a portent of the future form of social conflict. Most important, they have destroyed the twin tenets of Gaullism.

First of all, de Gaulle's foreign policy lies in ruins. When faced with a revolutionary assault, the regime immediately abandoned its anti-imperialist position in order to unite all the counter-revolutionary forces. All anti-American propaganda was dropped. The pro-American readers of Le Figaro could thus ally themselves with the Gaullist technocrats. Hence May destroyed the illusion of an autonomous France. But this does not mean that a more liberal home policy will be pursued. Quite the contrary. Valuable time and energy have been lost and must be recouped. Hence de Gaulle has been forced to accelerate his technocratic programme whilst maintaining the delicate political equilibrium between the traditional Right and the Gaullist movement. Hence at the moment he has donned a Leftist mask to woo the masses with the idea of a technologically-modernized society. It is a very delicate operation involving abandoning just enough support on the Right to gain strength from the Left. For example, the sacking of Pompidou, who came through the crisis with flying colours, symbolized the fact that de Gaulle is prepared to go to the utmost limit in his battle.

Secondly, internal policies have heightened antagonism. The cornerstone of Gaullism, its scientific revolution, has had the effect of increasing and broadening the political consciousness of the students and young workers. The contradictory demands made by modern society and the tensions they create between youth and other groups have become crystal clear. Without developing the argument in all its complexity,[1] the scientific revolution is based on the rapid expansion and equally rapid obsolescence of accepted forms of technical knowledge. What is required and rewarded one day is rejected the next. The bearers of such knowledge are thus subject to increased insecurity very similar to that experienced by workers during the great industrial expansion of the nineteenth century. Today young workers and technicians are required to adapt themselves constantly not only to new techniques and new qualifications but to a constant reordering of the organization of their work whilst in no way challenging the notion of hierarchical social controls in the factory and in society itself. These rules must remain unquestioned. Yet this is exactly what they begin to question. Moreover, the young worker masters new techniques much more quickly than the older worker. The traditional notion that seniority corresponds to age has been destroyed. The older worker also becomes vulnerable to technological unemployment. Inevitably the older worker and the organizations that back him up, the traditional form of trade unions, respond with hostility towards the younger workers. Therefore the increasing pace of technological innovation creates *a permanent quest for what might become marketable knowledge* and has thereby structured and perpetuated a conflict between the generations, giving it political content.

This conflict was at the root of the May Revolution. It is not surprising that students and young workers displayed a far more acute understanding of these events than did the established trade-union organizations. They clearly acted as a vanguard. The universities, the 'knowledge-factories' of the scientific revolution, became the permanent centres of the insurrectionary organizations. It is significant that Marxist ideas, once restricted

1. J. P. Vigier and G. Waysand, *Révolution Scientifique et impérialisme*, report presented by Vigier and Waysand at the Havana Cultural Congress, January 1968, '*Année du Guerillero Héroïque*'.

to the arts and social science faculties, spread not only to science faculties but to the law schools as well. The intellectual orientation of the university community has undergone a most remarkable change.

In terms of modern developments and institutions, French society has advanced further towards the 'new capitalism' than any other Western European society. It has developed more starkly the ideas of continuous consumption and the absorption of deviant elements into one bloc than any other country. From this picture of the economic and social situation in France we can conclude that whilst discontent amongst large sections of the traditional working class was high, the expression of their discontent took a very different form from the traditional strike and was expressed outside the existing opposition parties. May dramatically showed that something new and unexpected was afoot. It also demonstrated the obsolescence of the traditional opposition forces: the Left-wing political parties and the trade unions. They were unable to respond to or appreciate what was happening around them. Despite their resort to traditional rhetorical devices and their calls for structural reform, they were incapable of appreciating how this was to be done. Traditionally reform was brought about by working from within. But when it became possible to achieve significant changes by working from without, they failed to act and retreated in total disarray. If we are to propose new forms of actions, we must first understand exactly why these institutions failed.

In my view, the fundamental cause is that political and economic organizations, founded to oppose capitalism, have slowly acquired the same hierarchical structures and methods of acting as the system they claim to be attacking. In other words, except for their rhetoric they have actively attempted to integrate their supporters into the system. They have systematically minimized conflict and sought to make temporary compromise after temporary compromise. But these have never been compromises because the essential has always been conceded. They have adjusted to change rather than trying to define change. We can see this clearly by the fact that they no longer serve as fulcra to change. They have become incapable of proposing any meaningful alternative to the present hierarchical system. Hence their role has been that of securing compliance. The evolution of these movements has once again raised the problem that has dogged the Socialist movement since its foundation: how does one avoid the danger of integration? How does one turn acceptable modes of behaviour against the system? How does one raise the level of the movement's consciousness so that revolutionary change becomes its natural response?

The problem is partially historical. Political parties are products of a particular phase of historical development. In those situations they were revolutionary. Their leaders, structures, activities and ideologies took on the complexion of those periods. But since that time these organizations have not changed. Ideologically moulded and organizationally paralysed by the images of a past epoch, they have become obsolescent and, in fact, counter-revolutionary.

The May events highlighted the contrast between new possibilities for action and traditional approaches. For the first time non-economic demands were made on a large scale. The gap between the notions of economic rewards and the control of production traditional to trade unionism narrowed. Here we find the beginnings of a new form of consciousness with the possibility of transcending the old distinction between economic and political demands and the distinction between leadership and mass activity. Significantly these problems were raised by the non-integrated groups, the students and the young and foreign workers. On the other hand the traditional trade unions like the CGT could do no more than reassert traditional demands, accepted modes of economic and political action and use any means in their power to move the strikers in that direction. They resisted the movement so strenuously that in their bewilderment they looked to de Gaulle for a lead.

What is now clear to all who are serious about revolutionary change is that the parliamentary game is futile. For several generations the French bourgeoisie has used elections and the plebiscite to legitimize their power. But these institutions were meant to civilize the demands of non-integrated groups and make them more palpable. Parliaments recast demands in forms acceptable to existing society. This role of control in modern society is now played by the communications industry. The vicarious feeling of 'participation', no longer associated with the parliamentary system, is now engendered by the mass media. Hence we can understand the Government's swift and brutal reaction to ORTF strikers demanding no more than 'objective' reporting.

The collusion between existing institutions and the Left-wing political parties was laid bare by the May events. An agreement between the Communist party and Socialist federation spoke of a change in government whilst ruling out any fundamental change in the regime. In much the same vein, the CGT maintained continuous contact with Pompidou during the crisis, tried to prevent strikes and when they occurred, attempted to steer them towards the traditional demands for higher wages. The Communist party justified its behaviour by claiming that because the revolutionary struggle was not initiated by the working class or its representative organization, the workers were not revolutionary. This is, of course, an obvious *non sequitur*. That the workers were not immediately revolutionary does not mean that they could not be revolutionary. In fact the PCF's argument reads better when inverted: May demonstrated that given the correct impetus the workers would behave in an extremely revolutionary way. Had the PCF seized the initiative, it could have led to revolution. The PSU, now to the Left of the PCF, also misjudged the situation. A socialist transformation will not be the product of isolated incidents miraculously united with the PSU emerging as the replacement for the traditional Left-wing parties. This is pure utopianism. Indeed, the PSU's own subsequent failure at the elections testifies to its sterile parliamentary strategy.

The concept of 'double power'

The reasons for the failure of traditional organizations point the way to a new strategy. In essence it is very similar to the notion of 'double power' developed at the beginning of the Russian Revolution. It can be summarized briefly as follows:

1. A truly revolutionary movement must not only challenge existing social values and structures but must in a parallel movement create the embryo of the new society to which it aspires. It must destroy and create at the same time. Otherwise the movement will run the risk of eventually conforming to the structures it is combating. Hence the movement would be drained of its dynamism and creativity. The failure of the Russian State is a testimony to this problem.

2. Existing society must be challenged at all levels and in all the spheres of its activity. One cannot limit one's challenge to one sphere only. The reason is that these spheres have been defined by existing society. Activity in one sphere at a time is therefore acceptable. Hence society tolerates the economic activity of trade unions and the political activity of socialist parties. What it cannot tolerate is a form of organization that acts on both levels at the same time. Hence opposition must be total and permanent. One must choose one's own battleground and not accept existing battlegrounds. This is what is meant by *contestation* and *guerrilla tactics*.

3. The principal myth of capitalist society is that power is a function of different spheres: political, economic, cultural, intellectual, etc., and they are unrelated. For the first time we can envisage a total struggle for power which is not compartmentalized according to existing social norms. It follows that action must be open-ended so that one can effectively respond to any situation and more important define the situation. This power of definition is equivalent to the power of manoeuvre on the battlefield. He who possesses that power of manoeuvre has the advantage. The greatest fault in traditional opposition organizations has been their rigidity. Dogma is fatal to a correct strategic appreciation.

4. But since French society is so clearly atomized and one group is played off against another, another task is to *polarize* potential opposition so that the delicate equilibrium of the Gaullist regime will be destroyed.

5. Hence one of our first priorities in the light of the require-

ments of open-endedness, contestation, guerrilla tactics and a movement which springs from and responds to the rank-and-file is to foster what the Cubans have called *insurrectionary centres* (*focos*) which fester and spread like malignant sores.

6. Such insurrectionary centres are now feasible in Western societies. The scientific revolution has created a limited number of vital nerve centres which could be paralysed. Technical and intellectual workers are willing to undertake such actions. Mass discontent can be combined with strategic technical blows against the system. It follows that our tactics must be malleable, and ready to take advantage of any opportunity.

7. Similarly we must be able to catapult one action into another. Factory occupations and wage claims are not enough. We must put over the idea that power lies in the act of production, itself emphasizing ideas like those used by the workers in Nantes: 'A massive rise in wages without corresponding social, economic and political changes leads only to a massive rise in the cost of living and a return to the *status quo*.' Hence what we are calling for is a modern version of the Paris commune.

The action committees

The theory outlined above found its practical expression in the action committees which sprung up spontaneously during May. These committees represent the initial form of the new revolutionary challenge to capitalist society. May crystallized this new form of total opposition. What had hitherto been critique and theory became action. In that sense the May events mark a turning-point in the history of Western industrial societies.

There are three stages to the development of the action committees.

The first impulse naturally came from the young people. The movement started in the universities and slowly seeped down into the lycées and eventually even to primary schools. Not all the activists by any means came from working-class families. For the most part they responded as a result of their experience to the contradictory demands placed upon them – a condition analogous, as Alain Touraine pointed out,[2] to the early formation of the working class. These students manned the barricades in Paris, Lyons, Bordeaux and Toulouse and fought the battle at the Renault works at Flins. Their first form of organization was committees of self-defence based on their university bastions. These rapidly evolved into organizations which began to fill the void left by the collapse of existing university institutions. These replaced existing student organizations, drawing their power from the immediate, concentrated, continuous and direct involvement of all the participants. Already we saw a new definition of democracy. Rather than a notion of a formalistic democracy based on the representation of interests, democracy was based on involvement. Certainly the committees themselves were made up of representatives but their role was reduced by means of subtle forms of interlocking controls, a constant change in personnel and the continuous participation of the rank and file. The similarity between their own experiences and that of the traditional working class allowed them to move towards new forms of alliances and a total critique of society. Hence we find the first form of the action committees were those based on a particular stratum or profession.

In the second phase the student catalyst injected the young workers with an enthusiasm connected with the students taking over their universities and defining their own priorities. In relatively self-contained areas, with a strong local tradition, the movement spread with exceptional speed. This happened, of course, in the case of Nantes, where not only were action committees set up in factories but a central coordinating committee was soon established which became the veritable government of the entire *département*. This coordination was a form of worker–student–peasant power. Hence in some areas an embryonic socialist society was being actively substituted for a capitalist society.

The third phase is the crucial phase. It is marked by the substitution of the old hierarchical relationships by new forms of

2. Alain Touraine, 'Naissance d'un mouvement étudiant', *Le Monde*, 7–8 March 1968.

direct democratic control. The action committees would move from occupying factories to running factories and from accepting established modes of political communication to establishing their own. The embryo would become the new society. The old structures would become increasingly irrelevant and fictitious: the ideas they were based upon would become increasingly nonsensical and meaningless. With the initiative in their hands, the action committees would establish their hegemony over society. Only their proposals would be accepted as 'real' and commonsense. In the final stages the old State would crumble revealing an already-formed socialist society.

The May events corresponded to the first and second phases: catalytic detonation, a general strike and the first formulation of new means of action. The third phase never followed because the existing trade unions and political parties were interested in defending the existing social framework and were still powerful enough to resist. The traditional Left operated in one dimension. A multi-dimensional struggle was beyond their comprehension. They could only resist and by doing so favoured the re-establishment of the Gaullist regime. Had they pushed and cajoled the movement not towards traditional quantitative claims – wages, reduction in the working day, etc., – but towards taking over factories and running them, as the movement was beginning to demand in many areas, the outcome would have been very different. Clearly what was lacking was coordination and a new form of leadership. There had not been time for these to have evolved.

Hence the action committees find their historical roots in the May events and in the secular changes in French society. They represent the only contemporary political vehicle which can operate on the multiplicity of levels required to engage and replace capitalist society.

We have indicated that they must contain the potential to move from the destructive to the constructive phase. They are the embryo organizations of the new society. Hence the question of their current organization is extremely important.

There are several basic forms of action committees. There are those like the action committees in the university which specialize in one sector. Internally they radicalize the student body and externally act as liaison between other action committees. There are action committees in the factories. These are rank-and-file committees which cut across traditional trade-union divisions and crafts. In some areas the committees are organized according to workshops thus incorporating manual workers, *cadres*, technicians, engineers and draughtsmen. During May the rank-and-file committees were in almost constant session. It is interesting to note that they were very heavily attended. Whereas participation in trade-union activities is low and trade-union membership quite small the action committees were well attended and joined by a large number of non-unionized workers. The action committees elect a central committee which coordinates its activities. But there are also a multiplicity of committees dealing with different problems. In all cases a mandate is revocable at any time, and meetings are open and public. The third type of action committee is the local committee. In Nantes these were formed by the wives of strikers, initially to support the strikers but later to set up forms of communication with peasant action committees to obtain supplies and eventually to run many of the social services in the locality. Already they were beginning to replace existing institutions. In Paris they helped pickets, coordinated aid to strikers occupying factories and formed specialist committees. They provided a real form of local democracy which had never existed and, most important of all, politicized women and for the first time allowed them to play an active role. These three forms of organization: university and lycée, factory, and local groups, were coordinated together by liaison committees.

Action committees now exist throughout France. They are naturally concentrated in the most militant areas. Their concentration corresponds to the level of action during May. For example there are now three or four action committees in every arrondissement of Paris. They are strongly entrenched in the university faculties and the 'red belt' of Paris. In the provinces they are unevenly distributed. They are particularly strong in places like Lyons, Bordeaux, Rennes and Nantes.

Again the university action committees are very different

from the action committees in the factories. At the factory level, they cut through the traditional forms of trade-union organization. They include all elements, even those who were hostile to the May events and foreign workers who have hitherto been refused trade-union membership in many areas. By refusing to conform to the norms of factory organization, they constitute a challenge to the system. The university action committees service other groups and help to create centres of agitation in the factories.

From our brief description it is clear that the action committees are not and must not be politically homogeneous. Neither are they a mere scattering of fragmented groups. Their power is derived from a combination of concentrating on one particular field and their ability to show the interrelatedness of one field to another. Hence they differ from traditional political parties and soviets. Their single common characteristic is their crystallization around the problem of the struggle for power. The looseness of their organization is a great advantage. It not only permits different groups to work together but it also allows them to respond undogmatically and rapidly to a fast-changing situation whilst engendering many types of 'unconventional' action.

In many ways the action committees resemble the Castro model. As the Moncada assault was a prelude to the successful guerrilla war in Cuba so the May events are the pattern of future political activity in France. As Castro's forces adapted themselves to the political exigencies of their situation so have the action committees been formed with the same flexibility in mind. Just as the group of the twelve *Granma* survivors were able to raise a revolutionary army through a correct strategic appreciation so we hope that our centres of action will expand to encompass the revolutionary potential in contemporary French society. Like the Cuban *focos* the action committees try to create an explosive situation by setting off simultaneous sparks in industrial centres throughout the country. We will attempt to build *focos* of extra-parliamentary political activity and mass violence against the system. Our aim is to polarize the social forces to such an extent that the finely-balanced social fabric will be destroyed and those who destroy will, in a parallel movement, construct the new society.

Naturally this analogy with third-world movements is not comprehensive. In third-world countries, the force for social revolution is poverty or rather poverty to the extent that it allows people to see its political determinants. In neo-capitalist society, the force for social revolution is the contradiction between class rule and the real possibility of equality and affluence afforded by industrial potential. It is significant that the May Revolution occurred during an economic revival. The more we work towards automation and integration the more the basis for an equal society appears to be 'logical', the more the age/knowledge hierarchy breaks down. We are here to foster this 'logic'. It is the essence of revolutionary consciousness.

The Future

A great deal of reflection is necessary before we can take further action. For the first time we came near enough to power to know precisely what obstacles must be removed. Just as in 1905 when the Bolsheviks retreated into a period of analysis without abandoning their organizations, so must we follow a similar course of contemplation and perhaps self-criticism and introspection. Our numbers may temporarily diminish. This is only to be expected given the repressive atmosphere that exists. But our belief in the appropriateness of our present analysis assures us that we are on the right path.

The tactical need for action committees at the moment is to construct modes of mass mobilization along the lines I have outlined above to cut through traditional social divisions. The problem of combining mass discontent and latent discontent with effective technical blows suggests that some form of loose federation must be created. Many trade-union organizations are interested in such action now. The change in the Loire-Atlantique has been particularly electrifying. But the problem is how to coordinate without stifling initiative.

Again our decisions must be framed according to the line adopted by the Gaullist regime. The crucial problem is whether it will be strong enough to pursue its anti-American policy. There are indications that it may be forced to close down the universities until January and perhaps disband or 'reorganize' several faculties. The students would not take this lying down, to say nothing of the setback such an action would cause to the country's technological requirements. A more probable policy will be a 'speed-up'. That is, the economic crisis will be used as a pretext to speed up the transformation of French society necessitating a direct attack on the trade unions. Such measures could include the increasing concentration of industry, a cushion of high unemployment, devaluation, a reduction in the standard of living of the working class, all in an attempt to attenuate the fighting spirit of the working class. Where the next 'hot-point' will be we cannot predict. It could be the university. It could be the factory. In any case we must prepare for all contingencies.

These are the immediate problems that confront us. Our permanent aim is to establish committees for agitation, and self-education which popularize the idea of the new form of action. We will move in time from forms of spontaneous action which we have witnessed in the past to prepare for organized, large-scale action directed incessantly against the weakest point of capitalist society wherever it will be. Only through such activity will the bond of reason be snapped and the new society emerge simultaneously.

July 1968

Western Culture
and Revolution

11. Psychoanalysis and the May Revolution

Maud Mannoni

The Revolution started with the student movement. The working class did not entirely understand the meaning of the unrest which was portrayed as mere lawlessness by the press, the radio and some of the unions. That psychoanalysts could actually call this disturbance a return to health[1] was very badly received. However, there were always 'good' psychoanalysts prepared to describe the events in such classical terms as 'generational conflict', 'behavioural crisis', 'paranoid crisis', and who didn't hesitate to use the expressions 'group psychosis' and 'mass hysteria'. Once this diagnosis had been made (that is to say once the area of alienation and segregation had been defined), the authorities were able, in the manner of the orthodox psychiatrist, to call for 'understanding'. Never has there been so much talk of 'dialogue' and 'participation'.[2] Faced with the students' demands, the frightened adults tried to reply with hastily concocted solutions which, although displayed as a sign of understanding, were soon to reveal their deceptive nature.

The psychoanalyst knows that it is not up to him to make suggestions for the setting up of an ideal educational system or

1. *Un signe de santé* in a special issue of *Le Nouvel Observateur*, No. 183 bis, 20 May 1968.

2. Lacan's answer to this was: 'there is no such thing as dialogue, it is a swindle,' 19 June 1968, École Normal Supérieur. (Jacques Lacan, French analyst, founder of the École Freudienne de Paris, whose basic theory is 'the unconscious is structured like a language'. He finds that language pre-exists the appearance of the subject and so to speak engenders its appearance. Man's essence is not biological nor social, but linguistic. Lacan's teaching can be described as an increasingly profound probing on the effects of the *signifying* in the structuring of subjective life, hence the very birth of the subject as a talking being.)

even for the planning of an ideal state. As an analyst, what he should question primarily is the *desire* which governs people's choice of goals. For him the only real wealth is 'that which can pay the price of access to the state of desire' (Lacan). The reason why the most aware psychoanalysts[3] sided publicly with the students is to prevent the abuse of psychological-type explanations from distorting the meaning both of psychoanalysis and the movement. They insisted on emphasizing the political character of the unrest. It seemed obvious to them that every form of professional training (including psychoanalytical training) is so designed that it fully participates in an alienating system, the very system which the students were questioning. This questioning or *permanent contestation* had been initiated by the students at Nanterre long before the events of May. It was felt as a danger and, as in analysis, resistances arose. In his quest for truth the student came up against a barely disguised form of incomprehension and rejection. People were prepared to think *for* him and *with* him but they were *much less well disposed to the idea of his thinking and acting for himself*. The experts' critical examination of the student problem was distorted by their desire to find a solution for it. A study which purports to be objective but aims indirectly at reducing (or stifling) protest is naturally suspect; its approach is unscientific since it involves ideology and morals. An American psychoanalytical review suggested as a solution to the unrest of the younger generation the setting up of 'guideposts' for a 'good' society: faith, reason, truth, independence, love, should, according to its author,[4] be those 'keys' which would overcome all difficulties. This same theme was taken up in France: 'The other must be loved in all his difference because he is not another "myself"'.[5] To love others more than oneself is one of those 'reassuring' slogans which emanate from psychoanalytical literature of a moralizing and overcharitable kind. This is the sort of slogan which has always given free rein to any temporal power. The students were

3. *Le Monde*, No. 7264, 23 May 1968, publication of a manifesto signed by seventy, psychoanalysts.

4. G. SHOENFELD, 'Guideposts for the good society', *Psychoanalytic Review*, Spring 1968.

5. *Le droit de vivre*, No. 339, March–April 1968.

not taken in by what they felt to be a deliberate mystification. A Beaux Arts poster replied in approximately these terms: 'Be young (be good) and shut up.' This was illustrated by a policeman, a truncheon in his left hand, standing behind a youth whose mouth he is covering with his right.

Love, kindness, dialogue, non-violence, these are the themes taken up by the experts who would like to cure this 'cancer' from which the younger generation is supposedly suffering. But no one has taken any serious interest in the nature of student action, in its role and function. The problem of *action* is different from that of *'passage à l'acte'*[6] and of *acting out*. In *'passage al'acte'* and in acting out, it is as though something were placed on a stage.[7] *The act* precedes the subject when it comes to speaking; desire is not central to the problems of action, however. Action is a *moment* which is neither a part of a process of reform nor of a process of change. Its function is to bring into the open what was hidden or what one did not want to see (or know). What is brought to attention or revealed is directly related to a form of truth in the unconscious. Whatever emerges is always of a scandalous nature and cannot fail to provoke every possible resistance, every form of denial and insincerity: because the truth has been spoken, panic reaches its height and nakedness seeks cover. Action shows that authority is force; this may have been known but with action it is seen to be true; in themselves

6. The English term 'acting-out' was adopted into French but is different from the term *'passage à l'acte'* (although usually translated into English as acting-out.)

> *'acting-out*: term used in psychoanalysis to denote those actions usually characterized by an impulsiveness contrary to the subject's habitual motivation ... its hallmark is its connexion to this transference and the subject's attempt to ignore it.
>
> *'passage à l'acte*: used in clinical psychiatry and restricted to denote impulsive, violent, agressive and offensive acts (murder, suicide, sexual assault, etc.); the subject moving from a representation of a tendency to the act itself. Its clinical meaning is not necessary to describe a transferential situation.'
> J. Laplanche and J. B. Pontalis, *Vocabulaire de la Psychoanalyse*, P.U.F., 1967.

7. There is either a provocation with a call to the Other, or a vanishing of the Other; anxiety is then actualized in the uncovering of the fantasm. It is generally when all landmarks of identification have vanished that acting out occurs. The difference between *'passage à l'acte'* and *'acting-out'* is almost like the difference between *I* and *he*.

the representatives of the state are representative of nothing, they are mediocre and non-existent. The students' action has revealed the impotence and fear of those who claim to govern them; the embarrassment of the 'officials' contrasted with the self-confidence of the young who spoke the truth with a straight-forwardness which showed up the empty words and phoney tone of their elders. Politicians and trade-union leaders, whether Right- or Left-wing, were identified with the system, a system which had proved its incompetence. The students were criticized for refusing to join in any official reform movement thus showing a 'non-constructive spirit'. At this stage in their action they felt that permanent contestation was their most useful weapon and the only one capable of revealing the nature of their opponents and the ridiculousness of a system which could only perpetrate *immobilism*. The exposure of this untenable situation marked the beginning of the collusion between the university administration and the forces of political repression. The reason why this acted as a detonator is that suddenly there was a resurgence of repressed knowledge (one knew things were that way . . . but one didn't want to know about them) – hence the flash of truth. Truth became the *cause* of this true subject or subject of the unconscious. A new voice has come to life, gaining ascendancy, changing in a particular way the subject previously trapped in prejudice, that is to say in the many snares of the imaginary. Something akin to identification has happened (as in analysis), and the revolutionary act has actually ushered the subject into an entirely new order in a structural sense. It is significant that the students' questions revolved around the idea of *lack* and that they refused the linking operations offered by the reformists. According to Lacan's theory, lack is inseparable from desire and very relevant to truth and knowledge.[8] Where truth is concerned, lack becomes the unthinkable, it is also the element which is irrevocably *excluded* in the formation of the structure. The subject of knowledge opposes a resistance to this through the mirage of knowledge. Knowledge seeks to centre things, which in the operation of truth can only be perpetually excluded from the linking operation. A veil has thus been rent: knowledge

8. Yves Bertherat: '*Freud avec Lacan*', in *Esprit*, December 1967.

and truth are cut off from one another.[9] As we have seen, in the very midst of the ignorance and incomprehension in which everyone was taking refuge, this truth became something which could be demanded. Out of the confrontation between youth and the system sprang a current which created a need for a mutation of civilization.[10] For some time now students had been demanding changes in the way knowledge was imparted. They had been objecting to the type of knowledge which, like a coin, had to be rendered intact to the examiner. They were questioning a system of education which was strictly utilitarian, based on a boss/employee relationship, and prohibiting criticism. Two conceptions of knowledge were thus opposed, the first based on the notion of selection, the second anxious to remain open to the experience of truth, and aimed at decentralizing the subject.[11] Young people have demonstrated that adults were capable of accepting the university only if it remained a vacuum based on reassuring language. In a system where conformism alone is recognized, a word with any real meaning cannot be tolerated. Which is why student protest was immediately directed at the *language* which created a particular style: the style of women's magazines, advertising, and American catch-words. Against the anonymous clichés, the students upheld their right to be anxious; they countered with slogans, posters, a whole *new language*. A free idiom sprang up all over the walls and streets (there was talk of a 1968 version of Surrealism)[12] and the truth was spoken where least expected. After being restricted too long by a whole system of conventions, imagination and inventiveness burst forth, like symbols of a renaissance. A generation faced with a world based

9. Jacques Lacan: 'The symptom ever more loaded with its content of knowledge, is cut off from its truth. And that which severs them from one another is precisely what constitutes the subject'. Seminar, May 1967.

10. '*Le bonheur et la liberté*' in *Nouvel Observateur*, 3 July 1968. By Pierre Coulomb, Jeanne Favret, J. P. Peter.

11. Lacan reminds us that knowledge can be a sort of mirage. 'Knowledge is what comes instead of the truth, after the object has been lost'. In psychoanalysis the lost object is that which falls away in the process of signification, and the function of psychoanalysis is to maintain an opening and to refuse any linking operations.

12. One of the most poetic descriptions on the walls of the colleges was: '*La culture est une mandarine*' which does not mean that it is a sort of mandarin orange but that it belongs to the order of the Mandarins or pundits of the intellectual and university world whose authority depends on the system.

on *having*, rose to defend its right to exist in terms of *being*. What this generation has rejected is the mere satisfaction of needs which would deny them any possibility of retaining authentic and valid desire. This demand for truth which is alive in the protest movement represents a liberated language (very close to the language of the unconscious). The *power to speak* has always been a crucial point in every discipline. In the medical school the nurses joined the movement. 'We used to be *given* permission to speak. Those days are over, now we *assume the right* to speak.'

The experience of contestation, like the analytical experience, aims at the advent of a truthful idiom. This dialectical movement brought to light (as analysis does) the relationship between the subject's *ego* – seat of all misunderstandings and delusions – and the *I* author of a speech whose meaning the subject must understand before he can be freed from his (social) alienation. The students are attacking the stereotypes of a discourse in which the subject is spoken to rather than speaks; these stereotypes are nurtured by a particular style of teaching and by the very information media which surround the speaking subject from early childhood.[13] The aim of the protest movement was to shatter the absurd structure that fostered alienation[14] and produced what amounted to sclerosis in working life. For a long time in France people had ceased to work.[15] Students, workers and teachers are trapped in a daily routine hardly conducive to inventiveness and creativity. Chaos, it is said, gave birth to life.[16] Imagination and creativity made their appearance along with a new hope based on the rejection of traditional systems. The pleasure of creation, the satisfaction of responsibility, were feverishly assumed; students in every field have been taking

13. cf. Émile Copferman's book, '*Problèmes de la jeunesse*', Maspero, 1967. Here is an extract from a letter published in this book: 'Intelligence for all is the great enemy. Of course we need intelligent children, but not that many, a small elite, a selected group, the children of eminent citizens, landowners, civil servants. What would become of the others? They would turn into rebels, communists, bitter men, in short the sort of person who is a menace to the community.'

14. For example they denounced advertising slogans such as 'Shell *pense pour vous*' (Shell thinks for you), the mediocrity of the sensational press responsible for a generalized intellectual torpor.

15. '*Le bonheur de la liberté*', in *Nouvel Observateur*, 3–9 July, 1968.

16. ibid.

their affairs into their own hands and by their actions have rejected the psychological-type theories which contrasted youth (instability) with adulthood (so-called maturity). *There is no such thing as adulthood as opposed to youth.* Youth is not a stage of development, it is a state of mind. Adults have always felt the need to make the young infantile by keeping them in a state of prolonged irresponsibility. The 'instability of youth' is the symptom which the adult needs to feel well-balanced; the other is the sick one, not he. As has been demonstrated elsewhere,[17] the child also serves to support the adult's belief. Childhood and youth play the same role in relation to the adult as underdeveloped peoples played in the past. It is they and not the adults who embody all human weakness, helplessness and credulousness: God must exist since there is someone who believes in him. The 'Revolution', by allowing the young to take their affairs into their own hands, has at the same time deprived the adults of the prop they needed to feel secure and morally 'strong'.

This complementary aspect of the relationship between adulthood and youth also plays a part in the ritual of the transmission of knowledge. For a person's prejudices to have such a firm hold, someone else has to give them support. Everyone, whatever his field of work, will have realized at some point the extent of the restriction imposed on his intellect by the principles prevailing in his class or firm. This is why one of the unexpected effects of the barricades was to give people a more genuine access to science. It is also interesting to note to what extent the style of research is linked to the style of the regime. Students trained in the rigid traditions of classical French psychiatry were able to demolish, in less than two weeks, a fortress of medical traditions which was thought to be impregnable The natural concomitant of the adult/child and adult/primitive man relationships is the deliberate doctor/patient dichotomy. The students found it quite natural to start questioning overnight the style of this relationship. At the same time, the foundations of classical psychiatry were also implicated. The students felt the need to replace the systematic classification of entities by the study of the speaking

17. O. Mannoni: ' *Itard et son sauvage*', in *Temps Modernes*, October 1965.

subject, thus showing the same preoccupations as an important psychiatric *avant-garde* abroad (whilst seldom being acquainted with their work).[18] The question of the regeneration of psychiatry has thus been linked, as was mentioned above, with the contestation of the regime. Let us not forget that it is only the *politicization* of student action which allowed the uncovering of a truth which gurantees scientific progress. A movement of *depoliticization* necessary to the maintenance of the regime has already begun. Its intention is to make reforms and to silence contestation; and it is this contestation which has been responsible for the strong movement to destroy the myth of the doctor and his power.

Depoliticization can play into the hands of the mandarins; it flatters those who still cling to the idea of privilege. The existence of privilege fosters in the doctor a kind of mystical belief in his mission, a mission which makes him the rightful heir to a sacred function. There is actually a social need for this 'Boss' figure. Whether or not the doctor agrees to put himself in this position (even on an imaginary level) will determine the therapeutic relationship which he sets up with the 'unwell', especially in psychoanalysis. Before he even begins his medical training, the student is in danger of alienating himself in his fascination with the status of Boss (the danger is the same in psychoanalysis) and this can pervert a whole aspect of his relationship with his work. In refusing to accept this authoritarian training, the politically aware student knew that he was defending his only chance of remaining intellectually free and open to criticism. The doctor or psychoanalyst who adheres to the role conferred upon him by his status runs a great risk of turning his knowledge into a screen between himself and the other – a screen which makes him inaccessible to the messages of the unconscious. The patient who has not experienced these flashes of truth finds himself in a situation which is much closer to suggestion than to psychoanalysis. He is not struggling with his experience of truth but with the idea which the analyst has of 'his' truth or 'his' well being.

18. In Britain such important work has been carried out by David Cooper and Ronald Laing.

The situation is the same for the future psychoanalyst; his personal psychoanalysis might bring him, as a *pupil*, to identify with the persona or model of his analyst, which will then influence his whole training (i.e. his resistance to a dimension of truth).[19] Freud said that an analyst's training is only valid when it rests on his own capacity for identification with the patient. (This is the origin of the idea of a non-segregative relationship between doctor and patient. Medical training is nevertheless designed to defend the student against this kind of identification.) The fact that these crucial problems were brought up by the students in connection with the events shows the way in which they felt themselves directly implicated.

The Revolution has forced each person to define himself in relation to his own discipline. In the dialectic process of contestation, the subject (as is the case in analysis) found himself divorced from his usual consciousness of self. The search for identity became effective only when disconnected from the subject.[20] The latter then found himself within another structure, it is in fact from another place that his speech was able to become free.

Happiness is no more the aim of revolution than of analysis. There is no such thing as ultimate good.[21] The limit for everyone is the point at which the problems of desire come into play – and psychoanalysis is there to remind us that the idea of desire being adequately met by the object is a myth. The subject does not seek the object, it seeks its own experience of the gap between desire and object. By reducing our concept of man to a being made up only of needs, we lose sight of the speaking being, that is the desiring being[22] who is caught in a structure which revolves around no centre and which can only produce a split subject.[23]

19. The disturbance that an intervention by Lacan at a round table on 'psychoanalysis and medicine' created at the Collège de Médecine is an illustration of this. cf. Cahiers du Collège de Médecine No. 12,7 ième année. Expansion scientifique.

20. Lacan: *Écrits*, Édit. du Seuil, 1966 p. 292.

21. Lacan: 'Doing things in the name of goods, or worse still for the good of others, is certainly not going to free us from guilt nor from all kinds of inner catastrophes, particularly not from neurosis and its consequences.'

22. Who is situated beyond the point whence a call is addressed to the other.

23. Lacan's theory substitutes the scientific reference to a logic of the unconscious for any ideological reference.

If one refers only to the criteria of need outside any structural context, there is a danger of interpreting a situation, however revolutionary, in terms of ideological aims; the temptation is then to produce other myths to replace those things whose loss was necessary to the birth of the desiring subject.

One might well think that the students' intention was to use violence to back up their demands concerning the university, their liberties, and the respect due to them as persons. In fact the explosion which occurred showed what was hidden behind these demands and revealed the true nature of the problems. The question which became paramount was that of the relationship of the subject to knowledge and truth, a question which no one can solve for anyone else, which is why the student is asking for the freedom to solve it by himself.

July 1968

12. Sociology and Politics in 1968

René Lourau

The events of May 1968 have underlined the importance of sociology. Their distant origin lay in an initial phase of unrest on the university campuses and in the halls of residence – unrest caused by the restrictions imposed on the students' sexual freedom. The strike of November 1967 at Nanterre signalled a second phase. The strike was concerned with the problems of the application of the Fouchet reform and was inspired by, among others, 'docile' sociologists, sometimes Left-wing Catholics. The future *enragés* of May, the militants and leaders of small Leftist groups, participated only on a minor scale.

This dress rehearsal for the May crisis was, however, important for the future of the movement. Indeed, it not only permitted a certain syndicalization, a resurgence of UNEF ('Union Nationale des Étudiants de France'); it also rapidly revealed the limits and contradictions of reformist claims.

By establishing that the most reasonable claims concerning the organization of courses, teaching methods and the application of the Fouchet reform in general, were unacceptable to the university authorities and to the Government, both the students involved in the November strike and those who witnessed its failure were impressed and, moreover, *politicized* by the concrete problems of the university struggle. Such a result undoubtedly would not have been produced by the classic means of political education alone (propaganda, the spreading of slogans, lectures, the broadening of recruitment, the selling of newspapers).

From the beginning of the spring term in January up to the

eve of the Easter vacation, a climate of discontent was maintained by the paucity of results obtained the previous November, by the unkept promises, by the usual difficulties caused by the overloading of facilities and by the shortage of teaching staff. Even so, whilst this discontent remained apolitical as far as many students were concerned, it tended to grow into a more global questioning of the university institution. This was brought about, on the one hand, by the sense of disappointment caused by the failure of November and the lessons drawn from this, and on the other, by the diffusion by the small political groups of an ideology of *contestation*.

Claims grew into *contestation*; the games and the playful demonstrations of the anarchist–situationist mini-group gave way to more serious activity. This transition naturally assumed very different forms according to whether the students were recently politicized by the November strike, militants of political organizations, or those still in the process of gaining political education from the activities connected with the campaign against the American policy in Vietnam.

Within this movement of politicization and political education, discernible not only at Nanterre but also in most of the universities and lycées, sociology students did not play a major part – except, significantly, at Nanterre. Not that the *Comités Vietnam* were more active there than elsewhere. Nor was the social recruitment of male and female students more proletarian there than elsewhere (on the contrary!). As for the hostility between Left- and Right-wing students, this was probably more intense than at the Sorbonne, insofar as the Nanterre campus precipitates such clashes peculiar to itself: it is a small island of 'culture', surrounded by the worst manifestations of urban life (council houses – HLM, Arab shanty-towns, waste tips, muddy building-sites). In this no-man's-land between the capital and the industrial belt, a dreamlike area which seems to deny the opposition of town and country by displaying the most archaic features of both, there is no social space for social intercourse, for the many trivial necessities of everyday life or for the fulfilment of the roles which make up the pattern of urban living.

It is of course quite futile to seek to identify the key factor which would explain why Nanterre was at the root of the May troubles. It is easy to attribute it all to the general position of the French universities, to the current political situation, to the contradictions of the economy, to the world-wide unrest among the younger generations, to the international 'plot', to the presence of a German Jew, etc. Let us therefore limit our analysis to one of the variables, namely, the position and the problems of sociology (of which Daniel Cohn-Bendit, the 'German Jew', is a representative).

Let us make it quite clear that we are not attempting to discover THE cause or to be wise after the event. We shall merely sketch in the main lines of the teaching of sociology and the problems posed by this teaching. On the whole, we can apply the example of Nanterre to the sociology departments existing elsewhere in France.

When sociologists are accused in the Press and in speeches of bearing a large measure of responsibility for the events of May, or when the supporters of the movement attribute major credit to the sociologists, who or what is the subject of these remarks? Sociology students? Sociology lecturers? The way sociology is taught? Or that part of the discipline which is more or less subversive? Let us try to answer this question.

We shall begin by considering sociology as a university course taught for several decades within the framework of the philosophy degree, and for the last ten years as an autonomous discipline. For many years its standing as a science, on a par with other human or social sciences, has been the object of criticism. The Left holds it responsible for the diffusion of a reformist and neo-capitalist ideology, operating under the cover of scientific integrity and neutrality. Only in the last few years have the Communist countries concerned themselves with sociological research, created chairs of sociology and participated in international ventures. Roughly speaking, this thaw came with the end of the cold war and is beginning to make itself felt in all the social sciences. At the same time, in the large Western Communist parties, the after-effects of Stalinism caused many 'revisionists' to turn to sociology; these 'revisionists' had either been expelled from or had left their parties at times of crisis such as the Hungarian uprising of 1956 or the military *coup d'état* in France in 1958.[1]

The image that the Right has of sociology is the reverse: it is synonymous with dangerous criticism, destructive analysis and dependence on Marxism. As soon as law, religion and ethics become objects of sociological analysis, then the science becomes just as suspect as all the manifestations of modernism condemned by the popes. Strictly speaking, young girls from upper-middle-class homes are permitted to take one or two of the intermediate certificates in sociology, just as they learn tennis or underwater fishing.

So much for the *ideological status* of sociology in general. As far as France in 1968 is concerned, some clarification is necessary. Ever since the advent of Gaullism, our country has been striving to modernize its economic structures. Behind a façade of nationalism designed to conceal our dependence, industry has begun to imitate the USA.

This imitation has also taken the form of a change in the old technical and social division of labour. The place of sociology in the spectrum of human knowledge is no longer the same as when it was a mere extension of studies in philosophy. It has now taken its place in a *technical* division of labour prompted by the demands of productivity, competition and economic planning.

Similarly, the sociologist's position within the *social* division of labour, within the system of social status and social functions, is no longer that of a research-worker or disinterested academic, but that of an expert linked to other experts, participating in the process of integration into 'the bureaucratic society of channelled consumption' (as Henri Lefebvre has described it).

It is thus both the *theoretical status* of sociology and the *social status* of the sociologist that are brought into question. Its ideological status (i.e. whether it is revolutionary or reactionary) is consequently more ambiguous than ever; Right- and Left-

1. Among the principal representatives of French sociology are professors and research workers who have been members of the Communist party for periods of a few months to several decades. Those who are still members are, however, rare.

wing sociologists confront each other in a conflict of dubious validity, in which affiliations or references to this or that ideology, or the rejection of affiliation and reference, create a confusion which prevents any clear distinction between the two sides.

How can one be surprised that the communication of sociological knowledge suffers the consequences of such a state of affairs? – a state of affairs which, incidentally, is not confined to sociology. Nevertheless, due to various factors, the discipline is now the one which best satisfies many students' confused demands for political education, where once law, philosophy, history and literature performed this function. These have not lost their previous role of *support* for intellectual and ideological aspirations, but sociology is perhaps a better *support*.

Why sociology? Can it be because as a science it has been brought into question, because its theoretical status is precarious, because it is situated at the vague point of contact between intellectual curiosity and the emotional commitment of action?

And yet, it is argued, the sociology degree offers no openings. How can such 'conscious' students as the sociologists devote themselves to a subject which will turn them into intellectual unemployed or into workers with useless qualifications (well acquainted with Durkheim and Parsons although they are not required to know as much as this!)?

It is true that the state of the sociology market is confused: on the one hand, the teaching of sociology is blamed for producing practitioners of and seekers after integration and conformism; on the other, it is criticized for not being orientated towards serious openings. Is the contradiction to be found in the reasoning or in the reality?

It is to be found in the reality. Let us make it quite clear that if, as is the case, the teaching of sociology, like most other disciplines, tends to respond, if only unconsciously, to social *demands* (the demand of the dominating ideology and the commercial demands of the capitalist institutions), it is equally the case that these demands are currently so badly formulated, so ambiguous and so ambivalent that the division of labour cannot guarantee a clear view of the position of the sociologist. Neither can it pronounce on what is and what is not expected of him, nor on his training and his efficiency.

This lack of precision concerning the social demands[2] is not the result of chance, just as it is by no means peculiar to sociology. Modernist capitalism or, as is more often the case, industrial society in its bureaucratic phase (monopolistic or state-owned or with state-owned monopoly), has to promote social change as well as to arrest, canalize and direct this change towards a better functioning of capitalist means of production. Those who manipulate this change, whether they be the management (economists, administrators) or the 'spiritual managers' (as Lacan aptly describes psycho-technologists, psycho-sociologists and commercial sociologists) participate, with or without their consent, in an ideology and in processes of integration of individuals into the norms and aims of capitalist society.

But, as the analyses of Marx have very well demonstrated, the function of capitalism is to produce its opposite. At the beginning of an industrial revolution, the concentration of capital first in the manufacture and then in the factory produces cooperation. From the *technical* cooperation of the workers (of the 'collective worker') are born the *social* forms of cooperation. One of these forms is the cooperative of producers or of consumers. In Britain, the 'Rochdale Pioneers' replaced the old 'Union Shops' in 1844. Then, from 1863 onwards, there was rapid expansion in the English and Scottish wholesale societies. Similarly, the socialization of the process of production takes the form of trade unionization and politicization: the trade unions and the Chartist Movement represent the model (and the counterbalance) of a trend which was to cover Europe and America. Everywhere, the proletariat organized itself as it became larger; socialism, originally a visionary theory, gained in substance and its projected realization became one of the major historical forces of the modern age.

Cooperation in its second phase, characterized by the con-

2. These concepts which are used by certain sociologists are well formulated in an article in Althusser's periodical *Les Cahiers pour l'Analyse*, no. 2, article by T. Herbert on the social sciences.

centration of capital in banks and in other credit organizations, assumes a new form: emphasis is placed above all on the differentiation and compartmentalization of the tasks, on the scientific organization of work and on rationalization as envisaged by Taylor. Here again the dialectic of the system produces a feedback: over-rationalization and production-line labour, for example, are dysfunctional to the social relations within the enterprise, and are consequently dysfunctional to production. Psycho-sociology grew up to study 'human relations' and to remedy this new evil.

The contradictions of the third phase of industrial society are more visible in English-speaking countries than they are in France. Burnham and Galbraith herald modes of organization which only make their appearance much later in France. The denunciations of Riesmann, Packard and Marcuse are seen here as warnings and prophecies. Even so, certain aspects of these contradictions have been examined by sociologists. Henri Lefebvre, some time before the May unrest, wrote: 'What do we see? A society tactically and strategically orientated towards the integration of the working class. It succeeds in part (by a day-to-day life organized repressively by means of restrictions, by the persuasive ideology of consumer-power rather than by the reality of the consumption) but at the same time it loses the capacity to integrate its elements: youth, ethnic groups, women, intellectuals, sciences, cultures.'[3]

How does this situation manifest itself in the openings offered to the sociologist? On completion of his degree, he can follow a more advanced course of study in the master's degree (introduced by the Fouchet reform) or in the doctorate. This prolonged study can be carried out in conjunction with a project commissioned by an Institute, a Laboratory or a private research organization.

Since the reform, a different channel has come into being – that of teaching, either in the upper classes of the lycées or in certain Institutes of Technology. The number of positions is still, however, very limited and the sociologist who wishes to

3. See Henri Lefebvre: *La vie quotidienne dans le monde moderne*, Gallimard paperback, 1968, p. 152.

teach must turn to the university faculties or, if he has a reputation, to the *École Pratique des Hautes Études*. It is worthwhile pointing out that research-workers tend to take jobs as lecturers in the universities, thus combining two functions (partly for financial reasons).

As an expert capable of using his knowledge at least partially, the sociologist has not so far been in great demand. There are less commercially-employed sociologists than there are psycho-sociologists or psycho-technologists. As far as the civil service is concerned, while it may be beginning to follow the vogue for sociological knowledge (just as it has followed the vogue for juridical and economic knowledge), it is not yet prepared to put the cat among the pigeons. In a Ministry which is calling for large-scale research on youth, the sociologists are present mainly to decorate the credits of the reports.

There is, however, one sector which has seemed for some time now to offer greater scope – the study of urban development and large-scale planning. The sociologist can find employment either in the framework of bodies responsible for planning, or within public, semi-public or privately-operated services working under contract to such state bodies as the *Direction Générale de la Recherche Scientifique et Technique* (DGRST). Such a *demand* is easily explained when one considers that urbanization necessitates cooperation between different specialists. As long as no 'science of towns' exists, multi-disciplinary teams serve as a substitute: they group together architects, geographers, economists and sociologists, working under the direction of an engineer from the relevant Ministry or some other 'technocrat'.

The position of the sociologist in this multi-disciplinary cooperation is far from clear: if he sometimes imagines himself being asked to construct new towns, this is because he underestimates the role of political power in the organization of knowledge. Instead, he will be asked to furnish research on the 'needs of the inhabitants', on 'the image of the town', on 'the setting up of industries' or on 'the strategies of the various groups interested in planning'. He will also be entrusted with the responsibility of probing the possibilities of extending the 'cooperation' to the broadest sections of the public. A specialist in integration, he will become a specialist in *participation*, a grandiose idea which consists, at least at the moment, in making sure that the 'public' assists without protest at the impressive spectacle of its own alienation.

Is this picture too gloomy? The criticisms launched at sociology by the revolutionary Nanterre students in the months preceding the May explosion, were much stronger and much more radical. In Berlin and Rome, in Mexico and in Rio, 'global contestation', the strategy of rupture with the institutions, poses in strong terms the problems of the relationship between knowledge and power, between science and ideology, between teaching and politics. It is this problem which we in our turn shall attempt to pose.

In 1917, in the dual capacity of sociologist and teacher, Max Weber posed the question of 'axiological neutrality', that is to say, the question of the value-judgements which the professor of social and economic sciences brings to bear on the ideas which he transmits. Criticized for his own political commitments, Weber tried to distinguish between *practical evaluations* and *logical evaluations*. In the course of his professional activities the professor must limit himself, according to Weber, to logical evaluations, that is to say to analyses, criticisms and judgements based on the laws of reason. Outside his classes, he may go beyond this, allowing himself practical evaluations which are based on the exercise of freedom of thought and on the recognition of the right to differ. A distinction of this sort is not useless. But it presupposes the existence of social sciences and scientific theories which are perfectly adequate for the end in view; it implies not only that sociological knowledge is, as in the case of the exact sciences, a *cumulative* knowledge (offering at all times a body of demonstrable propositions) but also that this knowledge can be expressed in a rigorous *metalanguage*, in a precise code and in a formalized vocabulary.

Sociology does not demonstrate these characteristics. Neither do the other human and social sciences. The psychologist (Freudian or non-Freudian), the linguist, the economist, whether or not they deal with quantitative data, possess different models of analysis, rival or complementary; they do not possess a cumulative body of knowledge. The ever-increasing efforts to translate economic or sociological data into mathematical terms show clearly that one aspect of these sciences lends itself to calculation and quantification: it does not show them to be in the process of creating a metalanguage like those of physics or chemistry.

The sociologist and the other specialists of the human sciences deal in concepts which, although operating in a system of theoretical reference (when the sociologist is not a blind fanatic of empirical methods!), are also used in everyday language and are weighed down with implicit ideological connotations. Or it may be that these concepts have been borrowed, sometimes without much checking, from neighbouring or complementary disciplines.

It is slightly naïve to ask whether this represents a great handicap for the social sciences. As long as the so-called 'exact' sciences remain incapable of describing the objects of the social sciences or of fulfilling the function fulfilled by them, it is difficult to see why observation and theoretical work should be less respectable activities than quantification or mathematical formalization. There is no reason why the close relationship between sociology and ideology or political practice should constitute an original sin.

On the other hand, it is true to say that the sociologist, under the cover of scientific integrity and neutrality, has become, consciously or not, the tool of this or that ideology, *whenever he has overlooked this ambiguity which lies at the heart of his knowledge*. This is the criticism that the revolutionary students of Nanterre and elsewhere make of the sociologists who refuse to see the ideological and political implications of their teaching, their theories and their practice. These sociologists generally consider themselves to be apolitical, purely scientific and rigorous, and they accuse their Marxist colleagues of being 'doctrinaire': conservatives and reformists are well known for covering themselves with the cloak of neutrality and objectivity; under this pragmatic cloak it is easy to dissimulate, and to dissimulate from oneself, positions which are the most conformist, the most reactionary and the least 'rigorous'.

The main question concerning both the sociological theory and the social practice of the sociologist can be formulated as follows: how is it possible to *participate* in the technical and social division of intellectual labour by means of the profession of sociologist, without at the same time being *integrated* into the ideology and into the institutions of the ruling class? Taking as a frame of reference the knowledge which has been gathered, transmitted and sanctioned by university institutions, the question can be formulated in the following terms: how is the relationship to knowledge (i.e. the relationship of the teacher, the research worker, the expert as well as the student) at the same time a relationship to power? Or again: is scientific objectivity anything more than an honourable façade for the failed intellectual?

Sociologists and theorists have formulated this type of question: Lukács has demonstrated that the more a science formalizes its language, the more it becomes divorced from the social and material bases from which it sprang and grew. C. W. Mills, in his polemics with the structuro-functionalism of Parsons, has denounced the fact that 'integrated' sociology studiously avoids problems of power, of coercion and of manipulation by established interests. In France, we are beginning to understand that the *epistemological division* that Althusser and his school make between science and ideology is only an ideal (idealistic) demarcation, that it is never effective, and that the effective reality of knowledge resides in its relationship with the power structure, with the institutions responsible for transmitting this knowledge and with the social demand that permits research. Fairly old political groups, like *Socialisme ou Barbarie* and the *Internationale Situationniste* have denounced the integration of sociological research and practice into capitalist society.

It is a problem as old as sociology itself. Only the supporters of positivism deny that it is at the heart of theoretical thought. From the origins of sociology, Saint-Simon, Comte, Spencer, then Durkheim and Weber, have posed this problem. According to Saint-Simon, the new social science could be broken down into a 'social physiology, consisting of the material facts culled from direct observation of the society', and a 'social hygiene, consisting of the precepts applicable to these facts'. The mission of the sociologist was thus to diagnose and to treat social maladies.

Auguste Comte says much the same thing when he distinguishes between sociology proper and the art of politics, the second drawing its efficacy from the first. The self-appointed expert in sociology is the new magician, the successor to the great charismatic political leader forging the destinies of his people. Herbert Spencer mocks the belief that anybody can carry out administration: according to him, the sociologist is equipped with tools which are indispensable to the exercise of power.

As for Durkheim, writing at the time when Marxism had elaborated its revolutionary programme, he declares that socialism is not a science, but that it must be an object of science for sociology. The sociologist appears once more as the coordinator of fragments of knowledge and the shaman capable of resolving the conflicts born within the industrial society.

Generally speaking, it is possible to formulate the hypothesis that sociology, in various forms and sometimes using conflicting methods, represents an attempted liquidation of Marxism, in that Marxism claims to possess not only the key to the history and the functioning of society, but also the theoretical and practical ways of transforming it. If this hypothesis is perhaps over-ambitious, then at least it can be said that since its origin sociology has been vainly striving to introduce into its theory and practice a separation and connexions between itself and politics: in fact, it is not equipped to conceive of this separation and these connections, since its objective function is to fill or hide the breach which has been opened in the bourgeois universalist ideology by the Marxist dialectic and by the workers' movement. The contradictions, those parts of the economic and political system embracing sociology which are *unaccounted for* and *unaccountable*, can only be perceived by active means: either by radical criticism, which implies a rejection of close or distant participation in the society such as it is; or by the strategy or tactic of breaking with the institutions which maintain established order.

Does this mean that sociologists must look outside the universities for new forms of social fulfilment? Some have been tempted to do so. In the USA, for example, those who are disgusted with the integration of official sociology and who are unsatisfied by the successors of Mills (radical nihilism) seek in the most committed activity, in the black ghettos, a vindication and an active questioning of the basis of sociology.[4] Will these worker-sociologists be any more successful than the worker-priests trying to change their society from within?

If one looks for nothing beyond the content of sociology, one must ask oneself how it is that this science experiences such difficulty in accounting for the political action which has grown up in the student sector in France and in the rest of the world. Why are the concepts, theories and methods used so ineffective when it comes to analysing the functioning of revolutionary groups and organizations? The sociology which studies organizations has proved very fruitful when dealing with economic, political and cultural institutions; it excels in describing *established society*. But it is inadequate as soon as it is a question of studying the *society in the process of establishment*, social practice, social action and day-to-day existence. In this case, the concepts of systematized structure, function, organization, negotiation etc. are totally inappropriate. Concepts such as anomy, deviance, the typical and the atypical, intra-determination and extra-determination, cannot account for social dynamics. The lack of foresight and comprehension on the part of officially sanctioned sociology was exposed by the kinds of action, strategy and tactic adopted by the *22 mars* movement and by the other *groups possessing a revolutionary strategy*. One must not be surprised, then, if the students turn more readily for concepts and models of analysis to Marx, Engels, Lenin, Rosa Luxemburg, Trotsky, Gramsci and other more or less 'orthodox' Marxist theorists, than to the French disciples of American sociology. Here the link between sociology and politics, between knowledge and action, assumes its fullest importance: *The Class Struggle in France* by Marx, Lenin's *The State and Revolution*,

4. '*Manifesto for Sociologists – Institution-Formation – A new sociology*', by H. Etzkowitz and G. Schaflander, typewritten May 1967.

Trotsky's *The New Course* enjoy greater success than works dealing with social psychology or organizational sociology. Many of the students have understood this. The lecturers and the research workers, for their part, are beginning to understand that, although it is useless to look for a 'revolutionary sociology', it is by no means pointless to come to grips with the problem of revolutionary action and the new form of sociability that this action creates to coexist with or to replace the classical institutions.

Is sociology to content itself with 'explaining' the world, rather than 'transforming' it? This is impossible to predict or to anticipate. What is certain is that sociology, along with the majority of the other disciplines which are fragmented into partial bodies of knowledge, must re-evaluate the social conditions of its appearance, development, research, teaching, orientations and results. Even more so than other disciplines, it must become capable of perpetually analysing its *institutional implications*, the degree and the means of its integration into the power-structure, and the forms of its participation in the dominant ideology. In our society knowledge is a commodity: in this lies the 'truth' of science and scientific work. Kautsky, before he became a 'renegade'[5] bluntly depicted the situation of the research worker, the intellectual and the lecturer: 'In contemporary society,' he said, 'it is not, as it was before, the exploiters themselves, or at least a class of exploiters, who indulge in the sciences and in the arts. They have relinquished this task to a special class which they pay to do it for them. Instruction has become a commodity.'

One of the most beneficial effects of the minor revolution of May 1968 will have been to make sociologists understand that this situation is *their* situation.

August 1968

5. Karl Kautsky, *'Le programme socialiste'*. Commentary on the Erfurt programme 1892. Translated into French by Marcel Rivière, 1910.

13. Create!

José Pierre

I saw this remarkably laconic slogan signed by the JAC (Jeunesse anarchiste communiste) on a wall in the rue de Vaugirard just opposite the Senate. Yes, I said to myself, we must create or die!

But create what? How? For whom? The startling turmoil prevailing these last few days amongst the Paris revolutionaries, with their pens and paintbrushes, indicates that the answers to these questions are not immediately forthcoming. For my part I consider this state of affairs absolutely normal. The problem can be reduced to the question: does the complete restructuring of society, tacitly accepted in principle by many artists and writers, necessarily imply a global reconsideration of the pursuits of the cultural *avant-garde*?

I will be accused of improperly singling out only the socio-economic context which only partially determines artistic genres. This is not quite what I mean. I believe that a painter who completely changes his style because he is exhibiting in the Renault factory rather than in the Maeght Gallery is a charlatan. Equally, an author who suddenly decides that he must become readable when he moves from *Tel Quel* to *l'Humanité*[1] is or was cheating; either he was cheating in playing the part of the incomprehensible author or he is a hypocrite in his role of the proletarian author.

Having said this, I am aware that one does not write for a daily what one would write for a periodical, and that there is a world of difference between what one hears or sees on radio or

1. Respectively *avant-garde* structuralist review close to the PCF and the PLF daily newspaper.

television and what one puts in a fat philosophical treatise. I only wish to draw attention to those mugwumps who are prepared to burn what they adored yesterday rather than censure the present.

I do not disbelieve that many of these sudden conversions were quite sincere. All conversions are sudden, including those to the revolutionary cause. But I still marvel at the fact that yesterday I mixed with all these extremists without for a moment suspecting the flame of subversion was burning within them! I marvel even more to see an art critic whose followers are the Prime Minister's intimates, or an author well-known for his ultra-reactionary position (I will name no names so that this does not become a public denunciation) in the front row of the cultural barricades! Imagine, writers like Louis Ferdenand Céline and Georges A. Mathieu for example (one of whom died recently but I can't remember which one) summoning André Malraux to relinquish his authority to a soviet of revolutionary artists and writers and you will have a fair idea of the kind of shilly-shallying currently running riot amongst our intelligentsia!

Nevertheless, all suspicion and sarcasm aside, I believe that such phenomena are a sign, caricatures they may be, of a deep conviction; a conviction, dormant through these many years of despair and cynicism, that the emancipation of artistic and literary forms is linked indissolubly to the question of economic, political and social emancipation.

My reservations were only directed at those people who have been in public life for many years and who have had many opportunities to express their burning convictions had they felt the need to do so! On the other hand, nothing could be more healthy than the constant questioning of values and constant discussion amongst young artists and students of art schools even if they are inevitably doomed to falter on as rotten a rung of the ladder as that of 'committed art'. The explosion in the 'monkey factory' of the rue Bonaparte – 'the École des Beaux Arts,' is not a negligible achievement, that revolutionary posters should be churned out by artists like Brianchon is progress indeed.

The Revolutionary Ideal

What is the new framework in which the problem of artistic creation is posed? Should writers' and artists' pride be as wounded as that of political and trade-union leaders – and that is something? On this point the students have again shown us the way. They went further and said it clearer than any of us.

I feel it my duty to point to the remarkably pertinent report of the commission on 'culture and creativity' published last April by the *22 Mars* movement in its bulletin, 5494bis (*sic*), just a few weeks before the beginning of the May revolt.

Whilst waiting for this report to be printed, as I hope it will be, in giant letters on the walls of the lycées, I will extract a few revealing sections.

The report first studies the problem of creativity as it is posed for each individual from the moment of his birth.

Creativity is one of the most evenly distributed gifts on earth. Childhood proves this. The first gestures of the child are sheer poetry; he impeccably harmonizes the subjectivity they express with the discovery of a world in which his subjectivity can be objectivized. This harmony is our revolutionary ideal. . . . The child, in his relationships with the adult, sees his creativity condemned. (Instead of saying 'Don't do that' . . . you should say . . . 'You must'.)

The constant need for adult society to repress childhood creativity imbues the child with a permanent feeling of guilt about any future display of his own spontaneity. Parental repression of the child's creativity is thus both the interpreter and the sign of society's repression of his inherent spontaneity. Indeed, in the society of the grown-ups, one is not encouraged to play or to create but to work: 'The child plays but the adult works; between the two lies one's apprenticeship in society's cultural ideology . . .' whose 'rather unattractive role' is to '. . . convince people of the moral righteousness of the need to work whilst obscuring the real reasons why.'

Seen in the way: '. . . culture disinfects the creative impulse of its human element of past creativity (which at the time of its fashioning was the revolutionary challenge to society) and serves as a guarantee against future disorder . . .'

However, not only past but present creativity is threatened for '... all culture can be incorporated by those in power ...'

Thus all the *avant-garde* would sooner or later be absorbed by society's cultural ideology and emptied of their revolutionary significance. The last twenty years of art history provides us with a splendid confirmation of this. How can we escape from this systematic 'incorporation'? 'Culture must be subverted in such a way that it cannot absorb the subversion and use it anew as a lie.' For there is one thing, 'in the nature of culture which cannot be incorporated, and that is the violence with which it is expressed'.

Creative Violence

Here lies a contrast likely to illumine more than one intellect, the natural and qualitative differences between creative violence and fascism.

Fascist violence is the negation of the self as a unique truth whereas creative violence, on the contrary, is the acceptance of this subjective truth through the creativity it expresses.

And with admirable dignity the report concludes:

All artistic creation is violence, all political action is violence; violence is the only way for subjectivity to express itself against a power which tries to prevent it from doing so. Violent action is the negation of this power and the negation of its authority.

What I have tried to condense in this text is confirmed by events. The student movement has opened completely new perspectives in the fight against the bourgeois university, against police repression and against the neo-capitalist State. The political plurality within the *22 mars* movement, the predominance of revolutionary action over revolutionary theory, and the spotlighting of the notion of 'spontaneity' are clearly the offspring of this creativity. Both in the realm of ideas and expression, so long as they both liberate this creative will, artists, writers and intellectuals have everything to gain by the inspiration of such a generous definition of revolutionary creativity.

For them, as for all those resolved to 'change life', as Rimbaud put it, there is no doubt that the alternatives are either creation or death.

June 1968

14. Discourse on Birth Control

Ipousteguy

Citizens, my father was born and died a pope. Who amongst us persists in confusing the revolt of the intellectuals with the despair of the proletariat?

The revolt of the intellectual is his moment of moral awareness, promoted equally by an absence of material cares and an abundance of leisure. These intellectuals are extremely caustic and penetrating – marked, one might say, by 'scrupulous honesty' – but their revolt is never a question of life and death. Nor is its implication the immediate and definitive demolition of the world, but rather, its reconstruction.

Whereas for the proletarian – with whom these savants, in all good faith, claim bonds – despair is corporeal, visceral and deflected from a precise aim. Its immediate expression is devastation.

Undeniably, through his relations with the proletariat, the intellectual always seeks to substitute his ideas for the very basis of their revolutionary actions. An additional complication arises when, at the mustering of the forces, these rebel ideas fail to stir the submissive. And when the former must inevitably use the latter as their cannon fodder. For the hierarchy is reconstituted anew, and with a few scintillating exceptions, the lowly remain lowly and the eminent remain eminent.

The impossibility of extrication from the muck of the drill-field is the primeval curse heaped upon that ordinary foot-soldier – the proletarian. A number he is and a number he remains. Once again, the plural becomes the flock and the singular is the predator.

In 1936 my father mislaid his pay packet. He collapsed in tears. The larder was bare. That February he struck, ready to kill. At that time my eyes were sore, the Mayor of Pavillons-sous-Bois (Hautes-de-Seine) gave my mother money from his pocket as a gift. She bought me a pair of spectacles and returned what was left over. The Mayor was deeply moved. The people never cheat – yet another of their curses.

Society interrogates the people through her go-betweens, a thousand and one inquisitors, the first of whom is the concierge. The proletarian replies. But what should his answer be? The truth of course! And so he states the truth.

In turn he questions society. But society never answers. . . . Father, it was clear to me that the man sprung from the people who wants to break the spell of his curse must either remain silent or reply 'obliquely'. . . . Just like the boss who speaks 'obliquely' if he consents to speak at all to his minions.

But the intellectual cheats: hence the inverted commas around his scrupulous honesty above. In the name of mankind he tries to foil nature's most implacable tyrannies. Indeed, a welcome action because fascism is ready to rear its head in the name of inherent needs. The intellectual is an assiduous 'collector of knowledge' who uses his receipts to his own advantage. He is also an inquisitor and through his answers displays his prowess. Thus he cheats to please, to displease, to charm and to shock. And finally he cheats to be alone – to be *himself*. Here he reconquers, to an extent, the contours of truth. He reveals its only truth, the will to power. But if he rises from the people, his brute force can be demonstrated only outside society lists. Once inaccessible – if not blocked off from the start.

But I have neither cheated nor lied. I remained silent – which is the same thing.

For the people cowardice is the basic necessity of their daily existence. From time to time this allows them the privilege of a massacre. It is never beautiful – still another curse. It is horrible and sadistic. 'I sheltered a viper against my breast,' said the schoolmaster. 'It is cumbersome.'

If the attack is launched too soon and if it is felt that there is a profit (illicit!) to be made, then the people are stripped surgically of their courage and cocksureness at one blow. Hence: the Commune of Paris.

Where are our stripling sixteen-year-old soldiers? Noble, generous ... and alive, those not dead in the wars. Their lot is always the same. Read history. For the flock there is no choice; whether saints or murderers; whether Bara[1] the hero or the vegetating cut-throat.

The lot of them: Bara, cut-throats, saints and murderers had to make the revolution: unexpected conjecture. Unexpected conjecture, they had to make the revolution. For here is the only breach in the wall of curses these past thirty years. Not that there weren't the bumptious, the hoodwinkers ... and the niggardly. But the other side was worse, its patent absurdity stood out a mile off. But amongst those on the barricades not a trace. There was but one side.

I travelled to that point like a submarine, but false to the core, a real navigator, an instinctual engineer.

Our spirit comes from others but our ideas come from our guts. Thus glide to the depths, close your hatches! Don't rely on the hatred of the torpedo! Spend the eve of action in idleness. Be invisible. Keep still! Cut your hair and only surface with infinite precaution.

Coward! Swindler!

You are not like a fish in water but inside and outside are armed like a U-Boat. Water carries, retains and envelops. Be the density of water and solid steel, TNT, an atomic pile all at the same time.

Hypocrite! Clearly you are possessed by all the vices. Bara, cut-throats, murderers ... coppers.

Yes ... coppers. An additional curse, the people are cut down by the people.

You walk up to the CRS and say:

Will the sons of lawyers, doctors, industrialists and professors please step forward!

You can be sure that no one will. For here is a regiment which if it were not from the fields and factories would never advance. On the contrary, marvel of marvels, they charge. Father abuses

1. Joseph Bara, teenage hero of the 1789 Revolution.

son and son abuses father in the punch-up of the underdeveloped followed by all the bludgeons, wounds, and blows from behind that you would care to see.

Horror of horrors, the people are cut down by the people!

By killing my father as a pope and not as a fellow workman, I rejected the curse – the essence of the act perpetuated 2,000 years ago when the original father killed his son as a God – I irrevocably broke the perpetually regenerating vicious circle. You see, I no longer chase my tail. I emerge. I begin to emerge. The verb is lord and master. Language is the political expression of the verb. Savour the transparent images of thoughts of procreation and birth!

In fact, I seethed in my shell and have hatched only recently, in 1959 – having remained imperiously hidden for the above-mentioned reasons. A singular, extravagant and exceptional event, in 1959 I acceded to the most alluring and frightening of freedoms. That very mythical freedom incanted in political meetings whose sensuality has never been enjoyed by a proletarian on the face of this earth. Today, I think, man can no more conceive of this freedom than be believer of God. Yet it is to be feared that the all-powerful States will increasingly make us write the word 'freedom' just as the churches of old made man write the name 'God'. But in 1959 I actually understood. I understand. I understand freedom. But was I not a saint? Well . . .

Unhindered by the barriers, I entered into freedom. The luck of a Jean-Jacques Rousseau or a Lulli.

They could have left me alone and respected.

My apprenticeship was hard, and if a brother offered me freedom, the Father – here I speak of the spiritual Father, the master, the professor of design – imparted to me those terrible illicit rules, the iron laws of profit.

I say illicit rules because anything which touches art is illegal, illicit, and subversive.

Despite everything, Art, you are not dead. You will survive and we will once again be your corpses.

June 1968

What are the Lessons of the May Events?

15. What are the Lessons of the May Events?

André Gorz

The first major revolutionary crisis to have shaken capitalist Europe in the last thirty years has not exploded in some backward country, suffering from widespread misery, corruption, misgovernment and ruthless authoritarianism. It has exploded in the country that has invented modern capitalist planning, that enjoys consistent economic growth that boasts a *per capita* income that is higher than that of Great Britain or any Common Market nation, a sound and respected currency, a sizeable sector of State-owned industries, nationalized banks and insurance companies, and an advanced welfare system.

It has happened in the country which is the very model of neo-capitalism, which claims to have learned how to master the business cycle and whose official spokesmen like to say that affluence has wiped out political radicalism, that socialism and capitalism, as they see them, tend to become one and the same thing.

Of course, everyone knew that French society was riddled with serious shortcomings. Every year, more than 100,000 people, mainly young men, had to leave the farming areas to look for work in the cities. Every year, too, 850,000 youngsters were looking for their first job, compared with 725,000 people reaching retirement age. This increase of the potential urban working population was running up against various obstacles and bottlenecks. French industry and commerce were undergoing a process of rationalization and concentration; employment in industry had been levelling out since the early sixties; the housing shortage was dramatic, though 300,000 privately-built flats had remained unsold in early 1968; training schools were inadequate and had to refuse thousands of applicants every year. One third of adolescents looking for their first job had received no training at all. There was a general feeling of uncertainty and fear about the future.

All this was well known and widely discussed. But there was no sense of urgency about these issues. They had become commonplace. To a certain extent, the sharp increase in unemployment had been foreseen and even planned by the Government as a means of keeping wages down and stiffening discipline at work. The official line was that France had to bear the cost of rationalization and modernization, and that since the rate of profit of French industry was allegedly lower than in most other advanced capitalist countries (an allegation which was finally proved false in October 1968), the wage earners were the ones who had to make some sacrifices. To suggest that they might be unwilling to do so and fight back was a hypothesis that was usually laughed at. How could they? Who would lead them? What alternative was there to capitalist rationalization? Hadn't the working class become used to middle-class standards of living and of thinking? Weren't the labour unions and Left-wing opposition rather perplexed about what reforms to propose? And who could dream about something more radical than partial reforms since there was no real crisis, only the kind of difficulties, distortions, conflicts of interest that are quite normal in a period of rapid technical change and international competition and readjustment?

Still, to most contributors to the present volume, the explosion that blew neo-capitalist petulance sky high did not come as a complete surprise. The insurrectional general strike in Belgium in 1960–61 and the violence that had exploded almost yearly in Italian cities from 1960 onwards, pointed to the fact that a revolutionary potential lay dormant in this part of the world. There had been recent evidence to suggest that this potential was accumulating in France, too. At the Peugeot automobile factory, for instance, some 20,000 workers had gone on an unlimited strike for shorter hours in 1966. They had had shorter hours during the winter, while the factory was making preparations for a new model. They had come to enjoy the difference which a forty-two hour week (compared with the 'normal' forty-eight hours) can make in a man's life. When asked to return to the 'normal' schedule they found this simply unbearable.

Then, at the beginning of 1967, came the strike at the Rhodiacéta plant at Besançon. The workers occupied this synthetic fibre factory and willingly explained that they were not striking for higher wages. They were the best-paid workers in this region; none earned less than 850 francs. Many owned a car. Money was beside the point: what they wanted were tolerable working conditions; job security; housing conditions which would enable those on night shift to get some sleep during the daytime; cultural facilities which, with the exception of a small cooperative library, were non-existent; playgrounds for their children; in a word, the kind of environment inside and outside the factories which would make a man feel that twentieth-century civilization was not the sole privilege of the upper classes and that workers are not a labour force which corporations can hire and fire as they wish and 'squeeze like a lemon'.

Other long-drawn-out strikes, involving draughtsmen, technicians and engineers, occurred in the aircraft industry at Bordeaux, at Berliet (lorries) near Lyons, the heavy metal-working industry at Nantes, etc., in 1967. And early in 1968 the workers at the Saviem lorry factory near Caen walked out when management refused to discuss wage claims and working conditions, and demonstrated in the centre of the town, battling with police forces and pushing aside union leaders, who wanted things to remain calm and orderly.

The new common feature of most recent strikes was the disproportion of apparently limited claims and the almost insurrectional violence of mass action: occupation of factories; sequestration of directors; fighting back at police forces and, mainly at Caen and Besançon, participation of students, teachers, apprentices and unemployed youngsters in street demonstrations and violence. Also, none of these strikes was called by the unions; they were initiated by young workers, and local union leadership followed rather reluctantly.

The powerful CGT usually tried to channel these spontaneous movements towards wage claims to be bargained for at top level. CGT leadership on several occasions (at Besançon, Lyons, Nantes) seemed impatient with the workers' obstinacy at fighting things out at the local level. The CGT seemed in a hurry to end open conflicts and in some instances had to fight its way back into the factories against CFDT and 'Trotskyite'-influenced workers who were by no means satisfied with the settlement the CGT had reached. The reason the CGT adopted this 'soft' line over 'hard' methods was rather obvious: the Communist leadership of the CGT has always held that the political victory of the working-class parties was the necessary condition on which any improvement had to depend. Henceforth, union action had to be subordinated to political strategy. And the political strategy of the Communist party was to knit a close alliance with the social democrats and to work out a Government programme with them, which could lead to a peaceful parliamentary victory of the combined forces of the Left at the next elections. Pending these, long and massive strikes had to be avoided: they would frighten the voters and spoil the chances of the Communist party whom Government propaganda would blame for working-class violence. Thus, whatever the restlessness of the workers, they had to wait until 'true democracy', restored by Communist party participation in government, would make real social progress possible.

The line of the once-Catholic CFDT was much less prejudiced. Its younger militants propagated the idea that 'quantitative demands' (i.e. wage claims), important as they were, were no solution to the workers' problems: the bosses shouldn't think that they can buy our submissiveness in the factories and in society; that they can rob us of our dignity, pride, craving for responsibility and self-determination by 'putting golden bars on our cages'. No amount of money, many younger CFDT militants like to say, can compensate the worker for his daily oppression, for being the underdog. 'Qualitative demands' for workers' control, for increased union power in the factories, for a say about work speeds, training, hiring and firing, etc., are as important as wage demands if we want to live and work as human beings.

This emphasis on workers' control and union power on the work place was popular mainly with the younger technicians and the workers of rural origin. Whereas the CGT remained by far the most powerful union in the old industries of the Paris region, of Lyons and of northern France, where an ageing working class remained truthful to this class-conscious and once revolutionary organization, the young workers and technicians in the newer, 'decentralized' factories of Brittany, Normandy, eastern and south-eastern France were attracted by the CFDT which had become dominant in a number of key industries (electronics, petro-chemicals, electrical engineering, etc.) employing a majority of skilled personnel or first generation young unskilled workers. The latter, as well as young technicians and production engineers of petty bourgeois origin, were neither used nor prepared to accept the oppressiveness of the 'normal' production process, the prison-like discipline of the factories and the bosses' contempt for manual labour.

Why do people refuse one day what they have accepted so far? Replying to this question, a group of young workers in a factory where there had been no strike for ten years claimed things had worsened so much they had become intolerable. An older labour leader objected: 'Things haven't grown any worse lately. What has changed is people like them. They don't want the same things we wanted. They're impatient. They haven't yet suffered defeat.'

The fact is that for fifteen years the bourgeoisie had been buying off the lower classes by offering or promising more consumer goods, education, social promotion. Wages were kept low, but overtime was the rule. TV, household appliances, cars became urgent needs and symbols of promotion. The average work week was kept close to forty-eight hours and demands for shorter hours were persistently refused as being economically impossible. International competition, so the Government and the *patronat* said, called for a reduction in labour costs and an increase in profits. On the average, salaries and wages could not possibly rise by more than 4 per cent yearly, or France – so the argument went – would price itself out of the world market. A tight wage discipline was imposed by the Government on the employers and by the employers on the unions. When the demands of the unions became too insistent, employers would entrench themselves behind Government orders.

The system worked: in 1967, the average rise in real hourly wages was kept down to 2·9 per cent. To break the employers' resistance, the unions would have had to confront and to defeat State power itself. Any large strike would have meant a political attack against the regime. And since the regime kept explaining that the economy was totally rigid, with no margin for concessions, the economic system itself would have had to be attacked to make higher wages possible. For an attack against the State and the system, however, wage claims were not sufficient motivation. To make such an attack plausible and possible, more radical, political and qualitative motives would have to be brought into play. But these neither the parties to the Left nor the union leadership were able to imagine. Thus, France has only known, during ten years, either spontaneous local strikes or national work stoppages limited to between one and twenty-four hours. With no results at all: the Government stood firm, waiting for the fighting spirit of the union to wear off.

In the opinion of both Government and Opposition, workers, employees and technicians were not prepared to accept the risk and the cost of an all-out trial of strength. The masses, so the argument went, were depoliticized and interested only in short-term gains. And this is where the younger generation came in. To them, TV, fridges and cars were a natural thing that did not mean the kind of liberation and promotion it had meant to their parents. They felt that working like idiots to afford these possessions was a lousy life anyhow. They were speaking despisingly of 'the old man who only cares about his little house, his little car, and his little life'. They also spoke despisingly of the union and political leadership which would do nothing to change life.

This disgust of the younger generation – whether workers, technicians or students – with society showed mainly, before

256

May, in their almost nihilistic indifference to any kind of socially-accepted and available job or purpose. They would react with brutally hostile rejection to any attempt to persuade them into doing things. Politically, their interest had been aroused only to a limited extent, but nevertheless intensely, by Vietnam and Cuba, two symbols of military defeat and moral bankruptcy of so-called Western civilization. Support for Vietnam was organized outside the established political parties in the (strongly pro-Cuban) *Comité Vietnam National* and the fifty *Comités de base* (neighbourhood and factory committees) which were the main breeding-ground for a new revolutionary radicalism.

The new generation's rejection of the prevailing social order had some specific motivations that are common to most advanced societies. A youngster of between fifteen and twenty-five has usually been to a better school than his parents. He knows more than they do about technology, science and what's going in the world. Methods of teaching, though still backward and inadequate, have changed in many fields. Young people, instead of feeling more ignorant than their elders, feel the latter have nothing much to teach them about a profoundly-changed and still-changing world. They know that knowledge and professional values are undergoing rapid transformations, that no *lasting* values are left. They look down on older generations, including their parents, as on a hangover from the past, as poor chaps who were overtaken and overpowered by events.

Historic change has produced a break between generations and ruined whatever authority their elders may have held in previous times. This goes for relations between adolescents and their parents as well as for the traditional hierarchical relations at school and at work. Young workers inevitably notice that the foremen have poorer qualifications than themselves and that work and time are being wasted. In the secondary or higher schools, pupils or students notice the discrepancy between what they are taught and what the real problems and facts of life are in their own experience.

They also feel that society has no proper use for them; for their actual or potential capacities. Unemployment is rising sharply: 600,000 people were looking for a job in May 1968 (as against half that number two years earlier); 300,000 of them were under twenty-five. Unemployment was often explained by the inadequate or total lack of training of job-seekers. But public credits for more and better training schools were 'not available'. In fact, those with a good training too often have a difficult time in finding a job: they represent more than one third of the 600,000 unemployed. When they do find work, they often can't put to any use what they have learned: they remain intellectually underemployed. And they are asked to fit into a rigid hier-archical pattern in which power and authority do not rest on competence, but on birth, wealth or age.

The students specifically were directly threatened by the stagnation of the level of employment and by the rigidity of social and economic structures. Universities, so the government argued, were overcrowded with students unfit for higher studies and who, even if they were fit, could hardly expect to find work in their future capacities. Therefore, the Government pleaded, there should be a *sélection* at entry to the *Facultés* which would cut down the number of students by a good third. Those admitted would remain threatened with elimination. Those barred from the universities would be channelled on to technical and business schools (which hardly existed as yet). Moreover, as the previous Minister of Education, Christian Fouchet, stated, the University was to be 'industrialized': the number of students and their training was to be adapted to meet the needs of employers and not to exceed the prospective professional outlets and opportunities.

To the students, this policy not only meant the 'technocratiza-tion' of the University. It also meant that culture was to be subordinated to the jobs available in this hierarchical and purposeless capitalist society. Culture was to be downgraded to something utilitarian and to be denied to the majority. This policy was quite understandably resented by all prospective students (the *lycéens*) and the majority of actual students, as an attack on their right to have access to culture. They could not challenge the Government's position – which was by all means rational as long as one accepted the limits set by the capitalist system – unless they rejected the rationale of capitalist society and the pursuit of profit and privilege as being the determining motive. And that is exactly what the radical minority did.

They demanded that culture cease to be considered a class privilege; instead, it was to be seen as a historical need. Anyone was entitled to it. But if this was to be, culture, of course, could not confer any privilege any longer. Real social equality was needed. The University's function and the meaning of culture had to be redefined. Universal culture implied that anyone, and particularly manual workers, were entitled and could contribute to the creation of (a new) culture. One had to accept the prospect of intellectually-trained people doing manual work (as in Cuba and China) since one recognized the right of manual workers to higher education. In other words, all (bourgeois) social division of labour had to be abolished; the traditional technical division of labour – specialization binding some people to mechanical and repetitive work and others to purely intellectual work – had to be upset; one had to recognize and to prove (by no means an impossible task, as psychosociologists know) that the prevailing methods of organizing work merely reflected – and were mere devices of – a system of class domination intent on perpetuating itself by imposing – under the false pretence of efficiency and of 'technical' necessities – degrading and stupefying work on the mass of the people.

Refusing *sélection* and the technocratic university thus led straight to the demand for collective self-management, self-government and self-administration in all fields of social activity (in the factories, the workshops, the schools, the boroughs or municipalities). By refusing the logic that underlay *sélection* the students had to refuse also the docile, subordinate, profit-motivated and class-privileged position which capitalist society was offering to the 'good', 'capable', and 'successful' students. 'We don't want to have anything to do with this society; we don't want to work for it, to be used by it, to serve it in any way,' the *enragés* kept saying. And several hundred of them indeed interrupted or gave up their studies to work in factories and to try and win the working class for revolution.

However, the various theories about what was to be done and

what the ultimate purpose of action should be remained an obstacle to action itself. The sectarian quarrels of half-a-dozen revolutionary *groupuscules* presented a discouraging picture to the mass of potentially radical students, and tended to sterilize radicalism in endless doctrinal debates. It was Daniel Cohn-Bendit who best understood that the only way to break through the doctrinal and organizational divisions was to fuse all radical groups in direct action with immediate aims. Being contagious, action would mobilize growing numbers of students and the tendency of the *groupuscules* to put theory first and to act according to pre-established patterns would be kept in check by mass participation and direct democracy in action committees, strike committees, specialized working groups. The radical education of the mass of the students would be best obtained not by having them listen to leaders, but by involving them in radical action, in daily free assemblies, in deciding through collective debate what was to be done and how. The practice of direct democracy and action would produce a new type of self-organized vanguard, abolishing all authority and responsibility, abolishing the division into 'leaders' and 'led', submitting the theorists to the criticism and control of the rank and file.

It worked amazingly well. Agitation gained like a brushfire; hundreds of new militants sprang up, first at Nanterre, and from 3 May onwards, when action spread to the Sorbonne, everywhere else. The students proved able to re-invent, in a matter of hours, the tactics of street fighting and of demonstration which some of them had witnessed in Berlin. They proved able to beat the police, to defeat the Government, to challenge its policy in one decisive field and to compel it to retreat. An omnipotent State suddenly appeared helpless to cope with adolescents and even pre-adolescents. This fact, together with the stimulating example of the audacity of the students and *lycéens* sparked off the potentially revolutionary general strike. An unprecedented process of radicalization took place in which large masses of people belonging to a great variety of professions and classes suddenly became aware of the repressed needs and possibilities that lay dormant within themselves; of the alienations they had accepted so far; of the stupidity of a way of life that kept them immured in loneliness and defiant selfishness and in private versus collective needs. They gathered in the streets and at their places of work and discovered a new sense of community, discussing everything freely no longer feeling strangers.

One night, at the Place de la Sorbonne, a well-dressed man started shouting that he earned four thousand francs a month in an advertising firm, that he felt like vomiting, that his was an idiotic job, an idiotic life and that he'd willingly give up his salary to do something that had a meaning. In newly-built suburbs, dwellers' committees sprang up to discuss new plans for urban living, collective services and self-administration of their buildings. Assemblies of architects confessed that they should never have accepted Government rules that made them build 'rabbit hutches' and ugly neighbourhoods. At research centres of mammoth corporations like Péchiney, the whole personnel shut itself in for days after voting that no one would leave until everything (work relations, the purpose of research, wage differentials, the corporation's policy, etc.) had been discussed by all (engineers, scientists, technicians, workers, administrative personnel).

In many other large factories, engineers and technicians were the driving force behind the contestation of the management's authority of the hierarchical division of labour, of differences in income, of the logic of capitalist profits. A fact which can hardly surprise since those who hold professional skill and intellectual autonomy are the first to become aware of the limitations which the pursuit of financial profit imposes on research, technical improvements and the full utilization of human creativeness.

I heard research engineers declare to skilled workers that they would not object to an equalization of incomes; production engineers demanding that decisions regarding production pro-grammes and organization of work be collectively discussed by all concerned; that those holding responsibilities in a work-shop, a laboratory, team or office be elected from a list of 'possibles' by their 'subordinates'; whereas workers explained how work, money, expensive equipment and time were wasted through bureaucratic incompetence or sheer ignorance of workshop problems by those 'at the top'.

Elsewhere, at the aristocratic HEC (School of High Commercial Studies), the association of ex-pupils, all of whom hold leading and highly-paid positions in business, participated in the students' Revolution: they questioned the function they had to fulfil in the capitalist system, denounced a training that was meant to turn them into specialists exploiting employees and consumers and manipulating both the personnel of corporations and the buyers of commodities into submission to the logic of capital.

The same occurred in medical and engineering schools. Young *cadres* and doctors pointed to the fact that science and techniques were distorted from the outset by the class-oriented and profit-motivated function which they were expected to fulfil. They looked for a new definition of the *cadres'* or doctors' role – and for a new orientation of science, its preoccupations, and the methods of teaching – in a society of equals aiming at satisfying the people's needs. Even the students of agricultural schools came to the conclusion that their theoretical and abstract knowledge would remain useless unless they went to work on ordinary (and not model) farms, became familiar with real conditions and learned how to communicate with the peasants.

People also became aware of the human and social cost that was being paid for increased individual consumption. This suddenly appeared to be a society of cars versus culture, of maximal efficiency in producing consumer goods and tremendous waste of human creative capacities, health, and possible happiness. Never had people felt so free and so close to each other. And this was true not only with those *cadres* who came out for equal incomes for all; it was true also in the factories where a majority of workers rejected the 10 per cent wage increase offered on 27 May and strengthened their strike, well aware though that they were losing 2 per cent of their annual income every week. What they held out for, during two more weeks in several large industries, was not further rises but measures of workers' control that would give them a new kind of freedom.

To many of them – namely those who kept fighting in the car factories, the electronic and chemical industries, the schools and universities, etc. – elections appeared a farce. They were asked to delegate to professional politicians, by individual vote, the collective power they were holding in their hands; they were asked to say once again by whom they wanted the old society to be governed and the old State apparatus to be run, at a moment when they were discussing what society and what State they themselves should build. They were tricked into choosing between various brands of unimaginative politicians at a moment when they had become aware that true freedom does not consist in choosing individually among the various goods the ruling groups decide to offer you – whether soap powders or electoral programmes – but to decide collectively what is to be offered, produced or done, and then carry out the decision collectively.

This power – the power of self-management and self-rule – had seemed within their reach and they were unwilling to give it up, though they already had found out that neither they, nor the organizations whose business it should have been, knew how to take power, how to run the factory, the city, the seemingly crumbling society, and the economy, how to substitute popular power from below to authoritarian State power from above.

All they knew was that revolution would be of little value unless it meant this substitution; and that there was no organized political force capable of building this type of liberated and anti-authoritarian society. As a CGT worker remarked at Nantes to a CGT official there: 'If you won, you'd take the boss's place and run the factory just as he did; so we'd have to make another revolution to be free.'

This kind of awareness was the great novelty of the May Revolution. It was brought about by a movement sparked and led by a new *avant-garde* of young people who had not been marked by any previous defeat, nor by reformism or Stalinism, and who were in revolt not against any particular aspect of their situation, but against the capitalist society and way of life itself. They demanded not partial improvements, but global change so as to enable individuals everywhere to shape in free cooperation their individual and collective destiny. They rejected the traditional parties as being part of the established order and incapable of transcending it, since these parties were vitiated by the same bureaucratic and authoritarian degenerations as the society they rejected. What mattered to this new *avant-garde* was no longer which party or group would rule the State and exercise power on behalf of this or that class or stratum; what mattered was the destruction of centralized State power itself and of its bureaucracy, and the conquest of power 'from below'. The very basis and limitation of bourgeois democracy – i.e., in Marx's terms, the 'separation between civil society and State', State becoming the specialized and alien agency taking care of a 'general interest' divorced from the interests of the citizens – were questioned, not in the name of anarchy, as some pretended, but in the name of democracy, i.e. popular self-rule through permanent collective debate and decision-making.

The kind of massive popular mobilization which reformist and electoral programmes, wage claims and demonstrations for employment or higher pensions had failed to bring about, was sparked by a resolute minority asking for the 'impossible' and illustrating their demands by insurrectional deeds. Radical action by minorities proved a better means of communication and education, it politicized millions more deeply, in a few days, than electoral propaganda and Sunday speeches had been able to in decades.

Still, while the inadequacy of the traditional parties has become clear to large masses, no new political force of any significance has yet emerged from the May upheaval. The most clearly revolutionary episode in twentieth-century France has – as with the Paris Commune in 1871 – left no lasting gain in terms of power or organized strength. Some student groups hold that political parties have become useless altogether, that revolution can be brought about by the contagious example of radical minority action, that the forces able to defeat the capitalist State and to create a new society must grow out of revolutionary action itself and not be organized beforehand.

Other radical groups hold the view that though mass parties are discredited and useless, the need for a new vanguard party is clearer than ever: in advanced capitalist Europe, a revolutionary crisis and struggle can't possibly last long enough to forge a sizeable vanguard – as might be possible in parts of Latin America where guerrilla warfare is a political and revolutionary school. Victory must be won in a matter of a few weeks. And to win it, nuclei of well-trained militants must be available from the outset in the factories and cities. They must be able to coordinate local initiatives and to communicate with each other; they must be capable of proposing at the right moment the kind of action, plan and self-organization that can defeat the machinery of both the State and the traditional working-class organizations.

The author of this piece shares this latter opinion. May has shown both that centralized organizations are conservative and incapable of leading the masses in action, and that a new type of organization is necessary: an organization that would not want to direct and to rule the masses, but would help them towards self-organization, self-rule and the exercise of power from below. The new type of revolutionary militants that were born in May do not want to be ruled differently, they do not want to be ruled at all; they do not want to be submitted to a different central power – however socialist it may claim to be – they want power to rest with all those who work, act and think together. To them the true revolutionary is not someone who leads the masses, but someone who can express what they feel and favour situations in which they will act accordingly, and who then hands the power of initiative and organization over to them, that is to no particular person – to all of us. The first priority, in this perspective, is to favour a kind of political education that does not rest on indoctrination or submissiveness to a central authority (however revolutionary it may claim to be), but on self-expression in free collective debate preparing collective action. All self-appointed interpreters and official spokesmen of the deeper needs, motives and aspirations of the masses have proved to be out of phase with them. Before new attempts at political organization can succeed, these deeper needs, motives and aspirations must be encouraged to express themselves. Otherwise, new organizations will either fail, or resemble the old ones, or both.

September 1968

France after May

16. The Monetary Putsch or after the revolutionary movement of May: the crisis of French bourgeoisie

Action Committees of Paris, Vincennes and the Sorbonne

Introduction: The Sorbonne discussions: 22–4 November 1968

One thousand two hundred members of the action committees from the Paris region gathered in the Sorbonne for three days to discuss what the monetary crisis held in store for the revolutionary movement. Militants took part in the discussion as members of a broad movement rather than as members of sectarian organizations. The discussions centred on the economic and political crisis facing a French bourgeoisie equally confronted by the militancy of the anti-capitalist workers/students alliance. These discussions showed that the revolutionary movement ushered in by the May events can only grow by increasingly and radically challenging bourgeois ideology in the University, the mass media and in the reformist and revisionist trade unions and political parties. Through this struggle, the movement is developing its own ideology heralded in the originality of the slogans and posters that appeared during the May battles.

We decided to publish a summary of these debates in pamphlet form. Our text presents a general hypothesis about the class struggle in France after the May events. We hope that it will serve as the basis for further discussions which will amplify, clarify and challenge our ideas as part of the process of political activity which the revolutionary perspectives of contemporary France have made part of our daily lives. We hope that we have faithfully recaptured the essence of the discussions and the hypotheses formulated by the participants.

1. What the Present Crisis Tells Us About the Class Struggle in France

The crisis allows us to debunk the following myths and illusions: 1. the bourgeois myth of patriotism; 2. the reformist illusions so dear to all the 'Left-wing' and extreme 'Left-wing' political parties; 3. the illusions of political power upheld by the French bourgeoisie; and to find out 4. what cards they have in their hands.

1. From the lofty heights of his mountain of gold, de Gaulle pretended to conduct an independent foreign policy. Yet at the first sign of trouble, the bourgeoisie withdrew the gold he so zealously guarded. Between 1958 and 1968 France has been the international finance capital's safe-deposit box. Yet the French working class benefited not a whit from the 'nation's wealth'. Hardly had the working class wrenched a few concessions from the Government, when, as if by divine intervention, the gold vanished. The bourgeoisie reckoned that its capital was safer in countries undisturbed by a militant working class like Germany and Switzerland.

2. The efficient machinery of international finance capital sprang into action against the paltry concessions wrenched from a Right-wing Government. Had a Left-wing Government been in power, it would have moved even more swiftly. Such, indeed, was the fate of Léon Blum's Popular Front in 1936 when he refused to demolish the 'wall of money' and was forced to turn to devaluation. The same phenomenon was repeated in Italy in 1963 and in Britain in the period 1966–8, where 'Centre–Left' and Labour Governments were driven to milk the working class as vigorously as any conservative Government. The actions of finance capital abolished any remaining illusions about the possibility of a peaceful transition to socialism through the 'structural reforms' lauded by 'Left-wing reformists' and the 'parliamentary procedures' so dear to the PCF. With austerity and the defence of the national currency as pretexts, capitalism used international competition to nullify the gains so painfully won by the working class. The workers can retain their gains only by pushing the class struggle to the limit, destroying

international capitalism and establishing a socialist regime.

3. Looking at the French crisis as part of the international monetary crisis allows us to pinpoint those economic and political weaknesses of contemporary capitalism that could lead to a socialist revolution in France. A revolutionary outbreak in a Western European country like France or Italy would be a beacon to other countries under the yoke of imperialism. Such a breach would sharpen the contradictions of the capitalist system and weaken imperialism. When neither the national nor the international bourgeoisie can control the anarchy of the market system, one has the strategic opportunity to seize and hold power.

But as Lenin once said: '(*For the bourgeoisie*) *no crisis is insoluble.*' For if the revolution fails to turn the crisis into a revolution, one cannot expect socialism to come into being by spontaneous generation. Examining the world crisis allows us to discover the seriousness of its implications. For at the present time world capitalism can find no solution. Hence the revolutionary movement has a period of grace in which to develop, organize, and strike.

4. What cards the French bourgeoisie play depends on what the great powers do during the present crisis. De Gaulle and the French bourgeoisie nevertheless try to lead with the best cards. They may try to save the franc by passing its illness to the pound or the mark. They may call for help from the dollar, or in the last resort, from the rouble. The development of the international crisis will determine whether de Gaulle chooses the Atlanticists[1] or the PCF as his allies. Aware of these possibilities, the parliamentary 'Left' and 'extreme Left' have muffled their attacks and play a waiting game. Red May and Black November: the moments of truth arrived with increased frequency. The crisis shows us both the disposition of the armies and their plan of campaign. The resurgency of working-class militancy deepens the chaos.

The divisions in the enemies' camp become clear. The contradictions which undermine their strength are seen in the cold light of day. Vacant and blind, the impotent ideologues of the

1. A faction of the bourgeoisie who support the American alliance and Nato.

decadent Gaullist camp witness the breakdown of the force they so zealously built. May revealed the power of the working class. November demonstrated the weakness of the bourgeoisie.

The bourgeoisie are modest. They prefer to discuss and settle their problems in private, leaving their ideological factotums to transfigure questions of cash into 'national' and 'moral' problems. The Left-wing press, like *Le Nouvel Observateur*, reeks of gargantuan battles between 'technocrats' ('progressive' capitalists) and 'liberals' ('conservative' capitalists). But it is wary of revealing what forces hide behind these labels. Ill at ease, the Right-wing press blandly discusses the battle between the upright citizen and the odious gnome-like speculator. The flood of descriptions and depth studies *ad nauseam* cannot disguise the fact that the conflict is a real conflict and that the bourgeois camp is rent by division. Meanwhile journalists eagerly bury the conflict under a mass of verbiage which mars our ability to see what is really happening.

If it is, as they say, a battle between technocrats and liberals then who are the famous 'progressive' technocrats? Like every other Tom, Dick and Harry, the technocrats speculated against the franc when it served their interests. Are not the heads of nationalized industries, the top civil servants programmed by the ENA etc., also born speculators? Clearly the purpose behind this false distinction is to make us swallow the idea that the State is 'progressive' and the conservative bourgeois opposition is 'unprogressive'. The State is neutral and the terms Left and Right are obsolete. De Gaulle reigns supreme, enthroned above class conflict in the stratosphere. Couve de Murville dispenses justice flanked by Marcellin and Faure, that glorious mink-coated revolutionary. Spare us the holy images! The State serves the bourgeoisie. Its autonomy is a sham. This was proven in May.

Thus the November crisis was not a clash between the theories of *dirigisme*[2] and liberalism but was born of very real

2. A term used to describe a system of economic planning in which the State intervenes by coordinating investment policies. According to the theory, the State is a neutral body and uses its power to balance one claim against another. *Dirigisme* is supposedly the compromise between liberalism and planning as practised in the socialist countries.

contradictions. Hence we must examine the interests locked in battle and how the State behaved towards those sections of the bourgeoisie who held power and those classes and segments of classes deprived of power.

The much-vaunted conflict between capitalist-traitors and capitalist-patriots is also a sham. Analytically, patriotism is no more a useful term than *dirigisme*. The bourgeoisie know the score. Their wallet is their homeland and 'national' interest is calculated in terms of profits. Whilst one group stands to gain by clinging to the present parity of the franc and others stand to gain by devaluation, all are united in their defence of the 'homeland' . . . against the working class.

The Communist party is at sixes and sevens when it comes to coping with the meanderings of the mass media. The party has always seen Gaullism as the 'voice of the monopolies' – and when it wanted to be really sociological, it added, 'the voice of the major monopolies'. On paper the PCF's definition seems radical and the essence of 'opposition'. But it suffers from an enormous defect. By a touch of the magical pen, it causes all of the contradictions and weaknesses in the enemy camp to vanish. The PCF could never identify the weakness of the State against the working class in May nor could it begin to understand the contradictions within the bourgeoisie in November. De Gaulle obviously wanted to see a strong State but pipedreams are not reality.

According to the PCF the State is merely the tool used by the monopolies. This obviates the need to distinguish between different kinds of monopoly. The party hacks toss out the term 'monopoly-state-capitalism'. Are the rumblings of a conflict between commercial banks and the State just tall stories? Is speculation an old wives' tale? Who has the power to threaten the franc and strangle the Government's economic policy? These questions go unanswered.

Driven by fear, the petite bourgeoisie has been sending its capital abroad since May. Yet, despite the PCF, it does not rule the roost. According to official statistics, its funds accounted for no more than 20 per cent of all the capital that fled the country during the monetary putsch. The culprits: the major banks and big business who took all the important decisions. How then can one claim that the monopolies acted against the 'voice of the monopolies'? *Humanité*'s editors were caught napping. At first Germany was the bogeyman. And when that didn't wash, on 24 November *Humanité-Dimanche* roundly denounced certain 'circles close to the monopolies'. But who are these speculators close to the monopolies? Fighting words, but when the ruling factions of the bourgeoisie are merrily tearing each other limb from limb, such language deliberately obscures their real weaknesses. Spreading the fiction of an omnipotent State demobilizes the working class, reassures the bourgeoisie, and revives the PCF's political Malthusianism so prominent in May. Why this attachment to the illusory merger of State and monopoly? The answer is clear. Such a superficially radical definition suits *Humanité*'s purpose of denouncing the existing State as a Gaullist plot to allow the monopolies to rule the roost.

Using this definition, the PCF drew up a programme of reforms: get rid of the monopolist conspirators and take over the State to use its institutions for other ends or what the party called 'advanced democracy'. The Party believes that the State apparatus is neutral and can be used by all and sundry. Its definition of Gaullism as 'state-monopoly' was party to the bourgeois myth of the State which claims that the State can remain independent of high finance – a State as neutral as the State schools and as Left-wing as François Mitterand. The myth of the neutral State only shows how bourgeois is the bourgeois press and how revisionist is *Humanité*.

The idea of the unity of State and monopoly may be a good description of their common dream but to take one's opponent's dreams for reality is not exactly a working hypothesis. The monetary crisis showed just how impossible such a fusion was. Capital demonstrated, through the monetary putsch, that it alone is calling the shots. That it had to resort to creating economic chaos shows how the bourgeoisie are being undermined by the contradictions created by the May movement and how Gaullism has been dismantled.

While both the bourgeoisie and the revolutionaries agree that

May was the harbinger of a revolutionary movement, for the bourgeoisie May spelled danger incarnate. Their first objective was to attack the movement and steel themselves against a repeat performance. They proposed to attack the May events at the roots by conceding certain reforms and to attack the ideological and economic effects through co-option and repression. But these proposals are contradictory.

The bourgeoisie are deeply divided. On one hand, they dream of a French 'techno-structure' pieced together out of the remnants of Jacobinism and Bonapartism with the State as the underwriter of national unity. On the other hand, they find economic revenge and ideological repression alluring. They want to ram home the idea that revolt does not pay. Fighting against us is like ramming your head against a brick wall is their message, whilst they gaily proceed with their policies of 'deflation' and austerity. But the monetary putsch of November pulverized their notion of 'growth', demystified their reforms as nothing but the cynicism of exploiters and their 'science' as a metaphysic to show the inevitability of what is.

But these contradictions do not separate the 'good' from the 'bad'. They do not divide the bourgeoisie into two camps. They are *the contradictions of the bourgeoisie as a whole*. They have a common denominator: hostility towards and fear of the renascent working-class movement. Different sections of the ruling class reflect these fears in different ways. May shattered the edifice of bourgeois exploitation and accentuated these splits. The November crisis showed how the bourgeois State, classes and factions of classes are rooted in these contradictions. Since May the French bourgeoisie are governed by fear. Their nerve is failing. To analyse their splits is to prepare the attack.

2. From May to the Monetary Putsch

Before May 1968 the franc was strong and de Gaulle seemed omnipotent. Whilst the international monetary crisis sowed momentary panic in London in 1967, and in Washington in April 1968, France seemed miraculously impregnable. The *Banque de France* held one of the biggest gold reserves in the world. Foreign capital was flowing into France and de Gaulle conducted an independent foreign policy.

Abroad he could easily afford the luxury of challenging American imperialism. He was able to dangle the prospect of creating a French 'game reserve' independent of Russian and American influence. His attack on the hegemony of the dollar was aimed at loosening the grip of American imperialism and replacing it by a 'multi-national' form of world exploitation. At home, he encouraged the Bonapartist myth of the State-above-class-conflict. These games allowed the 'national hero' to place the bourgeoisie under the aegis of big business and, to sweeten the pudding, to buy off part of the working class thereby lessening the class struggle.

Yet within six months, the franc was on the operating table. Half of de Gaulle's precious gold had melted away and de Gaulle had to stoop to thanking Johnson for a friendly avuncular telegram of 'support'.

May sent the illusions tumbling. The haute bourgeoisie lost 'confidence' in de Gaulle. He was no longer its man of destiny, for the political and economic arrangements he had made were no longer able to curb the mass movement. De Gaulle was no longer the mediator and in this setting the class struggle kindled a savage battle within the bourgeoisie. Not only did the battle destroy de Gaulle's traditional aloofness but his precious foreign policy became the adjunct of France's international protectors.

Behind the vicissitudes of Gaullist policy lies the weakness of the French bourgeoisie. Between May and November, the Government vainly tried to organize a united front made up of the entire bourgeoisie. But the November monetary crisis signalled the unwillingness of big business to share its power and its profits. It showed that finance capital would not sacrifice its international interests to pay the costs of class struggle in France. Hence bourgeois France lost control over its political and economic policies. It was forced to live from hand to mouth whilst the differences in its own camp reached explosion point.

From May to November: the bourgeoisie try to create a united front

What the May events revealed was that the Gaullist state could not deliver the goods. A bevy of former *Résistants* and *Pétainistes*[3] responded to de Gaulle's appeal on 30 May and linked arms in an obscene procession from the Place de la Concorde to the Étoile which symbolized the new-found unity of the bourgeoisie. But somewhere en route the State was reborn as the counter-revolutionary instrument of the bourgeoisie.

1. Political tactics

As early as 24 May the political crisis of the bourgeoisie was already at its height. More than 100,000 demonstrators swept across Paris and in their wake they left the wreckage of the State's apparatus for repression and de Gaulle's referendum – that magical instrument designed to create national concensus around the 'national hero' ended up in the dustbin of history, thanks to the militancy of the movement. When class conflict reaches the heights of a general strike directed against capitalism, the bourgeoisie lose their vocation as protectors of the nation. France was not in danger, only the bourgeoisie were.

The survival of the Gaullist State required building a united front to rally the entire bourgeoisie. On 30 May de Gaulle, clearly understanding the situation, spoke to the bourgeoisie and not to the 'nation'. Hence he proposed a general election instead of a referendum. The State, above politics, was to be replaced by wedding parliamentary democracy, representing the traditional alliance between competing sections of the bourgeoisie, and Gaullism, henceforth cast in the role of a tradition.

The compulsory retreat to Western capitalism's institutions of yesteryear confirmed the victory of May. May led to the formation of a united front but henceforth the bourgeoisie had to enter directly into the fray without mediator and without intermediary.

3. Collaborators with the Germans during the Second World War and supporters of the Vichy Government under Marshal Pétain and Pierre Laval.

These were not the only losses incurred by the bourgeoisie in May, for they also had to pay the material and financial costs of the class struggle. In running a capitalist economy, class struggle is the most costly item. Finance capital's need to ally itself with other sections of the bourgeoisie led to the compromise of 30 May, a combination of an archaic system, parliamentary democracy, and a system better suited to the needs of finance capital, Gaullism.

But the most important effect of the compromise has been to sharpen the contradictions of the capitalist system and the institutions of the bourgeois State. By July, the bourgeoisie left the battlefield badly shaken by their collision with the mass movement.

2. The reforms: attempts to form a new alliance

Confronted by a potentially revolutionary movement, the haute bourgeoisie cannot govern on its own. The Third and the Fourth Republics were based on an alliance between the haute bourgeoisie and the peasantry. In those days, politically France appeared to be a Republic of small 'shopkeepers'; but economically, the haute bourgeoisie was at the helm and was responsible for all the 'incidental' costs. For example, 'modernization', the unbridled expansion of the economy, had to be retarded. The present backwardness of many industries, the outmoded commercial structure and the peasant crisis all have their origin in these forms of compromise made after every revolutionary crisis.

But de Gaulle's seizure of power in 1958 indicated a fundamental change in the way this process worked. May 1968 sealed its destiny. With the ground trembling underfoot, the haute bourgeoisie desperately needed a new political clientèle. Given the bankruptcy of the old alliance with the peasantry, it concocted a new alliance.

Last summer's reforms in the University and the factories, and the proposals for regional reform, all bear the mark of this compromise. Their purpose was to split the mass movement thereby ensuring the rule of the new bourgeois coalition. The old tactic of the stick and the carrot was used but as always it was a case of heads I win, tails you lose. Each reform contained an element of both stick and carrot. The stick comforted the petite bourgeoisie whilst the carrot ensured the 'participation' of the working-class aristocracy in the new system, as well as that of a section of the petite bourgeoisie, teachers, students and minor industrialists. This liberal façade hid the repressive reality. Regional reform deconcentrated but it does not decentralize. University reform meant introducing selection procedures into secondary education and industrial reforms meant destroying factory committees. The other side of Edgar Faure is Raymond Marcellin.

These new Gaullist reforms represent an attempt to redistribute power amongst the various factions of the bourgeoisie in order to guarantee the political hegemony of the entire bourgeoisie. For finance capital, they imply a partial ceding of power. But their duplicity is inevitable. The masses cannot be transformed into allies of the bourgeoisie, so they must be outflanked (hence the stick) and to buy time, their leaders must be bought off (hence the carrot). Meanwhile the petite bourgeoisie is not given a share of power. Its political and trades representatives play only a marginal role. Hence the failure of the reform movement.

3. The failure

Every aspect and every function of the State apparatus has been dislocated. Let us first examine what has happened to its ideological function. On 30 May de Gaulle had to shed his halo and descend from the Olympian heights above the class struggle. His compromise over how power was to be exercised did not quite transform him into a mere tactician of the bourgeois camp. Though no longer a Zeus, he was still no Cavaignac.[4]

Secondly, the Gaullist State is no longer the guardian of public order. Despite sacking the most militant workers, and stirring up a climate of repression, the movement in the factories

4. French general who put down the June 1848 uprising of the working class and then stood for the presidency against Louis-Napoléon.

and lycées continues. The Government had to postpone the beginning of the university term. The mass movement is far from broken.

Thirdly, its economic policies are as muddled and contradictory as ever. The grand design of a national imperialism based on a modern economy, i.e., dominated by French monopolies, is still a dream. Government subsidies have not been used by private firms to expand output and increase their competitiveness but merely to plug the most gaping holes left by sending their assets to Switzerland and Germany.

Finally, the apparent liberalism of the reforms was used to trick the masses whilst harsh police and industrial measures have been used to teach the militants a lesson and cut the costs of production. The Government has not been able to choose between these two methods. Because it used both at the same time, its strategy lost all coherence. Its economic policy became nothing but a series of contradictory day-to-day measures: death duties were increased while exchange controls were relaxed so that the bourgeoisie could easily send its capital abroad; borrowing was tightened up by increasing the bank-rate while credit for the building industry was eased.

After May no one pretended to conduct an orderly economic policy. The hand-to-mouth half-measures alienated every section of the potential alliance and turned the Gaullist dream into a nightmare.

Under these circumstances finance capital opted for a showdown to regain the lion's share of the booty. Between May and August it lost its patience: the economic reforms hindered its interests and it had to foot the bill of buying out the small outmoded parasitic shopkeepers and industrialists.

At a time when international competition was made more difficult by the Common Market and increased competitiveness was a first necessity, the Government measures led to a fall in profits and threatened the international position of the 'French' monopolies. Whilst the haute bourgeoisie tempered its economic hegemony, it got nothing in return because politically the reforms interfered with its industrial speed-ups and Gaullism failed to serve its purposes. The UDR had failed to organize a vast national–social–conservative front as quickly as was required.

In short, the alliance was no real guarantee whilst finance capital had only larger bills to pay for the counter-revolution.

The November Monetary Putsch

The November monetary crisis was a political operation staged by the haute bourgeoisie. It was political, for what economic difficulties could account for the massive diminution of capital? The 'expansion' of the French capitalist system was not threatened by an imminent catastrophe. It was thus a political operation staged by those who wielded economic power. The root of the crisis was the fundamental contradiction in contemporary capitalism between *finance capital*, whose activities are international and embrace the world market, and *national capital*, whose scope is national and whose activities are regulated by the State by means of monetary and credit policies. The State thus attempts to smooth out conflicts and regulate the appetite of the bourgeoisie.

The power of a few large commercial banks with international connexions to grant and refuse loans is enough to control most large industrial firms. By means of its interlocking interests, finance capital is extremely powerful both internationally and on a national level. Its enormous resources allow it to play off one currency against another and to impose its demands on the nation-State. By throwing its weight against the franc, it overwhelmed the small speculator and sent de Gaulle packing.

1. Why did finance capital blackmail de Gaulle?

On 10 November the CNPF issued an ultimatum:

Our country's future, our economic independence, our standard of living and the fight against unemployment require that the following measures be taken:

(i) That any action which weakens the authority and efficiency of public and private enterprise be rescinded;

(ii) That a massive reduction in all public expenditure save investment be initiated;

(iii) That the increases in death duties and income tax be revoked to restore confidence in savings;

These measures are of the utmost importance in maintaining the franc and restoring the confidence of the nation.

The voice of capital laid down its conditions.

The counter-revolutionary compromise of 30 May did not satisfy finance capital. The political compromise proved to be too expensive and the economic measures cut its profits. Finance capital demanded that its pre-May economic hegemony be re-established and that May should not be repeated.

So it demanded that its hegemony over the State be restored and, given that the strategy of reform repression was ineffective, the State should take such measures as were necessary to prevent a repeat performance of May.

Its solution can be called the 'tactic of the truncheon' and the creation of a powerful national-conservative party capable of welding the bourgeoisie into a coherent political force.

Finance capital thus set Gaullism the task of assembling this party and governing through and not without it.

2. The monetary crisis is a political crisis

Finance capital regained its hegemonic control of the economy. Since May the bourgeoisie have been unable to govern as they did in the past. Gaullism ceased to be an adequate form of political rule. Finance capital wanted neither de Gaulle nor Gaullism.

Yet finance capital cannot govern alone. Although its economic interests contradict those of the rest of the bourgeoisie, its political interests depend on a working alliance with those same factions. If the haute bourgeoisie were to confront the petite bourgeoisie, de Gaulle would be in the way. But since the bourgeoisie as a whole is confronted by a militant working class, de Gaulle must remain. Hence in the short-run finance capital cannot rule without a de Gaulle.

So finance capital's November ultimatum was intended to

subordinate de Gaulle to the new coalition. The 'guardian of the national interest' was to be transformed from the strategist to the tactician of the bourgeoisie.

The political crisis ushered in by May was deepening. A major factor was the inability of the bourgeoisie to change its hand. In the short-run its only hope was to subject de Gaulle to its will once and for all.

3. De Gaulle gives in: what else could he do?

Once the monetary crisis became a political crisis the national budget was shelved. To blackmail de Gaulle, finance capital cut off his supplies and bled him of his monetary resources. Hence de Gaulle was forced to declare:

If we are to safeguard our currency, we must clearly restore equilibrium to all sectors and in all respects.

From the economic point of view, this means that without rescinding the wages increases already granted this Spring, we must categorically refuse to impose any further burdens on the economy. . . . We must quickly develop our export capacity by relieving our industries of those taxes which adversely affect their costs of production.

From the financial point of view, the 1969 Budget deficit, estimated at more than 11.5 thousand million francs must be reduced to less than 6.5 thousand million francs by pruning the operating costs of our administration, cutting subsidies to the nationalized industries and reducing civil, military and university expenditure. From the point of view of maintaining public order – for the crisis would not have arisen had public order not been disrupted and crises will continue to arise if order is not maintained – requisite measures must be taken . . .

Defending the franc meant defending the hegemony of finance capital over the economy. Defending the political hegemony meant defending the power exercised by the bourgeoisie. Hence politically order had to be maintained and the mass movement destroyed. Reforms had to be sent back into the mini-brains of Capitant, Vallon[5] and other such jesters of Left-wing Gaullism.

5. Representatives of the 'progressive' wing of the Gaullist movement. Capitant was Minister of Justice under Couve de Murville and Vallon edited a Gaullist journal called *Notre République*.

Financially taxes on industry had to be reduced, State expenditure slashed and loans had to be secured from the United States and Germany. And socio–economically public tariffs had to be increased, public expenditure reduced, wages held back, taxes on consumption increased and unemployment allowed to rise. The workers and students were to foot the bill of finance capital's putsch and pay for its demands.

4. The class struggle continues ...

In November de Gaulle and the Gaullist regime lost control of the national economy. Hence the bourgeoisie faced further social turmoil.

At a time when the bourgeoisie were fighting for their lives, the contradictions between finance capital and the rest of the bourgeoisie continued to grow. They had to join with de Gaulle to maintain their political hegemony. Strange bedfellows indeed! Meanwhile finance capital managed to subordinate the national economy to its own profit-seeking interests at the expense of the other factions of the bourgeoisie.

So black month succeeded black month ... May, June, November, December ...

Since May the bourgeoisie have shed the ideological cloak behind which they assiduously exploited the working class – relatively untroubled by the amiable corporative tactics of the CGT. When the bourgeoisie lost the power to determine its own 'strategy' so the Gaullist dream twice went up in flames at the Bourse. On 24 May the students and workers set fire to the temple of capitalism thus destroying the referendum. On 24 November de Gaulle surrendered to finance capital's *coup d'état*.

5. Why didn't they devalue?

There were three immediate solutions possible: a 10 per cent devaluation; a 20 to 25 per cent devaluation; or no devaluation at all.

To devalue by 10 per cent, the so-called 'sledgehammer position', would have meant reducing France a few pegs to its true size under the American umbrella. It probably would have given the mass movement an opportunity to regain its impetus given the likelihood of a steep rise in the cost of living. In short, it would have been an open admission of the failure of Gaullism and an open declaration of the political crisis. Only finance capital would have gained anything.

To devalue by 20 to 25 per cent, which was Debré's cataclysmic proposition, would have caused the collapse of all Western currencies and led to the search for a new international monetary system. But it would have also meant recognizing the inherent weakness of the capitalist system at a time when it was being globally harassed by revolutionary forces.

Hence a refusal to devalue was the only possible solution. It allowed a temporary compromise to be struck between finance capital and the nationally-based monopolies. Hence monopoly capital gained what finance capital lost. The compensation for the interests that lost out most heavily from this decision, the agricultural and industrial petite bourgeoisie, was the purely ideological guarantee of law and order.

Given the problems of international competition, there were two possible economic solutions. *Either* finance capital should be allowed to play its trump card and be given exclusive rights to pursue its monopolistic policies, as in the mergers of Fiat and Citroën. Thus French industry must seek partners outside France. *Or* nationally-based industries must be given top priority. In this case if one were to compete successfully on the world market the costs of the class struggle could no longer be borne. National monopoly capital had no wish to support outmoded forms of production. Provided other bourgeois interests did not interfere, not devaluing kept this path open. De Gaulle was there only to make sure that these other interests were eliminated with speed – hence the C N P S's ultimatum.

On 24 November de Gaulle did not choose between the two alternatives. His speech was no more than an impromptu appeal for unity. But today these two forces eye each other in the battle for power. The situation no longer depends on the French State. International competition is the sole arbiter.

The anti-capitalist movement and bourgeoisie

May witnessed the first defeat of the bourgeoisie when they lost the ideological battle. They lost the power to feed the proletariat with their illusions. When the old bourgeois University collapsed so did the bourgeoisie's apparatus of ideological mystification.

They suffered a second defeat in November when they lost their grip on the national economy. Buying off the working-class aristocracy and reducing the class struggle to tolerable limits became more and more difficult.

The bourgeoisie's third defeat will be a political defeat. It is clearly on the cards as the bourgeois economy is tumbling into a state of permanent crisis. Having created May, the working class constitute a potentially revolutionary movement if an integrated anti-capitalist front under its leadership can be brought into being. The struggle will be prolonged. For even if the bourgeoisie are divided and can no longer claim to rule harmoniously, they will not commit political suicide without some help. The political defeat of the bourgeoisie can only be accomplished by the revolutionary movement begun in May.

3. Weaknesses and Divisions of the French Bourgeoisie

A decadent class enters history backwards. If November revealed the fissures within the bourgeoisie, the mass media turned itself inside out to hide the battle between conflicting interests behind a façade of 'pseudo-news'. Each faction of the bourgeoisie pines for its paradise lost and yearns for the snows of yesteryear. Small shopkeepers dream of the Fourth Republic and Pinay. The Gaullists hark back nostalgically to the centralized State and Bonaparte. The haute bourgeoisie see its future as a morass of interwoven yet contradictory national and international interests. It is realistic. It knows that time cannot march backwards.

Fairy tales spun by the mass media should not be allowed to obscure the true history of the French bourgeoisie. From the Fourth Republic to de Gaulle it is a tale of decline, divisions and conflict culminating in the November crisis. Herein we suggest a few points to open the discussion and pave the way for a more detailed study of the decline and fall of the French bourgeoisie.

The State apparatus

'All political revolutions have merely helped to perfect the machine (the state) rather than destroy it,'

said Marx in the *18th Brumaire of Louis-Napoléon*. May was not an exception to the rule. It saw the birth of the vast column that marched from the Concorde to the Étoile on the 30th to support its master rather than to take power. If November and the ineluctable consequences of May, appeared as the manifestation of a struggle between the State and the bourgeoisie, it is because the earthquake which shook the bourgeois State in May was also the most immediate cause of its reinforcement. History shows that absolute monarchy gave rise to the State bureaucracy, the 1789 Revolution accentuated centralization and strengthened the State apparatus. After using it against feudal power, the bourgeoisie turned the State against the proletariat and strengthened its apparatus against them. It is an irony of history that the growth of the State apparatus, the nationalized industries etc., products of the struggle of labour against capital, were immediately converted into weapons of capital against labour. For whilst *economically* the State fragments the petite bourgeoisie and unifies the working class, *politically* it reunifies the petite bourgeoisie and divides the working class. Hence the development of the State bears consequences which contradict the process of capitalist development. In its unceasing attempts to unify the petite bourgeoisie, the State is hostile to economic progress which tends to divide and abolish it. This is the present weakness of Gaullism. Ironically, when the working class was without a revolutionary perspective, it was once its strength.

The Fourth Republic died because the dominant faction of the bourgeoisie was unable to impose its hegemony over the entire bourgeoisie or contain and shackle the potentially revolutionary force of the working class by parliamentary means. National and international conditions demanded a change in the form and role of the State: the continuous erosion of the bastions of

French imperialism (the colonial wars), the relative instability of the balance of power between classes (the 1947–8 strikes, the general strike of 1953, the revolt of reservists in 1955–6), the problems that arose from the decline of the petite bourgeoisie (Poujadism in 1956–7), the accentuation of the conflict between imperialist powers in the wake of European economic reconstruction and the attempt to buttress weakening imperialist forces by building a European economic bloc, etc.

In the last few years of the Fourth Republic, defeat followed defeat. The State apparatus did not allow the hegemonic faction to launch a counter-attack. A parliamentary Republic seemed to be a luxury. A strong State above class conflict gives the ideological illusion of underwriting the unity and the best interests of the entire nation and of solving those problems which the Fourth Republic could never solve. There is no situation without its solution. But the perpetual procrastination characterized the parliamentary Republic. To attempt to master the situation demanded creating a type of State which could make the necessary decisions i.e., striking the necessary compromises. Algeria gave the excuse. The Gaullist *coup d'état* of 1958 used decolonization as a pretext for attempting to solve the wider problems in the interests of the bourgeoisie by instituting a Bonapartist type of regime. Bonapartism is a form of rule in which the dominant faction of the bourgeoisie attempts to hold the proletariat at bay by reconstituting a national front of the bourgeoisie. It does this by using the apparently neutral State apparatus and the prestige of a national figure.

To the haute bourgeoisie, Gaullism was the ideal instrument for the unobtrusive elimination of the petite bourgeoisie and the peasantry. It would be the instrument to transform France into a power that could compete on the world market.

May blew the feeble latter-day Bonapartist edifice sky high. In November the haute bourgeoisie decided to use the relics of the State apparatus to settle accounts with the petite bourgeoisie and the working class. But de Gaulle still remained skilfully clinging on to a modicum of power by attempting to paper over the cracks in the bourgeois camp and taking advantage of the contradictions in the haute bourgeoisie. It remains for the revolutionary movement to make the most of these contradictions and defeat the enemy.

The petite bourgeoisie

With its days already numbered, even when it still governed with other factions or by itself, the petite bourgeoisie staffed the Third Republic. Whilst politically bound to the dominant class, it could not avoid the consequences of the economic war waged against it by the haute bourgeoisie. With precision and success, it administered its own downfall. Endowed with a political spokesman, the *parti radical*, heir to the Republican ideology dispensed daily to millions of children by thousands of teachers, the petite bourgeoisie wrung compromise after compromise from the ruling faction by threatening to join forces with the proletariat. But the compromises were political and never economic. The petite bourgeoisie was unable to stem the tide of the monopolies, trusts, banks and industrial magnates.

During the Third Republic the gap between the petite bourgeoisie and its political representative widened, until in the twilight of the Third Republic the final blow was struck when the *radicaux*, in power as usual, became mere lackeys of the ruling class. From Herriot to Laval to Herriot,[6] the drama of the *radicaux* defending the policies of their adversaries drained the petite bourgeoisie of its political energy until it consciously abdicated any pretence of power or hegemony. The political and ideological bankruptcy of the *radicaux* in 1940 sealed the split and led to the party's annihilation.

Divided, dissatisfied and impotent, the petite bourgeoisie searched in vain for a political spokesman during the Fourth Republic. Returning to power in the wake of the proletariat in 1944, the haute bourgeoisie used the proletariat to eliminate its erstwhile ally.

Only that part of the haute bourgeoisie which collaborated with Fascism was absent from the grotesque coalition which

6. Herriot, the leader of the *parti radical* for about half a century, the epitome of the *radical* leader, perpetually a cabinet member and perpetually bending with the wind. Pierre Laval, Prime Minister of the Vichy regime.

came to power. Without relying on foreign intervention, the bourgeoisie had no way of keeping the working class in its place. The State lay in ruins. It had been destroyed, literally dismantled, by the August 1944 insurrection. Faithful to its historical mission of doing the dirty work of the haute bourgeoisie, the petite bourgeoisie took up the cudgels against the proletariat. Tricked by half-witted leaders, fallen victim to the general euphoria, the proletariat joyfully greeted the birth of a new era whilst allowing itself to be robbed of its arms. A sad caricature of a heroic struggle, June 1848 became the defeat of 1948 when the ministers of the PCF tip-toed out of the Government. Jules Moch[7] won the day, the strike was defeated and the revolution strangled. For its services the petite bourgeoisie was dealt a series of devaluations and then turfed out of the Government with nothing to show for its pains but a few sinecures for its most servile representatives. If the working class was but a caricature of itself, the petite bourgeoisie was the buffoon of a grotesque farce. Voting with amazing and obdurate consistency for deputies who once elected sold themselves body and soul into the arms of the haute bourgeoisie, the petite bourgeoisie once again demonstrated its congenital incapacity to seize the reins of power and impose its hegemony over the other bourgeois factions. The petite bourgeoisie amiably presided over its own ruin. It lauded the idea of 'reconstruction', trumpeted itself dizzy for the Marshall Plan but never saw a penny, lost control of the press and had to watch the spectacle of power falling into the hands of the haute bourgeoisie from the sidelines. Deceived by the Fourth Republic it helped to found, tottering between the temptation of adventurism (the RPF and Poujade) and faithfulness to its indestructible elder statesmen, the petite bourgeoisie wore itself out in internecine squabbles between its commercial, industrial, Voltairian and clerical interests. The Fourth Republic was endowed with parliamentary institutions galore, but real power was already outside parliament. There could be no compromise. The hypochondriacal convulsions of the petite bourgeoisie could hardly influence the hegemony of the

7. Minister of the Interior under Paul Ramadier, responsible for expelling the Communists from the post-war coalition.

haute bourgeoisie. Gaullism quickened the pace of the political destruction of the petite bourgeoisie. It took away the last vestige of its old prestige by eliminating them from the bureaucracy and exiling them to the sticks and their shops. In June 1940 the petite bourgeoisie lost its party. In May 1968 it lost its niches and prebends.

Why the lack of resistance? The answer lies in the ineluctable financial and economic contradictions that destroyed the bases of the petite bourgeoisie. Given the impossibility of using the State against the haute bourgeoisie, the 'ocean of small producers' either fell under the yoke of the monopolies (through take-overs and absorption) or lived on the fringes of the large firms by aligning its prices with theirs and by concentrating on luxury or specialized goods. The situation of the petite bourgeoisie is comparable to that of the artisans of the last century. In those cases where it held stocks and shares in large companies, these shares were not titles to property but certificates which hardly allowed it to intervene in the running of the firm. Finance capital's client was allowed to vegetate only when finance capital could benefit. The petite bourgeoisie screamed that the State spent too much, bellowed against taxes, but panicked and shut up when it came to disturbing the peace of its watch-dogs. The edifying experience of the Poujadist deputies, bought as soon as they were elected, who once preached against the bank and called upon small shopkeepers of all descriptions to rise against taxes was the upshot. Victims of their own ideology, instead of seeking an alliance with the small industrialists, they patched together an alliance with the artisans.

The petite bourgeoisie knows it has lost the game. Hence it tries to come to terms with the present that only their masters can guarantee. Trapped between the growing number of workers and monopoly capital the petite bourgeoisie is coming to the end of its history. Its death is slow for the contradictions within finance capital allow it a periodic reprieve. Soon the slowness of its death will be determined demographically rather than economically. This is why it hides the minuscule fruit of centuries of accumulation: its gold. It dares not convert its gold into banknotes, allow it to circulate or make a profit. It clings to its gold.

It hoards. To hoard! There is the touchstone of the French petite bourgeoisie, the most loathesome of its kind. France holds the record amongst capitalist countries for the most gold in private hands and for the quantity of dead capital.

The peasantry

The fate of the peasantry was even harsher. It voted for de Gaulle in 1958 just as it voted for all the parties of finance capital under the Fourth Republic.

Survivors of an obsolete form of production, the peasantry was reprieved for fifty years by its alliance with the haute bourgeoisie. The State maintained prices, prevented foreign competition, raised protectionist tariffs and subsidized 'cooperative' ventures. But no State can hold out for very long against the spread of capital from one sphere of the economy to another. The capitalization of agriculture, once limited to the Île de France, has now spread to the rest of France. In this respect, Gaullism is the opposite of the Bonapartist 'Empire of the peasants' for under its rule no class has been so oppressed and exploited as the smallholders. Pisani and Boulin[8] both explained that price supports have had to be abandoned for political reasons. Concentration and integration are the order of the day. The food industries compete with the so-called 'cooperative societies' for control of the market. For the peasantry there is no solution. The recently-developed contradictions between the peasantry and the State, the concurrent struggle between the peasant capitalist dependent on French and international markets, and the smallholder have been expressed in periodic revolts. De Gaulle's swaggering speech of 24 November will change nothing. The only question is whether these isolated smallholders will go down without fighting or if they will realize that their only solution is an alliance with the working class. The exodus from the countryside has created a network of bonds between the peasants and their relatives who have gone to work in the towns and cities. Urbanization or sub-urbanization of large tracts of the countryside may help to give the mass of

8. Ministers of Agriculture.

smallholders a true awareness of their interests. The development of modern means of communications have wrenched the peasantry out of its ancestral isolation. The help given by peasants to the workers of Nantes during May would have been unthinkable only twenty years ago and foreshadows future developments. Politically, by rejecting the traditional superstitious faith in the State, the peasants may soon help the working class overthrow the old society.

The haute bourgeoisie

The haute bourgeoisie holds supreme power. But by allowing the Gaullist adventure of 1958, it created a new series of problems. In no other regime over the last fifty years has the power of the haute bourgeoisie been so great. But its *inability* to rule through its own organizations has forced it to accept a series of compromises and a relatively autonomous State. But the State increasingly functions as the political organizer for the bourgeoisie. The bourgeois parties act as transmission belts for the State rather than for any one faction of the bourgeoisie. The State watches over the interests of the bourgeoisie as a whole. But this means it must, at times, fight against even those factions which spare power. The unity of the classes in power is thus contradictory. Equally obliged to mould the policies of the State to their own ends whilst allowing it greater autonomy of action in return for constraints placed on society as a whole, the bourgeoisie is thus suffocated by the very State it reinforces against the proletariat.

The State, the organ of the bourgeoisie, the oppressor of the working class, exalts the interests of high finance as the political interests of the bourgeoisie as a whole. To satisfy its appetite determines its line of action: to protect its interests when they are threatened and to provide its first line of defence. But the very performance of its duties exacerbates the contradictions within the bourgeoisie. This is exactly what has been happening since May. To defend the interests of the nationally-based monopolies has been the *sine qua non* of Gaullist policy since May 1968. Pigeon-holing anti-trust legislation, easing taxes on large businesses, providing massive financial aid for mergers, abolishing the petite bourgeoisie's prebends, expanding the scope of the T V A: all are measures which encourage the growth of monopoly capital.

The haute bourgeoisie has already recovered the economic power somewhat shaken by the nationalization of the means of credit after the Liberation. Under de Gaulle it waxed rich. Between 1961 and 1967 the principal commercial banks grew at a rate of about 15 per cent per year. The prohibition on short-term deposits, once only allowed to the nationalized banks, was revoked in 1966.

The banks became increasingly involved in the long-term financing of industries whilst new legislation on construction and urban development offered them a new field of activity.

But if the 'Who's Who' of the banking world overlaps with that of the industrial world (e.g. Bercot, chairman of Citroën is on the board of the Banque de Paris et des Pays-Bas), and the 'high society' of magnates is a closed society, contradictions are no less strong. 30 June not only marked de Gaulle's electoral victory but the official birth of the Common Market. The hell-bent pressure towards monopoly over the last few months grew from fear of failure and the impossibility of increasing prices due to German and Italian competition. The State, ever mindful of its golden rule over the last ten years, prevailed upon French trusts to organize themselves into *super-trusts on a national basis*. Alas! The iron law of competition had no pity, for Europe had embarked on a higher phase of economic organization. Europe, already bristling with giant industrial colossi, is on the eve of still more giant mergers. Within a few weeks of May, a wave of European mergers (Fiat–Citroën, E N I–Montedison, C F P–Gelsenkirchen, Hoecht–Roussel, U C L A F), enlivened the financial sections of the press. To their astonishment the bourgeoisie learned of the key role played by the commercial banks in these mergers. Clearly, a part of the *Who's Who* were putting their money in the *international* rather than the *national* market. Finance capital is more easily taken by this mania than is industrial monopoly. Finance capital is fickle. It merrily liquidates one enterprise and begins another. Its market is not national but international. Its ambition is to be like Lazard. A potentially explosive contradiction is brewing between the State's policy of supporting nationally-based monopolies and the interests of finance capital in developing international combines. At the moment there is no question of an open confrontation. But the conflict could become serious because it is just not an internal contradiction within capital but sets the nation-State against international combines. These international groups are human and do not work for some non-existent 'world' interest. They act at times through a particular State and the war between them is every bit as violent as their opposition to their 'national' competitors.

The final establishment of the Common Market is not only a pretext for de Gaulle to favour the setting-up of large national monopolies, it also marks the beginning of the great financial rush towards whatever country promises the best pickings.

Nation-States and international combines

The contradiction between the capitalist State and the international combine is clearly visible in the vagaries of national currencies. Printing money and fixing exchange parities are the prerogative of the State whilst the buying and selling of currency depends on the economy. For a prestige-conscious State a hard currency is an imperative. International combines care little about parities provided they benefit from devaluation or revaluation. *National* finance capital, however, finds that the international crisis presents the permanent possibility for blackmail through potential monetary crises. Since the division of the world among capitalist States does not correspond to the division of the world among capitalist enterprises, any pact or agreement is fragile and all currencies are weak. War or crisis or crisis and war?

4. The International Dimension of the Crisis

Finance capital thought that the correct way to deal with the revolutionary movement of May was to instigate a run on the franc. Since the French bourgeoisie had been unable to 'control' its working class, exploitation of the working class would henceforth be conducted in the name of 'defending the franc' or of the so-called 'discipline' of the world market.

So a bourgeoisie weak on the home front called the machinery of the world market to its rescue. But the aid given by the dollar and the mark 'to save the franc' were conditional on 'austerity', that is, the increased exploitation of the French working class. This is precisely how the Fourth Republic operated. Bourgeois parties of the Left and the Right took stern action against the workers in 1947, 1948, 1951 and in 1953 whilst, cap in hand, begging more alms from the Americans.

But today the situation is very different. The international bourgeoisie itself is weak and the entire imperialist system is under strain. The international monetary crisis has been growing in intensity since 1960. At that time the American hegemony began to weaken. Today the United States can no longer rule the capitalist world according to whim. The Americans have been weakened by the anti-imperialist struggle in Vietnam and Cuba, the struggle of the Negro at home, etc.; German, Japanese, French and Italian competition; and Russian competition. These are the roots of the present crisis.

Answering May with November was finance capital's attempt at curing one disease with another. By exporting its capital and weakening the franc, the bourgeoisie hoped to dress its wounds. Instead it only compounded its own ailment with the international ailment. In exchange for its capital, it has imported the shock-waves of the ever-deepening world crisis.

The international monetary crisis: the battle over the spoils

The monetary crisis is not a technical problem. It is part of an economical and political conflict. By claiming that only 'programmed' bourgeois economists dare fiddle with these problems, the bourgeoisie tried to distract attention from the incredible shambles caused by inter-imperialist conflict. While half the world starves, production in imperialist countries is curtailed, growth is checked and unbelievable sums of money are squandered in the wars. Conflict between the imperialist countries today takes the form of a monetary crisis. With the Americans, the British and the French all taking measures to curb their imports and increase exports, it runs the risk of being overtaken by a commercial crisis. A chain reaction is set off – each power instigates recessions amongst its imperialist bedfellows.

Imperialism is not only a war waged against countries like Vietnam fighting for their independence, or the shameless exploitation of other countries (the development of under-development in Latin America, India etc.), it is also the price exacted from all workers of the world because the imperialist countries cannot agree on how to divide up the spoils.

The monetary crisis demonstrates that the struggle for the division of the world is a struggle for its wealth, i.e., the fruits of exploitation. The crisis started in the early 1960s when capitalism had recovered from the effects of the War, international capital had found its feet, the financial markets, thrown into disarray by the War and its consequent crises and controls, were reactivated and capital began to flow freely around the Atlantic once more. At this point the American 'balance-of-payments deficit' made its appearance. Too many dollars left the United States, America was going into debt and spending too much.

Why? For three main reasons:

1. American policy was expensive. As the policeman of the world, America incurred the costs of buying governments, trade unions and other organizations. The war in Vietnam saddled her with a heavy expenditure of dollars abroad – in Japan, Formosa, South Korea etc.;

2. American capitalists invested in Europe because of the greater profit margins. Europe was technologically under-developed and the Americans reaped a harvest from their patents and inventions. Finally European salaries were still low;

3. Taking advantage of their privileged monetary position, the Americans printed large amounts of money which resulted in an inflation, paid for by other countries.

The monetary system worked to the Americans' benefit. In 1944 the United States owned almost all the gold in the world.

They decided that central banks, such as the Banque de France, could keep 'reserves not only in gold, as before, but also in dollars and pounds, (given the chronic weakness of Britain, the pound was dependent on and 'supported' by the dollar). This was the Bretton-Woods agreement between the United States and her allies.

Whilst Western Europe was engaged in its post-war reconstruction, it ran up debts to the United States. But after 1960 the tables were turned. The Americans went into debt and dollars began to accumulate in Europe. Then German and French capitalists began to exchange their paper dollars for American gold. Gold began to pile up in France and Germany and soon there was no longer enough American gold to guarantee the paper dollars scattered around the world. The pound was the first currency to be affected (the devaluation of November 1967) followed by the dollar itself (March–April 1968). The Americans suspended private banks' right to convert paper dollars into gold. They were forced to negotiate an agreement with the central banks of the ten leading capitalist countries to allow them to conserve their gold provisionally and under certain conditions. Hence they were no longer the absolute masters.

What is the heart of the matter?

The problem is how to divide the cake amongst all the imperialist powers. Imperialism *pays*: the exploitation of the so-called 'third world', and of the working class in the capitalist countries has led to a fabulous increase in the fortunes of a few huge international banks and monopolies. But imperialism is also *expensive*: war and policies of subjugation run up the costs whilst at home the bourgeoisie is occasionally forced to distribute a few crumbs to 'its' working class when they are combative. The monetary crisis stems from the inability of the capitalists to reach an agreement on who is to bear the costs and who is to get the profits. When a German banker says he doesn't want to pay for 'the American balance of payments deficit' i.e., American debts abroad, the Americans reply: 'We are spending all our money to defend the ''free world'' (imperialism) so you damn well have to pay your part – let's split the costs.' To which the European financier could always reply that if the Americans want the costs to be shared, they should share the profits – whereas, in fact, when the Americans buy a factory with their dollars (increasing the deficit) that factory belongs to them. There is no way out: the United States doesn't want to be the only country to pay for the defence of imperialism, whilst other capitalst countries don't want to subsidize American expansion. Hence the bitter competition and the monetary crisis.

The crisis is serious

There will be no quick and easy solution. It is not just a crisis of the dollar, the pound or the franc. All currencies are inter-dependent. If one goes under the others will follow as in 1930. Capitalism is becoming internationalized and no Western country can afford to remain outside international commerce and the world capitalist market. Hence the power of international finance capital, whose network covers all capitalist countries, and overrides national frontiers. Major American banks speculate against the dollar and American monopolies ignore Presidential decrees forbidding their investing abroad. The USSR is beginning to play a major role in the financial network through the Narodnyi Bank in London and the Banque commerciale de l'Europe du Nord in Paris. A free or black market of capital which escapes the control of national banks has been reconstituted. This is the so-called 'Euro-dollar market' in which major Japanese or French magnates can borrow enormous sums of money whilst avoiding exchange controls and official controls. 'Under our very eyes a world market as free as that which existed before 1914 has been reborn. For French business it opens entirely new fields of action,' declared the extremely powerful president of the Banque de Paris et des Pays-Bas.

The fellowship of capital is a fellowship of thieves based on the competition between capitalist powers and the battle for the spoils. The fundamental disequilibrium, identified by Lenin as the furious competition between imperialist powers, persists. The *unequal development of the forces of production* explains why American capital crosses the ocean and produces better results in Europe than at home – to the detriment of the American balance of payments. Moreover, the *unequal development of the exploitation of the working class* plays an even more important role: in the 'old' capitalist countries like Britain and America, the working-class aristocracy defends its privileges and capital has to 'buy' a section of the working class by making concessions. These are the overhead costs of the class struggle. American capital cannot afford an increase in the number of unemployed whites for fear of their combining with the Negro masses. Capital which refuses to pay these overheads emigrates to calmer climes – hence its visit to France before May and its untroubled stay in Germany. The Federal Republic has to pay neither the costs of the contemporary class struggle nor that of the past for the War and the reserve army of East Germans allowed a rapid reconstruction.

The development of the international network of finance capital is responsible for the global extent of the monetary crisis and proves that the bourgeoisie initiates and enhances 'the universal interdependence of nations', as Marx pointed out in the *Communist Manifesto*. The extension of international finance capital, transcending national barriers, quickens imperialist rivalries. The highest form of the quest for profit and maximum return on capital, continues apace. Moreover, finance capital benefits from its own instability using it to blackmail governments. Whilst scanning the world for the pick of investments, each country tries to entice the major banks. The monetary crisis is a universal form of prostitution practised by capitalist states in an endeavour to attract and retain investments by guaranteeing the highest returns and the greatest security. That is, by once again exploiting and deluding their working classes.

In Marxist terms, the stake of the inter-imperialist struggle is the international equalization of profit. The reasons for the crisis lie in the unequal development of the forces of production and the unequal exploitation of the working class (the unequal intensity of the class struggle). These two factors led to the unequal development of rates of profit. The problem cannot be solved technically for as Lenin remarked, 'only the sword' can be the ultimate arbiter. There is no such thing as a 'just' division, for each capitalist power tries to enrich itself to the detriment of the others: 'The law of capitalist production is characterized by the violence used by one capitalist against another.' (Marx, *Capital*, vol. III.)

Since the imperialist fight over social wealth is eternal, one should not be surprised if it is expressed through the monetary dispute or the gold problem: 'Gold and money are similar incarnations or expressions of the social origin of wealth.' (Marx, *Capital*, vol. III.)

Social wealth, born of exploitation, is what the imperialist powers seek to pluck from each other.

The crisis is serious. Johnson, Wilson and de Gaulle piously condemn the 'speculators' whilst doing their best to entice finance capital, capital which must speculate because, by definition, it seeks the highest rate of profit. The curse is only a verbal curse for every capitalist speculates. That the imperialist powers have chosen to deplore their own rules of the game shows that capitalist governments are no longer able to coordinate their home economies: the anarchy of the world market plays havoc with their 'plans' and 'reforms'. Hence despite the bureaucratic American trade unions and reformist and revisionist political parties, the class struggle is once more violent and savage (e.g. the unofficial strikes in Britain and Italy). The policy of full employment encouraged by growth and moderate inflation have been thrown to the winds. The dam built against the class struggle was on the point of bursting. De Gaulle wanted to trick the working class with his 'reforms' but he led them to the sacrificial altar of international capitalism. Like de Gaulle, Wilson sacrificed his party's programme, as Johnson did Kennedy's grandiose projects. When French bourgeoisie sought comfort in the embrace of international capitalism, one weakness engendered another.

The prospects: is there a technical solution?

The imperialist bourgeoisies are paralysed by fear. The more sordid and material their threatened interests, the more religiously they express their anguish. The meetings where bankers, financiers and ministers tear each other to pieces have been baptised 'conclaves'. As competition becomes more intense and the crisis deepens, the more difficult it is to divide the spoils and the costs of exploitation.

So they give way to dreams. Surely, they muse, there is a 'technical' solution which would end the dispute and arrange a 'just' division! Since 1960 the specialists have churned out a mountain of documents and reports bitterly defending and attacking each other. The cacophony is deafening. Bourgeois speculations on economics are as anarchic as the bourgeois economics of speculation.

Increase the price of gold? If the rise were substantial certain competitors like the Russians, the South Africans and the French would benefit whilst others like the British would lose out. So that would require an agreement to offset the consequences.

Then, what about junking gold and creating a world currency to regulate the distribution of credit and capital (Triffin)? But such an arrangement would inevitably support growth in one country and impose austerity on another. It would have to function like a world imperialist government. The fate of the United Nations proves that inter-capitalist quarrels are not so easily regulated through supra-national bodies.

The Americans like Kindleberger and the English through *The Economist* have long held the view that if the United States printed more dollars the problem would be solved since the US would thus play the role of a world bank. But they forget that the entire crisis arose because American hegemony is disputed.

An added attraction to the long list of utopias is the plan suggested by Mendès-France, Kaldor and Co. They suggest that a standard composed of a number of primary materials replace gold. Ideally this would benefit the 'third world'. But in reality it combines two illusions: first, that the international capitalists will eventually agree on how to distribute wealth; and secondly, that they would be willing to sacrifice their profits in the interests of humanity. Unfortunately for Mendès-France, the second coming is a more probable event.

It serves no purpose to list the other plans, floating exchange rates etc., because they all presuppose an agreement amongst the rival imperialist powers. The theoretical conflict (Reuff: gold is the basis of the economic system, versus Keynes: gold is a 'barbarous fetish') reflects the contradictions of exploitation.

'There are no crises without a solution.' To say that the solution is not a technical solution means that there can be no definitive and 'equitable' solution. The inter-imperialist struggle will continue. This does not rule out stop-gap and ephemeral solutions. But between who and whom? What will be the effect on the class struggle in France?

The inter-imperialist balance of power and de Gaulle

The conflict between the imperialist powers has two aspects: the battle for the division of the world; and the battle for the division of its wealth.

The Soviet Union openly intervenes in the first battle. Its aim is to secure markets and a clientèle irrespective of how reactionary the regime to which it offers 'aid' (its economic penetration of Latin America, very similar to its policies in India, Africa and the Mediterranean world, have aroused Cubin protests). Russian intervention in the second battle is heavily disguised (her purchase of wheat from the Americans in exchange for gold, her use of the Euro-dollar, her plan to join the International Monetary Fund). *Pravda*'s attitude during the French crisis showed that the Soviet Union intervenes directly in the monetary crisis. She, too, wants her share.

The conflict is polarized by the two financial and industrial super-powers. In the second rank is Germany whilst the most important economic power in Europe unable to wield her power due to her political weakness. The power of finance capital, banks and international monopolies to manipulate almost any State at will is a rebellious and ungovernable force. As long as national governments persist in their international struggle for capital, international capital will wax fat from their battles. Let them cry 'speculators!' Any compromise will be no more than a stopgap.

Before May, de Gaulle tried to play the role of the great

international arbiter. In fact, he was merely the instrument of the international financiers who deposited their gold in France. Extolling financial wisdom and the reform of the monetary system he was the spokesman of the world bankers frightened by the deficit accumulated by the American Government.

After November, de Gaulle could no longer pretend to be the arbiter. The outside capitalist interests will arbitrate the fate of de Gaulle. By rallying the Anglo-American interests he attempted to make Germany bear the brunt of the crisis. Hence his alliance at home with the Right-wing faction who support the Americans (witness the warmth of his welcome for Nixon and the extended hand to the 'centre groups'). But his policy runs into two obstacles:

1. At home, it accentuated the class struggle. The Government's overtly capitalist policies no longer allowed the trade union and party bureaucracies to hide their tendency to capitulation behind a policy of 'national unity' in defence of the franc;

2. Abroad, the sterling or dollar crisis could drag the franc down with them. The Americans might attempt an understanding with the Germans or Russians at the expense of the franc to bolster the dollar.

The French bourgeoisie and de Gaulle kept another card up their sleeve. It could only be played with great risk but it could have been used to pressure or blackmail. It is the alliance that the Left Gaullists parade as Jacobinism. If the dollar doesn't want to – or cannot – save the franc, France could have resorted to a savage devaluation, 20 to 25 per cent according to Debré, provoking the collapse of all Western currencies. The franc could only hope to have extricated herself from the chaos by leaning on the rouble. This would have entailed a more or less official alliance between de Gaulle and the PCF and between France and the Soviet Union. On 22 November, before de Gaulle's subsequent speech of the 24th, *Humanité* entertained such hopes with the headline, 'Bonn makes de Gaulle devalue the franc'. Only the wish for such an alliance can explain the PCF's refusal to denounce the responsibility of the haute bourgeoisie during the fifteen-day crisis.

Given the hearty competition between the USSR and Germany in central Europe, the USSR would have supported de Gaulle against Germany. But such an alliance would have stirred the pro-American faction in France. Hence it was relegated to the background. Moreover, there is no reason to believe that Russia would prefer France to the United States.

Between total submission to the Americans – with or without de Gaulle – and the highly improbable Franco–Russian alliance various compromises are possible. In every case, the decision is not that of the French bourgeoisie and its Government. The internal policy of bourgeois France depends directly on the competition between the imperialist powers ('peaceful co-existence') and on the vicissitudes of the world monetary crisis.

The French bourgeoisie is looking for a master. It will sell itself to the highest bidder. From now on its weakness will be the weakness of its masters. The bourgeoisie will be forced to import the shock-waves of the crisis and the division of the imperialist rivalry. The revolutionary movement does not confront a united block. In May the bourgeoisie lost its grip on the University. In November it lost its grip on the national economy. Today it lives from hand to mouth and the world crisis is now a French crisis.

December 1968

17. Postcript

May 1969. Almost a year has elapsed since these words were hurriedly written during the summer of 1968. What has happened to the May movement since that time?

A year later France seems to have returned docilely to her normal routine. The *pègre* appears to have trickled back to its sources, students to their books, revolutionaries to the world of the *groupuscules, blousons noirs* and Katangais to their haunts, the technician to his station, the worker to being the child of the assembly-line and the Communist party, the intellectual to the meanderings of the introverted literati and Paris the cauldron to the everyday chaos and violence of the Western city. The urban landscape has seemingly engulfed, absorbed and swallowed whole its detractors with its cafés, theatres, cinemas, reviews, and the asphalt neon-lighted jungles on to which the occasional demonstration – in the true style of the veterans of foreign wars – has been grafted with success. May 1969: Jacques Duclos parades through the streets of Nanterre preceded by a brass band and a team of American-style majorettes. Is May but a memory?

To many May 1969, a May of elections, a May of the Moderate resurgence, the May of Pinay-the-Minor, Alain Poher, marks the return to the tranquillity of the Fourth Republic. Wishful thinking. They have seriously erred. There can be no return. France 1969 is not France 1958. The Gaullist experiment of 1958 was undertaken in desperation and it failed. The gold that echoed its rock-firm stability is all but gone. Middle-class France is in a state of paralysis. Lucid to the last, de Gaulle realized the extent of the rout and, as in 1946, departed disdainfully, but in style. Behind him the rhetorical scramblings to capture the 'true spirit of France' and the inevitable calls to national unity are just an echo. Georges Pompidou, forever guardian of the wake, strives to maintain a Gaullist heritage whilst simultaneously seeking to pay his accumulated debts to the petite bourgeoisie and the world financial community. Like the fireside vagaries of MM. Poher and Duclos, his election campaign was Chekhovian. On the one hand, the idea of progress and reform is held aloft. France's Berkeley might yet be built at the Porte Dauphine or in the shadow of the army's testing grounds at Vincennes. On the other hand, the commitment to repression is just as great. M. Marcellin, the Minister of the Interior, has banned organizations, fired ORTF strikers, condoned Right-wing commando groups and deported hundreds of students and immigrant workers. By the time this book is published who knows how many shop stewards will have been fired, and how many trade-union branches destroyed, 'pacified' or disciplined? Industry will have chosen its own form of *participation*. And so, indeed, will the PCF.

May 1969 signals the advent of a new kind of regime. Shall we call it the Fifth and one-half Republic, a boisterous satire of both the grandeur of the Gaullist Republic and the modest corruption and chaos of its predecessor, the Small Shopkeepers' Republic? Far from being papered over, the contradictions of the past will sharpen. The homilies and the near hysterical references to a mythical France of a Pompidou, a Poher or a Duclos are no greater protection than was the Maginot Line.

The 'movement' now in disarray is held together by its trump card. It cannot forget those days when 'law and order', imposed reality, ceased to exist and when reality was what one could create. The juxtaposition of a possible future and a supposed return to the 'normal' is too great. Whereas organizations can be dissolved, trade unionists can be bullied, wage rises can be taken back by the tricks of monetary policy, and the most revolutionary leaders can be manipulated or turned into the 'stars' and *cinéastes* of the mass media or the anti-popes who believe in their own infallibility, such a vision cannot be erased. The cultural revolution is not a memory. It is a prelude. It is a prognosis.

To Walter Benjamin Paris was *Paris, die Hauptstadt des XIX Jahrhunderts, (Paris, Capital of the 19th Century)*. That Paris gluttonously absorbed the inventions and ideas of the epoch and reproduced them in their most ludicrous and highly-polished form against the backcloth of a swollen urban conurbation aping all the superficial qualities of the great industrial cities. That Paris produced the prototype of the workers' Revolution, that Paris gave birth to the Commune presaging the workers' councils and the Soviets of 1917. It was a prelude to a strategy. Paris today is twentieth-century urbanism gone wild: built higher than any other city, more expensive, and more crowded than any other city, more cars, more goods, the land of pure *kitsch*, an antheap magnifying the cultural values of a consumer's society *à outrance*. Paris found herself for a few brief moments in May when the theatre returned to the street, the cinema to everyday life, and art discovered its true vocation in the wall and the poster, and poetry in everyday speech; when the rationality behind the phrase, *prenez vos rêves pour des réalités* (treat your dreams as reality) became evident.

Paris the old is dead. Yet we still live in the carcass. The idea that May was a dress rehearsal for a 1917, the foundation of a new revolutionary strategy in the Western world, is far from absurd.

August 1914 silenced a flow of ideas in Western Europe and banished them to the University for two generations. These ideas have now begun to emerge. One of the victims wrote:

I remember when I arrived in Paris as a young man, more than thirty years ago. On that winter's night in that immense city, I was struck by a kind of social terror. It seemed that thousands upon thousands of men, passing each other by without a sign of recognition, an innumerable mass of lonely ghosts, were shorn of any human bond. And I asked myself with a kind of impersonal terror, how these beings accepted an unequal distribution of good and evil – how the enormous structure of society did not collapse suddenly and dissolve. I saw no chains upon their hands and feet. I said to myself: By what prodigious feat are these thousands of suffering and despoiled individuals submitted to such a fate? I did not then clearly perceive that the chain was upon their hearts – a chain whose burden the heart did not feel. Their ideas were enchained, but by a bond they themselves did not know. Life had imprinted its forms upon their spirits, habit fixed them in place. The social system fashioned these men. It was within them. It had, by some means, become their very substance against which they did not revolt, because they confused that reality with their own. . . . But they will transcend that reality by learning from it, and one can say, that they accept it in order to replace it all the more surely.

Jean Jaurès, *L'Armée nouvelle*.

Glossary of Abbreviations

CAL — *Comité d'action lycéen*. The Lycée Action Committee. Established in 1967 to fight for students' rights in the lycées, reform the curriculum, improve the working conditions and obtain the right to debate political and social questions in the lycées.

CDR — *Comité de défense de la République*. Committee for the Defence of the Republic. Founded by Gaullists, led by the Minister of the Interior and Right-wing organizations to combat the strikes and occupations during May and June.

CFDT — *Confédération française démocratique du travail*. The French Democratic Federation of Labour. A federation of trade unions, particularly strong amongst white-collar workers, engineers, draughtsmen, etc. Until recently a Catholic trade union. 25 per cent of unionized workers.

CGC — *Confédération générale des cadres*. The General Federation of *cadres*. A federation of managerial staff considered close to the Government.

CGT — *Confédération générale du travail*. The General Federation of Labour. Federation mainly composed of manual workers considered close to the Communist party. About 50 per cent of organized workers.

CGT-FO — *Confédération générale du travail – Force ouvrière*. General Federation of Labour. Federation mainly of manual workers considered close to the Socialist party. Split from the CGT in 1947. About 15 per cent of organized workers.

CLEOP — *Comité de liaison étudiants-ouvriers-paysans*. Students, Peasants and Workers Liaison Committee. Founded in May by students of agronomy and trade unionists.

CNJA   *Centre national des jeunes agriculteurs.* National Centre of Young Farmers. Part of the FNSEA (q.v.). Tends to be more radical and closer to the Socialist movement.

CNPF   *Confédération nationale du patronat français.* National Federation of French Industrialists. Roughly equivalent to the Confederation of British Industries except much more clearly dominated by small businesses.

CNRS   *Centre national de la recherche scientifique.* National Centre of Scientific Research. Research organization attached to the University.

CRS   *Compagnies républicaines de sécurité.* Mobile semi-military police force and riot police.

CVL   *Comité Vietnam lycéen.* The Lycée Vietnam Committee. Established during 1966, the first sign of politicization in the lycées.

CVN   *Comité Vietnam national.* National Vietnam Committee. Organization founded to support the National Liberation Front of Vietnam. To the Left of the Communist party.

EDF   *Électricité de France.* The French Electricity Board.

FEN   *Fédération nationale de l'éducation.* National Federation of Education. Federal body of all teachers' trade unions. Unaffected by the Communist anti-Communist split that affected the trade-union movement in 1947.

FER   *Fédération des étudiants révolutionnaires.* Federation of Revolutionary Students. Fundamental Trotskyist student organization preaching the impossibility of students as a revolutionary force within the University.

FGDS   *Fédération de la gauche démocratique et socialiste.* Federation of the Democratic and Socialist Left. Body to form a non-Communist Left made up of socialists, radicals, and reformist clubs. Near dissolution because of lack of policy and the policy of the Socialist party.

FGEL   *Fédération des groupes d'études en lettres.* Federation of Students in Arts. The students' union of the Arts Faculty in Paris (Sorbonne). Generally the motor of the student movements in France.

FNEF   *Fédération nationale des étudiants de France.* National Federation of French Students. Relatively Right-wing organization formed after split from UNEF (q.v.). But in recent times has been moving to the Left in order to avoid collapse.

FNSEA   *Fédération nationale des syndicats d'exploitant agricoles.*

National Federation of Farmers Unions. Roughly equivalent to the British National Union of Farmers but dominated by large farmers in the Seine region and in the North.

JAC   *Jeunesse anarchiste communiste*. Anarchist–Communist Youth.

JCR   *Jeunesse communiste révolutionnaire*. Revolutionary Communist Youth. Founded in 1966 after split from Communist party, one of the most active and important *groupuscules*.

MAU   *Mouvement d'action universitaire*. University Action Committee. Established in 1968 to coordinate activist groups amongst the students due to the weakness of UNEF (q.v.).

ORTF   *Office de la radio-télévision française*. French Radio and Television Service.

PCF   *Parti communiste français*. French Communist Party.

PDM   *Progrès et démocratie moderne*. Progress and Modern Democracy. Loose, mainly parliamentary, grouping of centre and Right-wing deputies.

PSU   *Parti socialiste unifié*. Unified Socialist Party. Left-wing Socialist party, the only organized political movement to support the students through the May/June events.

RATP   *Régie autonome de transports parisiens*. Independent Public Transport of Paris.

RTL   *Radio-télévision Luxembourg*. Radio service from Luxembourg beamed to France.

SFIO   *Section française de l'internationale ouvrière*. French Section of the International Working Men's Association. The French Socialist party, now part of the Federation of the Left.

SGEN   *Syndicat général de l'éducation nationale*. General trade union of national education. Affiliated to the CFDT (q.v.), close to the PSU (q.v.).

SMIG   *Salaire minimum interprofessionnel garanti*. The guaranteed minimum wage in industry raised 30 per cent to about 5s. an hour during the crisis.

SNCF   *Société nationale des chemins de fer*. French railways.

SNES   *Syndicat national de l'enseignement secondaire*. Affiliated to the FEN. The National Union of Secondary Education. Most lycée teachers belong to this union, currently close to the CGT.

SNESup.   *Syndicat national de l'enseignement supérieur*. National

	Union of Higher Education. Worked with UNEF (q.v.) during the crisis. Extremely active in proposing university and social reform.
TEP	*Théâtre de l'Est de Paris.* Theatre of Eastern Paris. Set up as an experimental theatre, specializes in forms of drama to make contact with social reality.
TNP	*Théâtre national populaire.* Established along the lines of the TEP by Jean Vilar, now run by Georges Wilson.
UDR	*Union pour la défense de la République.* Union for the Defence of the Republic. The name adopted by the Gaullist movement for the June elections.
UEC	*Union des étudiants communistes.* Union of Communist Students. Formerly an active organization but after its 'Italianization' in the early sixties it was taken over by the party.
UJC-ML	*Union de la jeunesse communiste – Marxiste–Léniniste.* Union of French Communist youth – Marxist–Leninist. Maoist youth organization.
UJCF	*Union de la jeunesse communiste française.* Union of French Communist Youth.
UNEF	*Union nationale des étudiants de France.* National Union of French Students. The main union of French students with about 80,000 members. Took a new lease of life during May.
UNR	*Union pour la nouvelle République.* Union for the New Republic. Pre-May name of the Gaullist movement.

Notes on the Contributors

Charles Posner is a lecturer in Sociology at the University of Essex and the Centre Universitaire de Vincennes, Université de Paris.

1. Edgar Morin is a sociologist attached to the CNRS. He is the author of several studies: *The Stars, Introduction à une politique de l'homme, Commune en France: la métamorphose de Plodémet*, etc.

2. André Jeanson is the president of the CFDT.

3. André Barjonet is an economist who formerly headed the social research department of the CGT and has published *L'exploitation capitaliste*.

4. Paul Gillet is an expert on police affairs and together with Claude Angeli has published *La police dans la politique (1944-1954)*.

5. Claude Angeli has written widely about the mass media, his commentary appears regularly in the *Nouvel Observateur*.

6. André Glucksmann is attached to the CNRS and is the author of two important studies: *Le discours de la guerre*, and *Stratégie et révolution en France: 1968*.

7. Jean-Pierre Vigier is a physicist attached to the CNRS, was a leading member of the Russell Tribunal and is active in the action committees.

8. Maud Mannoni is a psychoanalyst and has written widely about children: *L'enfant arriéré et sa mère, L'enfant sa 'maladie' et les autres*, and is one of the leading lights of the *Recherche* group.

9. René Lourau lectures in sociology at Nanterre and has written widely on problems of self-management in industry and education.

10. José Pierre is a poet who has published a number of works including *Le futurisme et le dadaïsme, D'autres chats à fouetter*.

11. Ipousteguy is one of France's leading sculptors.

12. André Gorz is an editor of the *Temps modernes* and has published some illuminating works on modern capitalism: *Stratégie ouvrière et néo-capitalisme, Le socialisme difficile*, etc.

13. The Vincennes–Paris–Sorbonne group which produced *The monetary putsch* is composed of many of the leaders of the May/June movement.

Bibliography

Background Books on France

In recent years the English have been particularly inept in their understanding of modern France. For this reason we have included a short but by no means exhaustive list of those books which are useful in understanding the basis of the May/June events.

PIERRE BAUCHET, *La planification française*. Still the best book available on French planning.

PIERRE BELLEVILLE, *Une nouvelle classe ouvrière*. Discussion of the change and lack of change in the work force.

P. H. CHOMBART DE LAUWE, *Images de la culture*. Important study of working-class *Weltanschauung*.

GUY DEBORD, *La société du spectacle*. The new forms of social alienation in consumers' society.

JOFFRE DUMAZEDIER, *Vers une civilisation du loisir*. Problems of the world of non-work.

J. ENSEMBLE, *Le contre-plan*. A counter-plan drawn up by trade unionists and Socialists.

ANDRÉ GORZ, *Stratégie ouvrière et néocapitalisme*. First theory describing the need for new kinds of opposition in the new industrial state. *Le socialisme difficile*. The need for new approaches in the Socialist movement.

MARC KRAVETZ, 'Naissance d'un syndicalisme étudiant' in *Temps modernes*, February 1964. One of the first studies of the student in the new industrial society.

P. LEBRUN, *Questions actuelles du syndicalisme*. Quantitative and qualitative demands and the need for a new kind of trade-union strategy.

HENRI LEFEBVRE, *La vie quotidienne dans le monde moderne*. An important study of the forms of social and political control in present-day France.

Le droit à la ville. The possibilities of the urban community.

HUBERT LESIRE-OGREL, *Le syndicalisme dans l'entreprise*. The present legal position of French trade unions.

SERGE MALLET, *La nouvelle classe ouvrière*. A pioneering study of the development of the movement amongst technicians, *cadres*, etc.

JULIETTE MINCES, *Le Nord*. The life of miners and manual workers in the most industrialized region of France.

DANIEL MOTHÉ, *Militant chez Renault*. Trade unionism in the Renault plant.

PIERRE NAVILLE, *De l'aliénation à la jouissance*. The possibilities opened up by the new work processes.

ALAIN TOURAINE, *La conscience ouvrière*. The relation between work situation, consciousness and action in the new industrial setting. 'L'évolution de la conscience ouvrière et l'idée socialiste', in *Esprit*, May 1956. The first outline of the three-stage theory of technological development and trade-union consciousness.